P9-APW-494

LANGUAGE AND LITERACY SERIES
Dorothy S. Strickland and Celia Genishi, SERIES EDITORS

ADVISORY BOARD: RICHARD ALLINGTON, DONNA ALVERMANN, KATHRYN AU,
EDWARD CHITTENDON, BERNICE CULLINAN, COLETTE DAIUTE,
ANNE HAAS DYSON, CAROLE EDELSKY, JANET EMIG,
SHIRLEY BRICE HEATH, CONNIE JUEL, SUSAN LYTLE

(Continued)

literacy matters

writing and reading the social self

Robert P. Yagelski

foreword by Victor Villanueva

MONTGOMERY COUNTY PUBLIC SCHOOLS
PROFESSIONAL LIBRARY
850 HUNGERFORD DRIVE
ROCKVILLE, MARYLAND 20850

WITHDRAWN

1131646

7-00

TEACHERS
COLLEGE
PRESS

teachers college
columbia university
new york and london

Published by Teachers College Press, 1234 Amsterdam Avenue, New York, NY 10027

Copyright © 2000 by Teachers College, Columbia University

All rights reserved. No part of this publication may be reproduced or transmitted in any form or by any means, electronic or mechanical, including photocopy, or any information storage and retrieval system, without permission from the publisher.

Library of Congress Cataloging-in-Publication Data

Yagelski, Robert.
    Literacy matters : writing and reading the social self / Robert P. Yagelski.
       p.   cm. — (Language and literacy series)
    Includes bibliographical references (p.   ) and index.
    ISBN 0-8077-3893-X (cloth : acid-free). — ISBN 0-8077-3892-1 (paper : acid-free)
    1. Literacy—Social aspects—United States.   2. Language arts—Study and teaching—United States.   I. Title. II. Series.
    LC151.Y24   1999
    302.2'244—dc21   99-36582

ISBN 0-8077-3892-1 (paper)
ISBN 0-8077-3893-X (cloth)

Printed on acid-free paper
Manufactured in the United States of America

07 06 05 04 03 02 01 00   8 7 6 5 4 3 2 1

*For Cheryl,
whose love and confidence never waver*

Contents

Foreword

In the mid-1980s, literacy theory and literacy instruction entered center stage in our publications. I'm not sure why. Maybe it was a reaction to *Newsweek*'s "Johnny Can't Read" issue; maybe it was a reaction to the "Nation At Risk" report. Researchers and theorists like Father Ong, Scribner and Cole, Shirley Brice Heath, and Linda Flower were ubiquitous in literacy publications. As was, of course, Paulo Freire. We read tales of literacy from bell hooks, Mike Rose, and others. In the universities, discussions were turning on "postructuralism," with Michel Foucault emerging as the academics' favorite. Exciting stuff. New pedagogies. We were rethinking literacy.

Some, like Richard Ohmann, worried that the popularity of literacy discussions, like those in *Newsweek* or the Carnegie report or the great popularity of E. D. Hirsch's *Cultural Literacy*, was an indication of something big changing on the political–economic horizon. And no matter what one thought of Ohmann's politics (which I sympathized with, but of course not all did), there were changes: the rise of an awareness of a new globalization with the United States as the center; the proliferation of digital technology, especially e-mail and the World Wide Web; the digital creating great wealth for some and obsolescence for others. There have been changes. Professor Robert Yagelski considers those changes, bringing back those major figures from the discussion on literacy of the 1980s, but looks at them with turn-of-the-century eyes.

I don't remember who wrote it—or who said it (since I don't even remember if I read it or heard it)—but someone said (or wrote) that the Black Power movement of the 1960s was divided among assimilationists and nationalists. I remember thinking how that particular division—assimilationist or nationalist—reflects two larger ideologies, the two dominant ideologies of the world throughout the twentieth century: liberalism vs. socialism, the individual or the collective. But postmoderns (and common sense) tell us to beware the binary, beware the either/or. In what follows, Professor Yagelski addresses both —the individual within the collective.

Then again, Freire, no matter what political label one puts on him (since he's been labeled a Marxist by many, a liberal by some, a liberation theologist by me), is playing out this same kind of a breaking down of the binary that Bob Yagelski will do in the pages that follow. Freire's "problematizing of the existential" is an argument for a localized politic through literacy. What that cumbersome, jargon-laden phrase means is something like realizing the desires of the individual with the individual's social context. And that is what this book is about: a look at how one negotiates students' (and teachers') entrenched notions of literacy as simple (or even complex) cognitive will and effort, of literacy as the single, key path to economic well-being and self-actualization (to use a now archaic term), literacy stripped of what Lloyd Bitzer terms "the rhetorical situation" (situational context, greater context, culture, or ideology).

And in doing so, Bob practices what he preaches: In the pages that follow we are let into his epistemological base. We see his own rhetorical situations, the sets of experiences which lead him to accept some theoretical and pedagogical positions and question others, as well as the writers on literacy of the eighties, the writers of their own literacy experience, Mike Rose and Malcolm X and others. We're in his working-class home, playing ball with his brother; we're in his classrooms, his conferences with his students; and we're privy to a representation of his mind, his thoughts, fumbles and all, as he reads his students' papers, and as he reads his students. And even if we hadn't taught high school seniors, college first-year students, non-traditional students confined within prison walls, we have all somehow known the students he confronts, works with, thinks through. And having known, we are drawn into rethinking how we have known those students by following Bob Yagelski's intellectual trail. Bob problematizes his existential situation. As we read, we problematize our own.

You're about to read a good book, well-written, refreshingly personal without being melancholy, decidedly thought-provoking. Enjoy it. I have. Think through your practices. I have. I am still rethinking.

Victor Villanueva
Pullman, Washington

Preface

Literacy remains a human invention contained by social contract, and the maintenance of that contract in education betrays our ideas of humanity as surely as our use of literacy enforces them.
—Elspeth Stuckey, The Violence of Literacy

In the spring of 1993, J. Elspeth Stuckey, teacher, literacy worker, and author of *The Violence of Literacy* (1991), visited Purdue University, where I was working at the time, to deliver a talk as part of a series sponsored by the Rhetoric and Composition program. I first encountered Stuckey's book a few years earlier and assigned it during the previous semester in a graduate course on literacy. It is a book whose angry argument about the complicity of literacy educators in an unfair economic system provoked my students and me, and we spent a good deal of time addressing Stuckey's question, posed near the end of her passionate critique, "What to do? What to do?" Stuckey's visit seemed an opportunity for us to voice our concerns about her book directly to her.

She is a slight woman whose gentle voice carries the lilt of her South Carolina home, and she endured our questions during her visit with charm and good humor. Her smiles and soft voice must have taken some of us by surprise, since the angry tone of her book might have led us to expect a severe, scowling person. Perhaps that's why few of us challenged her about her troubling book. We wanted to know how to get out of the dilemma she presents in her book: that as literacy educators we help perpetuate the very system that we believe we can change through progressive literacy education. We wanted to demand that she make the choice she offers in her book between "greater literacy" or "greater humanity" (p. 124). We never did. There were some hard questions, but she engaged us with her stories of her ongoing literacy work among poor adults in isolated rural areas and her obviously deep commitment to their well-being. Afterwards, several students confessed disappointment that we had not really pushed Stuckey to answer our real question: "What should *we* do as literacy educators?" At the time, I shared that disappointment, but I now suspect it was inevitable, given the complexity of the issues Stuckey raises in her book. Nevertheless, the uneasy sense that Stuckey was right and yet somehow not quite right remained long after her visit, and many years later it evolved into the impetus for this book.

In a sense, this book is my attempt to provide the answer that my students and I so genuinely wanted Stuckey to give us to her question about what literacy educators should and *could* do in the context of an inequitable economic system that depends in large measure on the very literacy we teach. As such, it is less an academic argument or theoretical discussion about literacy and literacy education than it is an exploration of the nature of literacy and its ambiguous role in our lives. Such an exploration prompted me to deviate from the conventional academic argument I thought I wanted to make. As a result, much of the book will likely disappoint academic readers seeking a neat theoretical answer to the problems Stuckey identifies. At the same time, I do wish to make a theoretical argument about the contingent nature of literacy as a local act of self-construction within discourse. This argument is central to my treatment of literacy in this book, even if my method is somewhat unconventional. My hope is that my approach enables me to make such an argument at the same time that it does some justice to the complexity of the issues I take up.

A NOTE ON METHOD

The discussion that follows encompasses much personal reflection on the ways in which literacy has played out in my own life and how my experiences as a literate person have shaped my ambivalent sense of the nature of literacy. I offer these reflections as a way to examine our beliefs about literacy and literacy education in the hope that such an examination can enhance our collective understanding of how we, as literacy educators, might best serve our students' needs. In this respect, I hope this book will find among its readers secondary school English and language arts teachers as well as college instructors who will see in my experiences as a writer, reader, and teacher some of the challenges they also have faced in their own work.

Nevertheless, my "personal" approach will worry some readers who wonder about the validity of my own experiences as "evidence" for the arguments I make about literacy in this book. One reviewer, for example, astutely pointed out that my implicit approach to "truth" as a function of my own experience is undermined by my professed adherence to a poststructuralist view of language and discourse (which I discuss in Chapter 3). That is, my poststructuralist perspective calls into question my own truth claims. This strikes me as a valid complaint, and one that deserves some comment, especially since similar criticisms have been voiced about various methods of inquiry (such as ethnography) that have emerged in recent decades as important methodologies in education research, literacy studies, and rhetoric and composition.

While I understand—and embrace—the notion of the contingency of all "truth" and meaning within a poststructuralist framework and therefore must acknowledge the contingency of my own truth claims in this book, I also argue, with theorist Paul Smith (1988), that one can still claim agency and construct shared meaning within discourse. That is, discourse inevitably shapes meaning and makes all meaning contingent, but it does not *determine* meaning; meaning—and truth— are thus always a negotiation among and within discourses by individual writers and readers who are in turn shaped by those discourses. I espouse the stance of some ethnographers who argue that one can make meaning only from one's own perspective, a perspective that, of course, is shaped by the discourses within which one writes and reads and works. In this sense, Paul Smith's notion of *self-interest*, which I discuss at length in Chapter 3, provides a way to understand the intersection between the "individual" agent and the broader discourses that inevitably shape that individual and his or her truth claims; Smith's notion thus opens up a space for the individual agency on which I rest much of my argument in this book. In short, I acknowledge the limitations of my method of inquiry at the same time that I assert that I have no other way to make the claims I wish to make in this book.

I also must emphasize that I have not attempted to construct a strict philosophical argument or to draw conclusions from a carefully constructed empirical study. Rather, I examine beliefs about and practices of literacy in the context of my own experiences as writer, reader, and educator, and in the context of a wealth of other studies—theoretical and empirical—of literacy that have informed our collective understanding of it. Indeed, my own writing here is an example of what I argue is true of all student writing: that it is a self-construction within discourse. Some readers, I hope, will see validity in the conclusions I draw; others inevitably will disagree or reach different conclusions based on their own experiences as teachers and literate persons. But in both cases I hope that my examination of literacy and literacy education will be thought-provoking and thus enrich each reader's understanding of the complex nature of literacy and its role in our lives.

A NOTE ON "DISCOURSE"

It will quickly become apparent that *discourse* is a key concept in my understanding and discussion of literacy. Indeed, my definition of literacy rests upon the concept of discourse: *literacy is a local act of self-construction within discourse.* Because so much of my discussion will depend on an understanding of discourse and because discourse is such a slippery yet important term in current professional discussions, I need to say something here about how I will be using the term in this book.

My understanding of discourse relies on poststructuralist thought and especially on the work of Michel Foucault. In *The Archaeology of Knowledge and the Discourse on Language*, Foucault (1972) writes that he has used the term *discourse* in at least three different ways: "sometimes as the general domain of all statements, sometimes as an individualized group of statements, and sometimes as the regulated practice that accounts for a certain number of statements" (p. 80). Sara Mills (1997), in her lucid and helpful book *Discourse*, offers this explication of Foucault's three definitions:

> The first definition that Foucault gives is the widest one: "the general domain of all statements"; that is, all utterances or texts which have meaning and which have some effects in the real world count as discourse. . . . It may be useful to consider this usage to be more about discourse than about a discourse or discourses, with which the second and third definitions are concerned. The second definition that he gives—"an individualized group of statements"—is one that is used more often by Foucault when he is discussing the particular structures within discourse; thus, he is concerned to be able to identify discourses, that is, groups of utterances which seem to be regulated in some way and which seem to have a coherence and a force to them in common. Within this definition, therefore, it would be possible to talk about a discourse of femininity, a discourse of imperialism, and so on. Foucault's third definition is perhaps the one which has the most resonance for many theorists: "a regulated practice which accounts for a number of statements." I take this to mean that, here, he is less interested in the actual utterances/texts that are produced than in the rules and structures which produce particular utterances and texts. (p. 7)

For the most part, I will use the term *discourse* quite generally in the first two of these three senses of the term. But often I will use the term as Foucault defines it in the second of his definitions to speak about particular discourses that shape the writing of the students I will describe—for instance, in describing the discourses of race and language and schooling that figure into the writing of Celina's essay in Chapter

4. In these discussions of student writing I also will at times use the term in a way that is consistent with Foucault's third definition in order to call attention to specific *practices* governing the writing and reading of texts within specific contexts—such as in my discussion in Chapter 4 of the divergent uses of language that Celina engaged in at school and in her home community.

My use of the term also draws on Diane Macdonnell's (1986) overtly social conception of discourse. Discourses, Macdonnell writes, "differ with the kinds of institutions and social practices in which they take shape, and with the positions of those who speak and those whom they address" (p. 1). In this sense of discourse, Macdonnell elaborates on Foucault's third definition, emphasizing that discourses are always "set up historically and socially" (p. 2) and that they are not homogeneous nor are they equal. "In any institution," she asserts, "there is a distribution and a hierarchy of discourses" (p. 1). In making this point about the relationship among discourses within a particular setting, Macdonnell also highlights the notion that discourses function—that is, circumscribe meanings and assign subject positions—not only unilaterally, as it were, but in relation to other discourses such that "a discourse takes effect indirectly or directly through its relation to, its address to, another discourse" (p. 3). This is a key point, since I often will discuss different discourses that are in place within a specific rhetorical situation and attempt to illuminate how those discourses function in that situation in relation to one another. My discussion of Celina's writing in Chapter 4 is perhaps the best example of this understanding of discourse.

A careful reader will notice slippage in my use of the term so that at times I will be calling primarily upon Foucault's second definition, while at other times I may be drawing more directly on his third definition. My use of the term is further complicated by the way in which *discourse* is sometimes conflated with *ideology*. Mills invokes Terry Eagleton to distinguish between discourse and ideology:

> It may help to view ideology less as a particular set of discourses than as a particular set of effects *within* discourses. Bourgeois ideology includes this particular discourse on property, that way of talking about the soul, this treatise on jurisprudence and the kind of utterances one overhears in pubs where the landlord wears a military tie. (Eagleton, 1991, p. 194; quoted in Mills, 1997, p. 46, emphasis in original).

This complex interrelationship between ideology and discourse, wherein each shapes the other and each exists only in relation to the other, perhaps will emerge most obviously in my discussion of Hannah's essay in

Chapters 2 and 6. However, as my examination of popular notions about literacy in Chapter 2 should indicate, my understanding of discourse, although it distinguishes discourse from ideology in ways that Mills argues for, nevertheless encompasses ideology in the sense that a particular discourse (as in Foucault's second definition) is always ideological in how it circumscribes meanings and in what it values or ignores or marginalizes. As Macdonnell (1986) points out, "Any discourse concerns itself with certain objects and puts forward certain concepts at the expense of others"; moreover, "different discourses elaborate different concepts and categories" (p. 3). As my discussions of the writing of Mr. Green, Hannah, Celina, and other students will suggest, this assumption about discourse and its relationship to ideology is a key one in my understanding of how literacy functions in students' lives.

Some readers will no doubt find reason for concern or complaint in my definitions and usage of the term *discourse*, but my hope is that my use of the term does not inhibit but rather enriches an understanding of literacy.

Acknowledgments

It is customary for authors to note in their acknowledgments that there are too many people to thank adequately for their help in completing a work such as this. It's true in this case as well. But there are nevertheless those whose influence and assistance were pivotal in the conception, development, and completion of this book. Some of those people never saw a word of this book as I was writing it, but their influence, which was effected through conversations and through their example as writers and scholars over the years, was critical in shaping the understanding of literacy that informs this book. Donald Murray perhaps will recognize little of what I have written here, but his implicit confidence in me as a teacher and a writer, together with his example as both, helped shape my attitudes toward teaching writing at a crucial early stage in my career. Andrea Lunsford pushed me but always allowed me to be the writer and teacher I needed to be; she provided a peerless example of teacher/scholar that helped me imagine this project. James Porter, friend, mentor, and colleague who will disagree with much of this book, nevertheless graciously read my work and engaged me in productive discussions that profoundly shaped the ideas herein, especially with respect to poststructuralist thought. Steve North and Amy Lee read versions of the early chapters, providing advice in the project's early stages. Kathleen Yancey was always willing to listen, question, argue, and ultimately validate my ideas and efforts. Victor Villanueva has become a supporter, colleague, and friend in recent years; I am deeply grateful to him for writing the Foreword to this book and for his generosity and unflagging good humor. Roxanne Mountford and Scott Leonard, valuable colleagues and wonderful friends both, offered support for this project, implicit as well as explicit, that helped me continue during doubtful times.

Many secondary school teachers graciously allowed me into their classrooms and meetings and professional lives in ways that enriched my understanding of literacy instruction. Among those, Joy Seybold and her colleagues at Jefferson High School in Lafayette, Indiana, deserve special mention and gratitude. Kim Marker of Queensbury High

School in New York State also deserves many thanks for her willingness to share her time and thoughts with me and to listen to my views. Other colleagues who indirectly shaped the ideas in this book include Tom Newkirk, Keith Walters, Roger Cherry, and Jim Berlin. My thanks to all of them.

Even more than these colleagues, the students I have known over the years have shaped this book. I thank all those who not only were willing to allow me to write about them and their own writing but who taught me more than they will ever realize about writing and teaching: Abby, Celina, Larry, Sammy, Hannah, Lynn, Mr. Green, Melissa, and others who do not appear directly in these pages but whose presence was nevertheless important as I conceived and carried out this project.

Special thanks go to Teachers College Press editor Carol Collins, whose soft-spoken enthusiasm for this project and confidence in me as writer were vital as I worked through the manuscript; and to Cathy McClure, who provided a thorough and empathetic reading of the manuscript.

Finally, I thank my family. My two sons and best buddies, Adam and Aaron, provided me with countless opportunities to explore literacy and helped me keep perspective with their studied indifference to the project and their disconcerting questions about it ("How can you *write* that much about writing?!"). My parents, Ron and Joan Yagelski, provided me the opportunity to become the student and, later, the writer I wished to be, for which I am ever grateful. And most important, my wife, Cheryl, has always been the patient listener, unshakable supporter, and sincere friend I needed from the very beginning. I cannot thank her enough.

Practicing the shallows wholeheartedly,
we may discover the ocean.
　　　—Bonnie Myotai Treace, "Dogen Cubed"

Chapter 1

Abby's Lament

Does Literacy Matter?

Write as if your life depended upon it.
                                    —Adrienne Rich, poet and activist

Never write anything; you'll only regret it.
                                    —Don Whillans, mountaineer

Abby doesn't believe she matters. She is 16 years old, a junior in a rural high school in upstate New York, and she doesn't believe that, in the larger scheme of things, she "can make a difference." She doesn't believe, in fact, that anyone her age can make a difference. She's irrelevant. They are all irrelevant. They don't matter in "society."

Abby told me all this during a visit I made to her school, Queensbury High School, a large public high school located in a small town in the Adirondack Mountains. I had been invited by her teacher, Sue Marker, who was then the head of the Queensbury English Department, to talk to her colleagues and some of her students about the possibilities for literacy learning with computers, which I had been studying with both college- and high school-age writers. I had spent the day at Queensbury cheerleading for the great communications revolution represented by the rapidly evolving use of computer technologies and the growth of the Internet and World Wide Web. My pitch was something like this: You're in the midst of the Information Age, a time characterized by an explosion of information fueled largely by computer and video media; if you're going to have any control over what happens in your lives, especially your political lives, you need to be able to participate in what's happening around you. That means you'll have to be able to confront this new information technology, to find a way onto the much-heralded Information Superhighway and its many byways, and to make critical decisions about what information matters and what to do with it. Otherwise, those with the knowledge of and access to these emerging communications technologies will make the decisions for you. You'll be left behind, on some dead-end off ramp.

It was, at its heart, a classic American argument for self-determination, and I pitched it as a kind of New Age exigency, a step toward a futuristic technological revolution that opened up untold possibilities for those with the knowledge and skills to participate. And for many of those teen-aged kids, who sat politely and (for the most part) attentively through my animated presentations, it seemed to resonate. At the very least, it was a mildly interesting diversion from the daily grind of English class (about which much more later). But Abby wasn't buying it. When you're irrelevant, you're irrelevant, computers or not, she was saying. The people who make decisions don't listen to kids, she argued: We have no say in what gets decided. I countered that she *did* have a say, that her views could be expressed in all kinds of ways: through letters to editors and political bodies such as town councils and school boards, through petitions and rallies, through student publications. You *can* make your voice heard, I asserted, especially through writing. The Internet and World Wide Web offer even more opportunities to make that voice heard and to gather information that can give impact to your voice. And when you're old enough to vote, you'll have a powerful way to register your views. "What difference would that make?" she asked in what was more than an affected adolescent dismissal. I didn't know this young woman, but it seemed clear to me that she wasn't putting on a show for her classmates. She was in earnest. Here was a twist to the Generation X apathy regarding political affairs that the popular press likes to describe. This young woman wasn't uninterested; she was angry about being perceived as unimportant and she was skeptical about my claims that she mattered. And she wouldn't give me an inch.

At the time, I was glad for Abby's feisty engagement with my ideas. After all, this was the kind of discussion I often try hard to foster in my own classrooms: lively dialogue about important issues intended to engage students and get them to think hard about those issues. I suspected that Abby spoke for many of her silent classmates, some of whom followed our exchange closely. This was, as I saw it, an opportunity for me to make my case that those kids did matter, to try to convince them that they could take some control over their social and political lives through a critical understanding of literacy and the careful and savvy use of the written word. It'll soon be your world, I told them, if you want to take charge of it. And you can do that through literacy. Abby's complaints fueled my own animated pitch, and I wasn't about to leave that day without convincing at least one of them that I was right—that they *did* matter and that literacy was the vehicle for their claims to the world.

In essence, I was offering Abby and her classmates my canned and somewhat oversimplified version of the kind of "emancipatory literacy" that theorist Paulo Freire, among others, advocates. As Henri Giroux (1987) explains it, Freire's view rests on the assumption that literacy is "a necessary foundation for cultural action and freedom, a central aspect of what it means to be a self and socially constituted agent" (p. 7). For Freire, "literacy is fundamental to aggressively constructing one's voice as part of a wider project of possibility and empowerment" (p. 7). From the time I first encountered Freire's views on literacy in his book *Pedagogy of the Oppressed* (1970/1984) as a young graduate student in the early 1980s, I began to see my own teaching as based on some version of a Freirean critical literacy as a means of social change and individual empowerment. Such terms as *social change* and *individual empowerment* are slippery, especially given the sometimes problematic ways that they are used in the professional jargon of scholars and educators. But for me they refer generally to the crucial role that reading and writing can play in our individual and collective lives within a democractic political system and a capitalist economy. Like Freire, I see reading and writing as acts of participation in a wider project of possibility and empowerment, as a way to construct our roles in that project, as a vehicle for participation in the discourses that shape our lives, and as a means of making sense of our lives in the context of others' lives. Literacy is central to the ongoing struggle for democracy and self-determination. It is a matter of individual empowerment in the way that it can enable one to negotiate the complexities of life; it is empowerment in a broader sense in that literate acts are always inherently social within the political, cultural, and economic contexts within which we lead our individual lives. And literacy represents a kind of joy as well: the joy that comes with using language to structure your world, to give voice to your ideas, to create a space for yourself in an endless stream of discourses, to work toward change, to reflect, to expound—to act.

It was that set of beliefs about literacy, in a watered-down form, that I was sharing with Abby and her classmates at Queensbury High School. I was genuinely interested in the ways in which those students were "socially constituted agents" and literate beings with the potential for committed political action. I was interested in helping students gain access to a literacy that opens up opportunities for them to claim agency for themselves, to participate in the many discourses that shape their lives—including those in evolving electronic media. And like Abby that day, I was in earnest.

I am still. But not without reservations. And it is in large measure the tension between my continuing belief in the potential power of literacy, on the one hand, and the many reservations I have come to hold about literacy and especially about how we teach it, on the other, that energizes this book. Since that visit to Queensbury High School, I have thought—and spoken—often of Abby and what literacy might mean to her and students like her. And like many educators who have devoted their professional lives to the teaching of literacy, I have begun to wonder uneasily about what I do in working with those students. I have begun to wonder, for instance, about the relationship between Abby's view of the world—and her participation, or lack of it, in that world—and my role as a teacher of writing and reading, a researcher committed to broadening our understanding of literacy, an educator who has helped train the English teachers with whom students like Abby study. How much of what I do actually empowers students in ways that Freire and other theorists describe? How much of what I do actually works *against* such empowerment?

ENGLISH EDUCATION AND THE VIOLENCE OF LITERACY

Elspeth Stuckey's angry book, *The Violence of Literacy* (1991), articulates some of my own concerns about literacy education. In her book, Stuckey argues that the "usual speculations" about literacy and its importance are wrong "because the assumptions about economic and social forces on which they are based are faulty" (p. vii). Literacy, she says, does not lead inevitably to economic success and social opportunity, as our social mythologies would have us believe; rather, it is implicated in an "entrenched class structure in which those who have power have a vested interest in keeping it" (p. vii). Moreover, literacy is "destructive" in the sense that it helps perpetuate that unjust class system. She documents that "destruction" in the form of exclusionary educational and social practices in which literacy figures centrally, unequal access to economic and social opportunity for citizens from certain classes, and institutionalized racism and sexism. And she attempts to describe "the extraordinary power of the educational process and of literacy standards not merely to exclude citizens from participating in the country's economic and political life but to brand them and their children with indelible prejudice, the prejudice of language" (p. 122). In these ways, she concludes, "literacy and English instruction can hurt you, more clearly and forcefully than it can help you" (p. 123). It is a sobering analysis—particularly so for those of us who have worked within the belief that "literacy really made us human" (p. 124). No, Stuckey unequivocally says, "literacy was never this way, and it was wrong to think it was" (p. 124).

Like Stuckey, I have come to understand some of the ways in which, "far from engineering freedom, our current approaches to literacy corroborate other social practices that prevent freedom and limit opportunity" (p. vii). I don't believe that Abby's rejection of my optimistic arguments about literacy and technology were driven by a careful analysis of literacy and its relationship to class and political power in the way that Stuckey's argument is. But I do believe that Abby, like so many students in English and language arts classes in this country, sensed some of the ways in which Stuckey may be right about literacy. And I believe Abby and some of her classmates may be onto us. Her ambivalence about her own literacy learning, which emerged in some of her statements that afternoon, grows, I'd argue, out of experiences with literacy that belie the mythology of possibility in a classless democratic society, a mythology that, as Stuckey points out, continues to drive our views about literacy and is reinforced continually by traditional curricula, popular media, and cultural practices. In other words, Abby's experience in the world contradicts much of what her English teachers—and other representatives of the educational and political establishment, including me—tell her about the importance of writing and reading, about the difference it can make in her life; moreover, as I hope to show in this book, most of what Abby is asked to do as a writer and reader in school has little relevance to her social, political, cultural, and economic life outside school.

I have come to believe that in some unsettling ways Abby is right: She is largely irrelevant. As a young citizen about to enter the adult world that has determined so much of her life, she is in many ways far removed from the political and institutional structures that shape her life. Her experiences teach her that she does not figure in any significant way into the political workings of the society she inhabits, and, regardless of what her teachers say, her encounters with literacy have done little to challenge that. The texts that she confronts daily—those "sanctioned" classroom texts like Shakespeare and Edith Wharton alongside the more prevalent cultural "texts" available to her on MTV and network news broadcasts with their hi-tech "town meetings"—do little to encourage a sense of participation in the political life of a society that seems so familiar to her yet out of her reach. Indeed, the texts she encounters outside the classroom encourage a different sort of participation—that of consumer—in ways that reduce political awareness to simple desires like having more disposable income or owning a particular kind of car or pair of athletic shoes, material goods that are presented as the measures and rewards of success in an economic system that defines Abby as a consumer. Worse, so many of those texts deny the existence of a political life in ways that reinforce Abby's sense of disconnection and encourage her lack of participation. Think of the not-so-subtle images that accompany the consumerist mantras like "Life is good" (from a popular ad for beer in the mid-1990s) that we are exposed to continuously in television and print (and now Internet) advertising for all kinds of products. Think of the daunting numbers of these images and slogans and the numbing regularity with which consumers like Abby are exposed to them. Think, too, of the messages about what matters that are contained in those images. Pop singer Bruce Springsteen's cynical indictment of cable television, "57 Channels and Nothing's On," recalls the famous TV-as-wasteland metaphor from the 1950s. But something *is* on those 57 channels: an endless stream of slightly different versions of the same text, the same continuous advertisement for a consumer culture in which agency is defined as the ability to choose which products to buy. How does one "read" such texts, which suggest that the only real power a student like Abby has is her purchasing power? The sanctioned texts like Shakespeare and Wharton that she encounters in her English classes—and the passive ways in which she is likely asked to engage those texts—do little to help her learn to negotiate those popular consumerist images and slogans and to consider what they might mean in her political and economic life. Given what she typically encounters in her official literacy learning in school and what she encounters outside that institutional setting, it's no surprise that she feels irrelevant.

But I don't believe it needs to be that way. While Stuckey may be right about the relationship between literacy and the maintenance of an unfair and often oppressive political and economic system, literacy *does* constitute power. It is not the "personal empowerment" implied in much of the professional jargon that educators and theorists use, or the simplistic literacy of "economic empowerment" that political leaders invoke as they announce new initiatives to fight the literacy crisis; rather, literacy represents a kind of power to participate in extraordinarily complex ways in the social, cultural, and political discourses that shape people's lives. That power resides not solely in the capacity to understand political discourse in what is supposed to be a democratic society or the so-called basic skills required for adequate employment in a capitalist system, but in a myriad of more mundane ways that often have a far more direct and profound impact on our lives. These include the ability to

- understand a lease or notice from a public agency;
- negotiate a car loan agreement;
- make sense of a curriculum document from a child's school;
- submit a petition to a town council or school board;
- respond to a request to sign a petition;
- understand the risks inherent in a mortgage document;
- engage a philosophical argument about welfare reform based on an article in a local newspaper;
- register for a course at a local college;
- request information from a government agency about local water quality;
- decipher a report from a therapist who has examined an aging parent;
- decide on an insurance policy;
- lodge a complaint about working conditions at a place of employment;
- understand the minimum wage law announcement posted on a bulletin board at a workplace;
- find a site on the World Wide Web with trustworthy information on a local toxic dump cleanup;
- place the editorial of a local newspaper columnist in critical perspective;
- be skeptical about the subtle messages contained in an advertisement for athletic shoes;
- delight in the subtle language of a popular song;
- compose a letter describing a divorce proceeding to a distant family member.

Such local acts of literacy do not at first glance seem to carry the political weight that theorists like Giroux and Freire suggest literacy represents; indeed, they seem almost petty in light of the theoretical arguments and political debates about literacy and school curricula that occupy elected officials and academics. But these acts of literacy amount to the very kind of political and economic participation about which Freire writes; they are local manifestations of the broader ideological struggles inherent in literate acts. And they represent the many complex, sometimes overlapping, often conflicting discourses within which people function every day, within which they negotiate the constraints and challenges of contemporary life, within which they make the many small decisions that can determine how much control they exercise over their lives. In this sense, an understanding of literacy in the context of those many discourses, and the ability to participate through literacy in those discourses, represents power. Moreover, as Eli Goldblatt (1995) has noted so poignantly, written language serves a "realizing function" (p. 28) by making "real" the institutions that shape our lives: "At the same time that writing confers an institutional validity to both our public and private lives, writing done by individuals effectively creates and maintains the reality of social institutions" (p. 29). In other words, individual writers and readers shape our collective reality through written discourse. To participate in those discourses is thus to shape our lives and the cultural and institutional ground on which we live those lives.

For me, then, the task of the literacy educator is not simply to teach students how to write and read or to help them see meaning in a literary text deemed great or even to encourage them to engage in cultural critique, but to enable them to understand how literacy functions as a means of participation in those ever-shifting discourses that shape our lives and to find ways to give students like Abby some measure of access to that power—even as we, like Stuckey, continue to acknowledge and examine and elucidate the ways in which literacy *is* violent.

REEXAMINING LITERACY AS A LOCAL ACT

To sort out this task is in large measure the purpose of this book. What follows is an examination of the ways in which we understand and discuss literacy in the broader political and cultural arenas in this country and in our own professional discourses. That examination— and my indictment of many of our educational practices that grow out of prevailing beliefs about literacy—rests on the assumption that the popular beliefs about literacy that drive public discussions of education reform as well as the professional efforts for curriculum reform, such as have been under way in many states since the early 1980s, are based on narrow and sometimes conflicting conceptions of literacy. In the popular mind—and in the minds of many educators— literacy is a set of basic reading and writing skills possessed by individuals; English as a school subject is the learning of those skills alongside the cultural knowledge gained from exposure to great works of literature (see Hirsch, 1987). These beliefs about literacy and literacy education, which I will examine in more detail in Chapter 2, are not only outmoded but, in a complex and increasingly technological society, often counterproductive. To continue to understand literacy primarily as basic skills that reflect individual cognitive abilities simply cannot lead to curricula that will enable students to develop the kind of understanding of literacy and the writing and reading abilities that I refer to above. What's more, these simplistic beliefs about literacy can be downright destructive. Because they ignore the complex and ambiguous nature of literacy and its social and political uses, they can result in the very kind of oppression—of economic and political "violence"—that Stuckey so compellingly describes. And for Abby and her classmates and the millions of other students in classrooms throughout the country, such beliefs can lead to a superficial kind of literacy that leaves them without the critical abilities they will need to negotiate their worlds. Moreover, such beliefs will likely leave many students with a sense that literacy really has no central relevance to their personal lives, aside perhaps from helping them secure employment. I am not referring to that old argument about teaching kids to like books; the common pronouncements in curriculum documents about fostering a love of reading and producing lifelong readers, while seemingly good ideas, also rest on narrow and limited notions of what reading is and how it can function in the life of a student like Abby. As David Bartholomae (1990) has shown, such pronouncements also imply a set of values about "good" and "bad" behavior, and "good" and "bad" literature, that are troubling at best. I hope Abby *will* feel compelled to read novels and poems—for personal enrichment and enjoyment. But if that's all her literacy education leaves her with, then we've failed her. And I believe we routinely fail students in precisely this way.

But my indictment of literacy instruction is not simply about arguing against particular approaches to teaching writing and reading or about assigning blame for the apparent shortcomings of education in this country. Rather, I want to argue for a conception of literacy that rests on the notion of participation in the discourses that shape our lives, a notion that implies individual and collective possibility. Thus, in Chapter 3 I will lay out a conception of literacy, based on poststructuralist analyses of language and discourse, as a local act of self-construction within discourse. Literacy, I will argue, is at heart an effort to construct a self within ever-shifting discourses in order to participate in those discourses; that effort is always local in the sense that any construction of a self within discourse, although inherently social, is mediated by a variety of factors unique to a specific act of reading and writing within a specific situation. My purpose in offering this conception of literacy is to provide a framework for constructing meaningful pedagogies for the teaching of writing and reading that address both the limitations and possibilities of literacy. To do so, I will draw on the ideas of postmodern theorists like Michel Foucault who have illuminated the ways in which meaning arises through discourse. Foucault (1972) understands discourses not as "groups of signs (signifying elements referring to contents or representations) but as practices that systematically form the objects of which they speak" (p. 49). He and other postmodern theorists thus help us see some of the ways in which discourse constitutes our world. Moreover, postmodern explorations of language and discourse reveal not only the unstable nature of meanings of words and discourses, but also the fragmented and contingent nature of the self. This insight into the nature of the self and identity is crucial, since popular conceptions of literacy rest so heavily on the idea of individuality and a conception of a unified and identifiable self.

I do not, however, want to foreground the political and social in a way that obscures the complexity of individual acts of writing and reading and the possibilities for individual agency. So much of our ongoing scholarly discussion about literacy has focused, I think, on the oppressive nature of what we now refer to almost unthinkingly as the "dominant discourse" and the need to protect students, especially those from nonmainstream groups, from the effects of this discourse, that it can become difficult to keep sight of individual student writers and readers trying to carve out space for themselves in the discourses they confront daily—in school, in the media, in their neighborhoods, among their peers. In addition, our collective obsession with difference, which often refers in superficial and even totalizing ways to class, race, or gender, obscures the many complex distinctions among individual writers and readers within these very broad social categories. As Maureen Hourigan (1994) has pointed out, the "political categories" of race, class, and gender "must and do combine in almost every instance, but it is difficult to predict, in everyday life and in classroom situations, the self-presentation of gender, race, and class identities" (p. 73). It is also difficult to predict—and equally difficult to describe without oversimplifying—how these complex identities will manifest themselves in individual literate acts. And so I will draw on the work of theorist Paul Smith (1988) to help explain how our students might be understood as "selves" or "individuals," constructed within broader sets of discourses, with the possibility for agency within those discourses.

All this discussion is intended to put forth a vision of literacy that helps us understand the specific acts of reading and writing that our students engage in and how we might best help them understand and accomplish those literate acts in ways that enable them to claim agency for themselves. In Chapter 4 I will describe my experiences with specific students, writing in a variety of situations, to illustrate how such an understanding of literacy as a local act of self-construction within discourse can play out in individual lives. I take up the same task in Chapter 5 in the context of emerging online media that have begun to shape how we engage in acts of writing and reading in ways that may profoundly alter not only what literacy is but also how it is valued in our increasingly technological society. In both these chapters, the focus is on understanding how individual texts come to be as students construct themselves through their writing and reading in ways that matter in their lives.

I have come to believe that such an understanding of literacy is essential to our efforts to create effective literacy pedagogies in schools, where literacy remains, in my view, poorly understood—at least the literacy that is enacted in typical school curricula. Thus, in Chapter 6 I will draw implications of a conception of literacy as local for the teaching of writing and reading and discuss ways in which I believe we might make literacy instruction more relevant to our students' lives. In the past decade I have worked alongside many English teachers at all levels and I have participated in various efforts to reform literacy instruction in states in the northeast, midwest, and west. Those experiences have convinced me that in order to foster any kind of meaningful change in literacy instruction, conventional beliefs about literacy must be reconsidered. In their book, *Critical Teaching and the Idea of Literacy*, Cy Knoblauch and Lil Brannon (1993) underscore the importance of educators' awareness of their own ideological assumptions regarding literacy, arguing that for educators to be unaware of their "ideological dispositions"—of their own beliefs about literacy and culture and political power—is tantamount to complicity in the kinds of "violence" that Stuckey describes (p. 24). In other words, to teach Abby to read and write in certain ways without a critical understanding of how those ways may compromise her own political and economic well-being is to do a kind of violence to her. It is crucial, then, for literacy educators to understand their own ideological assumptions about what they do and the implications of those assumptions for their students. And this is not just a matter of abstract disagreements about, for example, how to define literacy or what constitutes a "great book." As Knoblauch and

Brannon point out, competing beliefs about literacy "vie for power in political and educational life" (p. 17). That struggle plays out "in legislative assemblies, school board meetings, newspaper editorials, and classrooms throughout the country" (p. 17). In short, theoretical assumptions and ideologies shape the decisions that affect how and what we teach in English classrooms and, in turn, how our students come to understand and use literacy in their lives. It is imperative, therefore, that teachers understand these assumptions and ideologies.

Part of my purpose, then, in teasing out a particular theoretical perspective on literacy, is to challenge the limited and limiting beliefs about literacy that continue to drive much of the conventional English curriculum in American schools and to address what I see as inherent contradictions in how we understand and use literacy. I have no illusions about my role in such an effort. As is clear to anyone who has spent any time reading the volumes of scholarship on literacy, theoretical perspectives on literacy and literacy instruction are as numerous as the grammar worksheets that are still a mainstay of teaching in so many English classrooms. One more theoretical argument from one more educator will not by itself change the ways in which we understand and teach writing and reading. Moreover, even as I argue for the importance of reconceptualizing literacy, I am mindful of the complex ways in which literacy relates to broader social and political and economic structures that remain largely outside the control or influence of educators. Education researcher Jean Anyon argues forcefully in *Ghetto Schooling* (1997) that substantive reform cannot occur in our most troubled schools without broad-based changes in the social and economic character of the neighborhoods in which those schools are located—an argument that intersects with much of Stuckey's critique. All of which is to say that theories of literacy must be understood as one part of an immensely complex project of possibility and empowerment, to invoke Freire again, and they must be understood *as* theories with their own limitations and potential problems.

LITERACY AND CHANGE

Nevertheless, the need to understand writing and reading remains as pressing as ever, especially as we near the end of a decade in which there are more children in our schools than ever before. The neverending political battles over education reform (evident in the recent reading wars over phonetic and whole language pedagogies) and the explosion of research and scholarship on writing and reading in the past 3 decades have had little discernible effect on the ways in which those children will learn to write and read, yet the society in which those children live has changed dramatically in those decades. More than 30 years after Braddock, Lloyd-Jones, and Schoer (1963) called for more research into composition and 40 years after the passage of the National Defense Education Act, which defined reading and writing in terms of national security, we now routinely communicate in something called cyberspace with technologies that must seem to many elderly citizens more fantastic than the gadgets depicted in popular sci-fi films of the 1950s. Those same technologies now provide instant access to information and events that are themselves a function of those technologies. For instance, in a bizarre kind of irony that seems to prove French philosopher Jean Baudrillard's (1983) arguments about appearance and reality, modern political conventions, so long a crucial part of the election process in American society, are now shaped by television and print media in astounding technological efforts to use those same media to shape public opinion: Television represents television representing reality. It all becomes, to use Baudrillard's term, simulacra. And these events take place in a world that hardly seems to resemble the past so often invoked at those same political conventions: a constructed present constructing a past. Furthermore, the east–west divide that defined the international political landscape for most of the twentieth century no longer exists, and even as old nationalist tensions reemerge in places like Bosnia, the staggering growth of capitalism is making national borders virtually obsolete. The paradigm that seemed to give shape to our understanding of the world for the past 50 years— the paradigm within which the modern discipline of English evolved— no longer holds. As Richard Ohmann (1995) writes in his essay, "English After the USSR,"

> The world will be very different when our students are middle-aged, but the course of its change will not follow the master narrative of old marxism or the Cold War narrative of democracy victorious in an epic battle against communism. If we and our students are to be agents rather than dupes in the process, we'll need to invent a new narrative. (p. 237)

Many commentators have offered their versions of what that narrative might be. But the only agreement seems to lie in the sense that the world is very different now than it was when educators and lawmakers linked literacy to national security, and included English as one of the school subjects considered vital for protecting American geo-political interests, in the National Defense Education Act of 1958.

What does it mean to write and read in such a world, and in a complex, changing, economically defined society such as ours? What do students need in order to be able to negotiate effectively the kinds of local acts of writing and reading that I described above? What does literacy mean to Abby as she enters this often frightening world? How can literacy help her make sense of and negotiate—and change—that world? More than anything else, those questions motivate this book. The longer I have taught writing and reading, and the more I have puzzled over how my students—middle and high school kids, college undergraduates, adult men in a prison classroom—write and read, the more I have come to believe that literacy is inescapably local. To ask how a student came to write an essay or how she or he came to understand a text in a particular way is to begin to uncover the stunningly complex and specific ways in which literacy functions in the lives of our students and in our lives as well. It is also to begin to reveal the ways in which the larger historical contexts about which Ohmann writes might play out in our students' specific acts of writing and reading. Yet this specificity of literacy too often seems lost in the discussions about literacy and pedagogy and theory and the discipline of English studies that now dominate professional journals and conferences. Proponents of "critical pedagogy" have taken up Freire's project of literacy for empowerment in ways that have helped us see that our conventional pedagogies for reading and writing can too often oppress and marginalize rather than liberate and empower. At the same time—for reasons too complex to examine here—such efforts to construct "enlightened pedagogies," in bell hooks's phrase, can turn into academic fashion and foster new dogmas that can totalize students as surely as does the dominant discourse. If the power of critical pedagogy and the usefulness of cultural studies are to be realized in the teaching of writing and reading, we cannot lose sight of those individual readers and writers—like Abby—who struggle, in the local contexts of specific acts of writing and reading, to enter the so-called dominant discourse, to confront a world that needs to be changed.

And so I will ask that question—"How do these texts come to be?"—of some of the variety of texts that I have encountered as a teacher and as a citizen and as a parent, texts that reflect individual efforts to make sense of the world through literacy and that represent acts of engaging in the discourses of that world. In each case, my hope in examining such texts in this way is to illuminate the local nature of literacy in the context of its inherently social functions.

LITERACY AND INDIVIDUAL POSSIBILITY
IN A CAPITALIST ECONOMY

At the end of my visit to Queensbury High School, Sue Marker, who was Abby's English teacher at the time, told me a little about Abby's life: a brief and all-too-familiar tale of strife at home, disaffection, conflict. Abby, Sue said, was struggling with a lot more than writing papers for her English class. Her older brother had had a variety of troubles that led to his dropping out of school, and Abby seemed headed in the same direction. Moreover, Abby was preparing to enter a local economy that seemed excluded from the much-heralded American economic recovery of the 1990s. Her prospects for participating in that recovery seemed limited. What, I wondered, did Abby's English papers mean to her in such a situation—in the midst of her personal struggles and her sense of herself as an adolescent in a society run by adults? What did writing in general mean to her? How did her struggles to negotiate the complexities of her life affect how and what she read and wrote—or even *whether* she read and wrote? Such questions highlight for me another insight that often seems lost in public and professional discussions about what students like Abby need in terms of literacy skills: that in profound ways Abby is different from her peers whom she nevertheless so obviously resembles. I have been referring to Abby as if she represents a specific generation of students facing a bewilderingly complex and changing world, and to a great extent she does. As an adolescent at a particular moment in time and in a particular place, Abby confronts the same discourses that somehow shape the lives of all students: cultural, social, economic, political discourses. But Abby also confronts those discourses—and reads and writes herself into them—*differently* from her peers. That is, she confronts those discourses from a specific position—as a young woman from a specific family situation in a specific time and place—and with a specific personal background that sets her apart from her peers even as it identifies her as like them. To acknowledge this uniqueness in the position from which Abby encounters the world is not simply to embrace a superficial notion of individualism and self-determination; rather, it is to glimpse the complex ways in which Abby's writing and reading relate to her identity and the experiences that have somehow shaped that identity. To account for how the complexity of that identity might figure into Abby's literacy is in large part the central challenge of this book. I am interested in exploring the intersections of Abby's "self" and the discourses she confronts—both in and outside school. In other words, how can we understand Abby's self as she writes and reads her way into these discourses?

To try to answer such a question inevitably leads, I think, to some of the sobering insights that Stuckey shares in her discussions of the "violence" of literacy. It can lead as well to an understanding of Abby's insistence that she is irrelevant—a sense of her powerlessness and her belief that writing won't change it. A young woman in an undergraduate tutoring class I taught at the State University of New York at Albany, who was a proficient writer and successful student and who very much believed in the power of writing, asserted during a class discussion about remedial students that what really counted in our culture was not writing ability but money. "Successful people can hire writers if they need them," she said. Her comment was a kind of straightforward acknowledgment of what Stuckey and many other critics have argued: that we cannot divorce our understanding of literacy and its teaching from an understanding of the economic and social structures within which we live and write and read in American society. Freire (1988) addressed this connection directly: "Merely teaching men to read and write does not work miracles; if there are not enough jobs for men to be able to work, teaching more men to read and write will not create them" (p. 401). And as social critic Andrew Feenberg (1991) reminds us, the role of work is central to the lives of citizens in this capitalist society and thus must be at the center of any efforts to change inequitable social, political, and economic circumstances: "[I]n an industrial society, where so many social and political choices are made by management, democratization of work is indispensible to a more participatory life" (p. 17). Perhaps more sobering still is the fact that, while it can be argued that teaching people to read and write is a crucial part of the effort to create a more equitable economic system, we have ample evidence that literacy does not guarantee either economic or political power. In his impressive historical work, *The Legacies of Literacy*, Harvey Graff (1987) traces the development of literacy, identifying trends among various segments of the U.S. population from the seventeenth century through the present. Graff concludes from his analysis that "the contribution of literacy to economic welfare is a major issue" (p. 346). He cites example after example of specific ethnic and regional groups as they made gains in literacy and school and shows that literacy itself did not guarantee economic or political power. For Black Americans in particular, Graff writes, "the contradiction between the promise of literacy and its reality was stark" (p. 363).

We may not need Graff's extensive study to conclude that there is no direct cause-and-effect relationship between literacy and economic or political power in American society. Abby seems to understand that from her own experience. Any teacher interested in helping students gain access to the kinds of power of literacy that I described earlier must acknowledge the limitations of that power and understand how literacy functions within our culture, often in ways that marginalize and disempower. At the same time, an examination of what writing and reading can mean in Abby's life also can lead to a sense of possibility, a means of confronting the economic realities that Graff documents and that Stuckey describes. And here is where I part with Stuckey, who leaves us almost with a sense of despair at the end of her book. Referring to the impasse at which her argument about the oppressive nature of literacy instruction has left her, she writes:

> We promote greater literacy, or we promote greater humanity. The first choice is easy. The second choice is not. Perhaps one of the consequences of humanity is literacy. Perhaps one of the consequences of literacy is its failure to end the violence of an unfair society. Perhaps the consequences of both are to return the responsibility for violence to its rightful owners. That is who we are. (p. 124)

Stuckey asserts depressingly that "literacy is a blind alley" (p. 125), although she does conclude with a sense of the possibility of change as "incremental, local, one person at a time" (p. 126). Such change, she suggests, can lead to reforming the system that she sees as perpetuating the violence she describes; such change is, she writes, a necessity. But while I share Stuckey's outrage and remain sympathetic to her sense of the need for local as well as systemic change, I want to resist her sense of despair and her suggestion that teachers who simply teach within the system inevitably do violence. I also want to resist her separation between literacy and humanity, a problematic dichotomy that Freire attacks in his efforts to articulate a more critical literacy and a more empowering pedagogy. Freire (1970/1984; Freire & Macedo, 1987) has argued compellingly that to be fully literate—critically literate—is to take control of one's world and how it is constructed through language; it is, in a sense, to destroy the false dichotomy between the world and "the word." For Freire, the world is not static but is constantly in the process of being made through the word. Thus, to be critically literate is to control one's world; to be critically literate *is* to become fully human. His pedagogy targets the very kind of oppressed people for whom Stuckey is concerned, and is intended to help them in their "incessant struggle to regain their humanity" (1970/1984, p. 33). It may be impossible to avoid the dilemma Stuckey defines in her book, but Freire helps us see that it is also misleading to suggest that individual teachers of literacy working within the system cannot help individual student writers and readers claim agency for themselves through literacy and thus gain a measure of the power needed to effect the kind of change Stuckey calls for. Ultimately, literacy matters precisely because it is inextricably bound up in what it means to be fully human.

Adrienne Rich's statement that "we must write as if our lives depended upon it," quoted at the beginning of this chapter, grows out of her experiences as a feminist and political activist and as a writer whose work resists the kinds of oppression that concern Stuckey. Rich made that statement in 1992 at an awards dinner at Purdue University honoring the work of student writers at that university. I remember the uneasiness that her remarks caused some of the students' parents, who had come to celebrate the recognition their daughters and sons were receiving as authors. Writing to resist oppression, to claim political agency, which is what she emphasized in her talk, did not seem to be the writing that was supposed to be celebrated that evening. Yet I thought about the many students who were not honored that night as authors, students for whom writing was every bit as vital since it is part of their interaction with the world. Students like Abby. For Rich, it isn't enough to write for oneself; writing is about how that self interacts with—and improves—the world. I'm interested in understanding what such a stance might mean for Abby and other students who don't see the possibilities for agency that Rich finds in writing. Rich won't let Abby off the hook by allowing her to deny her own responsibility for taking action in her life—and perhaps working to change that which limits or excludes or even oppresses her. Part of what struck me so deeply about Abby was that she really wasn't apathetic at all, and despite her protestations to the contrary, she didn't want to give up. She desperately wants to be relevant. But she cannot see how literacy can make her relevant.

This book, then, is finally about my sense of how literacy *can* help Abby become relevant in the ways she so desperately wants—and needs. It is about a vision of literacy that sees Abby as at once social and individual, at the center of discourse and yet created by discourse. It is about the ways in which literacy reflects contradictions and complexities in how we understand the world through language—and in how we understand ourselves and construct roles for ourselves through language in that world. It is about the ambiguity of literacy. And it is about how we, as literacy educators, might use such an understanding to create classrooms in which students can acquire a literacy that enables them to claim agency and to write as if their lives did indeed depend upon it.

In the following chapters, I will introduce some of the other students I've met whose struggles and encounters with literacy represent, for me, both the limitations as well as the possibilities of literacy. Many of those students believe fervently in the power of writing; others, like Abby, are less certain. But at some level all of them engage in local acts of writing and reading that reveal the daunting complexity of literacy and represent the means for entering the discourses that inevitably shape their lives. My hope is that their stories and my attempts to make sense of their acts of writing and reading will deepen our understanding of what's involved in helping students overcome the limitations of literacy and gain access to the possibilities that I believe literacy represents.

Chapter 2

Literacy in Our Lives

Contradiction and Possibility

Everything resolves itself in contradiction
—*Soren Kierkegaard,* Concluding Unscientific Postscript

And that same sun that warms your heart will suck the good earth dry.
—*Indigo Girls,* Shaming of the Sun

It is a bright July afternoon, the kind of day we luxuriated in: slow, sunny, lazy. A sluggish, sweaty baseball game on a rocky lot at the edge of the neighborhood. Bottles of almost-warm Coke in the meager shade of the low sumac trees that bordered the lot. A good trade for a Hank Aaron baseball card. A half-hearted argument about who was the best player in the local little league. A bit of coal, a relic from the area's past, tossed absentmindedly over an adjacent dirt embankment. In the background, the monotonous drone of unseen lawnmowers from the next block pushed along by fathers just arrived home from work. A mother's distant call for dinner.

I enjoyed many of those days as a child and then an adolescent growing up in a northeastern Pennsylvania neighborhood that was not entirely blue collar, not quite professional, outwardly middle class. I did what boys were expected to do: play ball, hang out, be mischievious from time to time; I learned how to handle guns and how to hunt; I played war; I collected cards; I complained about dressing up for church. As often as not, though, I spent those summer afternoons reading on my bed, window open wide, a slight muggy breeze rustling the curtains. I read a lot, and a lot of it was typical fare for a boy in such a neighborhood: war stories, adventure stories, hunting and sports magazines. Later, as I entered the Jesuit school where I spent my high school years, I gave up those adventure stories for "Literature": Shakespeare, the Romantic poets, Jane Austen, Hawthorne, and Melville—a familiar canonical list that opened up for me worlds beyond the issues of *TV Guide* and the local newspaper that lay here and there in my home. And as I explored these new worlds, I spent more afternoons with books in my bedroom; and those afternoons sometimes stretched into nights as I pushed further into stories and novels and histories.

My father pushes open the door and sticks his head into the bedroom. I heard him climb the few steps from the living room to the landing outside the door of the room I shared with my brother.

"Whatta ya doing?"

"Reading."

"Why the heck don't you go outside and play some ball? It's beautiful out there today. Go find your brother and get a ballgame or something."

He leaves the door ajar as he goes out again before I answer. I want to finish the chapter I'm reading in Tolkien's *Lord of the Rings* trilogy. I'm thoroughly engaged in the book, a grand story of conflict between good and evil that appeals both to my boyish obsession with adventure and to my developing sense of the literary. It seems worlds away from my day-to-day existence. It is pleasure and escape. But now my stomach tightens as I consider whether to continue reading—which will earn my father's disapproval—or go outside to try to get involved in a ballgame that I don't feel like playing at the moment.

Outside, my brother is throwing a hard rubber ball against a low cinder block wall that rises from one side of our driveway. One of the neighborhood boys tracks down the ball as it angles onto the surface of the driveway and then caroms off the wall toward the grass on the opposite side of the driveway. They are playing one of the many forms of baseball we invented. My brother spent hours playing that game, but he wasn't especially good at it. He preferred playing real baseball, at which he excelled. He was an outstanding athlete, a three-sport letterman in high school who earned numerous local and state honors for his feats on the baseball diamond, the basketball court, and especially the football field. Those feats also earned him a full scholarship to play football in college. But it wasn't an easy road for him. Along with the many hard hours of practice and weight-training, he had to get through school—something that was not nearly as appealing to him as playing sports. My parents, especially my father, were deeply proud of his athletic accomplishments, but report card day was rarely a very pleasant one for him. He never failed a class, and he always earned sufficient Cs and Bs. But he didn't often bring home As, and there were enough Ds to generate the requisite notices from his teachers and to worry my parents. Report card day seemed always to include the inevitable lecture about "applying yourself" in school, doing your homework, reading more.

I never received those lectures. My grades were always good, although my performances on the football field and the baseball diamond weren't. We were almost alter egos, my brother and I: he, the accomplished athlete with little serious interest in school and almost none in books; I, the diligent student with a love of books and something less than mediocre athletic ability. On report card day, I received proud smiles from my parents. They had little direct interest in my academic work itself, I knew, and as I progressed through high school and delved more seriously into philosophy, theology, and literature, I felt further and further removed from them on those days when my grades came home. Yet they were happy about my grades and proud of me for having earned them, despite the sense, not always hidden from me, that I was too bookish, that I spent too many sunny hours reading in my room. In their eyes—and mine—I was positioning myself for college even as my brother was, although we were taking very different routes to get there.

I don't remember seeing any contradictions in these experiences at the time. But I remember—vividly—moments that now reveal the often conflicting messages I was receiving about being a boy, about school, about work, and especially about literacy. I remember the sting of my father's criticism after a lackluster performance at football practice when I was 13. I could never be quite good enough on the football field, and my father's disappointment, despite his well-intentioned attempts to support my efforts, was often obvious. Years later, however, he spoke with unmistakable pride in describing how I had worked so hard to earn the starting quarterback spot on that eighth-grade team, despite my obvious limitations as a player. Hard work and commitment. It was a kind of Vince Lombardi, blue-collar, Puritan work ethic. It applied to football, and it applied to school. Sometimes. I remember the even more obvious pride with which my father spoke of my brother's accolades: the "Athlete of the Week" awards in the local newspaper, the all-state honors, the phone calls from college coaches. But there was always criticism of the lack of effort in school, anger at the phone calls from teachers. Sometimes there was a not-so-subtle suggestion that, with regard to school at least, my brother should be more like *his* brother.

I never heard my father tell my brother to "go read a book" on those lazy summer afternoons. But once or twice, when he was angry, he called me a bookworm. It was a name that implied both a bit of pride and a subtle shame. It was a name that fit me well, and it stung deeply.

MIXED MESSAGES: LITERACY AND CULTURAL CONTEXT

In his autobiography, *Hunger of Memory*, Richard Rodriguez (1983) writes movingly of the increasing distance he felt from his Spanish-speaking family as he achieved academic honors in the Catholic schools he attended, where English was the language of success. For Rodriguez, there was a paradox in his parents' unwavering insistence on diligence in school: The academic success they valued was accompanied by a loss of familial intimacy; the more successful their son became in an English-speaking academic world, the less he was their son. Other academics, notably bell hooks, have written of this distance. hooks (1989) describes the way in which her parents "have always felt wary, ambivalent, mis-trusting of my intellectual aspirations even as they have been caring and supportive"; she describes her "longing to remain close to the fam-ily and community that provided the groundwork for much of my thinking, writing, and being" (p. 75).

I have experienced that longing. And I understand the paradox Rodriguez writes of: My parents' deep commitment to my academic success helped create, in complicated ways, a distance between them and me. Even as they praised my grades in high school, I was explor-ing ideas and literatures that they had no direct access to—or interest in. My reading and writing took me to places that sometimes seemed impressive to them: the worlds of Shakespeare and Virgil, for instance. They were also places that were unfamiliar, sometimes uninteresting, even intimidating to my parents. I remember sitting in my senior AP English class in high school, enthralled by a lively discussion of Thoreau, a writer whose ideas about self-determination and nature drew me, and wondering what my parents would think if they could hear that dis-cussion. Even then I understood that they would have felt like outsiders if they had been in that classroom. And the insider status I felt I was acquiring was heady, perhaps in part because it was a way for me to gain some independence from them, to define myself—through writ-ten language—in a way that I was never defined at home. My bookish-ness, which seemed to compromise me at times in my home and com-munity, earned me respect and opened doors for me in school. My parents knew nothing of the conversations I had with friends about the poetry we were writing and the books we were reading, and they might even have frowned upon such activities, although I doubt they would have actively opposed them. And indeed they never flinched when the headmaster of the high school suggested to them that they might consider getting a subscription to a magazine like *Time* or *Newsweek* or even the *New Yorker*. They purchased that subscription to *Time* because, like the headmaster, they believed that reading such a magazine would help prepare me for college. But by the time I entered college, our worlds seemed very different indeed. The literacy that they saw as a vehicle for my academic success seemed to be carrying me further from the home we shared.

It would be too simple to explain this distance as the result of having gained academic success, of having acquired an academic literacy that differed in significant ways from the literacy of my home and community. Rodriguez's (1983) account of his becoming a "scholarship boy" suggests that acquiring such literacy requires a loss of cultural identity, or at least of cultural intimacy, and a loosening of connection to one's home community, and other scholars have illuminated ways in which academic success can indeed entail personal loss (Tokarczyk & Fay, 1993; Zebroski, 1990). But my entrance into the academic world, largely through my growing competence with the kind of literacy valued in school, was, like Rodriguez's, a complicated process shaped as much by my gender, my ethnic background, and my status as a member of a blue-collar yet middle-class community as it was by the specific circumstances of my family life and my own desire to separate myself in some deep way from those circumstances. It was shaped, too, by larger discourses: of education, of capitalism, of work and material success, and of gender and class and American individualism. Like many contemporary scholars, Maureen Hourigan (1994) emphasizes these "roles that class, gender, and culture play in students' abilities to negotiate the conventions of academic discourse" (p. xv) and reminds us that "conflict as well as cooperation is an effect (and quite often a 'teeth-gritting' effect) of literacy activities" (p. 22). For me, there was initially more excitement than struggle in negotiating those conventions, but one effect of my entering the discourses of academe so enthusiastically was not just greater distance between my family and myself but increasing conflict between their ways of seeing the world and the ways of seeing I was being exposed to in academe. What I did not appreciate then was that developing competence in academic literacy and gaining access to discourses that were unfamiliar to my family began to reshape the ideologies I had brought from my community. For Rodriguez this process was complicated by the fact that Spanish was the language spoken in his home, while hooks (1989) discusses the role of race and class in this kind of academic "home-leaving." But although I was White and spoke English as a first language and lived an ostensibly middle-class existence, academic literacy represented a foreign world for my family just as surely as it did for Rodriguez and hooks.

As I think back on this personal literacy history, I am struck by how little we seemed to recognize the role of literacy in these conflicts and contradictions. Literacy was almost always referred to as important, as a "good," as essential for future success (which generally meant economic success). And yet the messages I received regarding literacy (especially school-sponsored literacy) and educational success in general were decidedly mixed. I was at once praised for earning good grades and criticized for being a bookworm. I was pushed to do well in school, but my brother's average academic record, although outwardly criticized, was implicitly tolerated as primarily a necessity for his football scholarship; his lack of interest in reading was accepted with a kind of boys-will-be-boys attitude at the same time that he was castigated for not doing his schoolwork. Publishing a poem in a literary magazine was a genuine accomplishment, even as writing and reading poetry were seen as somehow less than masculine. Earning high honors for a grading period in high school inevitably brought praise for me, yet as I grew older, I sometimes was charged by my elders, during tense family arguments about issues such as unionization or civil rights, with having only book learning. Everyone knew that although grades were important, you still needed common sense. And we all knew many sensible people who never went to college but made a lot of money and had comfortable lives.

Gender roles complicated these mixed messages about literacy and schooling even further. My three sisters, for instance, although always encouraged to do well in school, were never pushed in the same way that my brother and I were. When my sister Mary decided to drop out of college during her first semester to be with her fiancee, my parents were deeply upset. Eventually, however, she married into a comfortable situation in which her husband's successful business allowed her to remain at home as a full-time homemaker and mother. Everyone was pleased for her, and her situation seemed satisfactory. Only rarely was there any sense of regret that she did not pursue a career or engage in academic study or earn a degree (that is, until many years later when she was left—divorced, with two daughters, and without an income or a degree—to find a job). She seemed to fulfill expectations for a young woman in that community admirably. Her penchant for romance novels—a characteristic she did not share with my other two sisters—was seen as normal as well. Another of my sisters attended college and

lived the life of a successful "working girl" for a number of years before returning to our hometown when she was in her early 30s to settle
into a marriage. And my youngest sister also dropped out of college
after a few semesters, eventually marrying and raising three children.
All these women achieved success in school, earning good grades and
appropriate praise for their efforts, writing and reading appropriate
texts, but none fell short of expectations by deciding not to pursue
further academic study; none was castigated for not reading enough
or for being a bookworm.

For my sisters, and for most of the women I knew in my hometown,
these attitudes about women's roles in school never evolved into the
kind of loss that Rodriguez describes, nor did they create the difficulties
experienced by working-class women in the academy whom Michelle
Tokarczyk and Elizabeth Fay (1993) describe as feeling torn, women who
"wanted to maintain their ties to their families, but wanted to fit into
the academy as well" (p. 3). My sisters and the other women I knew as
I was growing up never confronted these "institutional prejudices against
women" (p. 7) that Tokarczyk and Fay describe, since they never left our
home community to enter the academic world as I did—nor were they
expected to; nevertheless, the sometimes intense scholarly debates in
the past 2 decades about "women's ways of writing" (Cooper, 1991; see
also Ashton-Jones & Thomas, 1990; Cooper, 1989; Flynn, 1988, 1991)
suggest not only that gender can be "another marginalizing aspect of
literacy" (Hourigan, 1994, p. 53), but also that literacy relates to gender
and social class in complex and often contradictory ways that are not
always obvious or well understood. To say that literacy practices, especially as they related to schooling, marginalized my sisters as a result of
their gender is to oversimplify matters.

Margaret Finders (1997), in her illuminating study of literacy
among adolescent girls in an Iowa town, describes how the complex
interconnections among gender, adolescence, social class, schooling,
and broader cultural attitudes related to education and gender influenced the literate behaviors of the seventh-grade girls she studied. Finders shows convincingly that literacy practices relate to gender, but to
understand that relationship requires sorting through a bewildering
array of other factors. In this case, the girls she studied were able to
engage in various literate practices—some sanctioned by the school,
others not—in order to pursue varied and sometimes conflicting social and personal agendas. To explain their uses of literacy by pointing
out that the sanctioned literacies of school may have marginalized these
girls in various ways because of their gender does not enable us to account adequately for the many ways that writing and reading figured
into their lives and enabled them to participate in social networks, in-

stitutional activities, and the broader discourses of school and adolescence, or to construct social identities for themselves. Nor does it illuminate the paradox that while certain literacy practices may have indeed marginalized these girls, literacy also empowered them and enabled them to accomplish personally and socially important goals. Indeed, if I received mixed messages about literacy as a young boy in a middle-class town, the girls Finders describes were sending other kinds of mixed messages about the uses and importance of literacy in their lives as adolescent girls. For those girls, literacy was a way to demarcate and declare social identities as they related to socioeconomic and institutional status as well as to peer groups. What and how they read and wrote—and the meanings of these literate activities to them—were a function of their social identities, which were always "female" yet never the same; how literacy helped determine those identities was a function of much more than their gender. Similarly, my sisters' uses of literacy grew out of their own social identities and the many factors that helped shape those identities as girls in a blue-collar yet middle-class community and within a formal parochial educational system. The interesting paradox I see as I look back on their adolescence through the lens of my own gendered memory and family identity is that although their uses of literacy may have empowered them in certain ways within their social networks and their classrooms, it also may have been a mechanism by which they were limited outside those networks and those classrooms. If my sister's reading of romance novels was a way for her to declare a social identity among her peers, as Finders' study would suggest, it was also a literacy practice that reinforced limiting social roles for her as a woman in her community—and perhaps to an extent in the broader culture as well.

Beyond gender and social class, the mixed messages I received about literacy were also, for me as I think they were for Rodriguez (1983), related to an immigrant legacy: the desire of my great grandparents, who arrived in this country from Poland in the late nineteenth century, and of their children and grandchildren to earn a place in American culture. Like Rodriguez's parents, who demanded that their children do well in school in order to succeed in American society, my parents inherited a belief from their parents and grandparents that success in education was a way to shed the status of immigrant and find a legitimate place in American culture. But this was a belief tempered by skepticism toward formal schooling and intellectual life, a skepticism complicated by widespread notions of "common sense" and wariness about too much book learning. (It is worth noting that such skepticism was intensified by the treatment many immigrants received in the context of formal schooling.) For Rodriguez, the high value placed on success in school by his parents was seen as a way to gain acceptance in American culture. Yet that acceptance—and that assimilation—meant a loss not only of immigrant status but of cultural identity as well. Or at least partly so. hooks (1989) resists the notion that assimilation is the only option for those from marginalized backgrounds. Although she speaks primarily about African Americans entering academe, her point seems germane to Rodriguez's experience as well: "The most powerful resource any of us can have as we study and teach in university settings is full understanding and appreciation of the richness, beauty, and primacy of our familial and community backgrounds" (p. 83). Even if it is possible to resist assimilation in the way hooks suggests, her point highlights the contradictory ways in which literacy relates to ethnic, racial, and gender identity.

And if gender, race, class, and ethnic background complicate our understanding and uses of literacy, these factors manifest themselves in unpredictably local ways. I have already described the differences in the ways in which writing and reading functioned in my life and my brother's life, even though we are both male and were both raised in the same community and in the same household. We were subjected to the same discourses—of education, of gender roles, of sports, of work, of economic possibility. Somehow, the ideologies inherent in those discourses seemed to play out very differently for each of us as literate people, and we entered those discourses differently. Ultimately, we engaged in different but sometimes overlapping professional discourses: I became a high school English teacher and, later, a college professor, whereas my brother became a high school coach and guidance counselor. But more to the point, we now each engage the discourses to which we are both subjected—the broader discourses of education and the social and political and cultural life of contemporary American society—in very different ways as readers and writers. Again, these differences cannot be explained adequately by reference to broad categories such as race, gender, class, and ethnicity. Nor can they be explained by examining our "family literacy" or our schooling. Literacy is, happily and maddeningly, more complex than that.

THE MISLEADING "SIMPLICITY" OF LITERACY

Perhaps the most stunning contradiction regarding literacy is that, although we have all to some extent experienced the kinds of complexities that I have been describing, literacy seems to be commonly understood in our culture in remarkably simple terms; that is, literacy often seems to be understood in ways that reflect none of the complexities and contradictions I have been describing. Despite so much scholarship to the contrary and many compelling personal accounts, there remains a seemingly indestructible belief, so commonly expressed in our public discussions about school reform and literacy crises, that literacy is a relatively straightforward matter of learning a set of rules by which to communicate through written language. As many scholars have pointed out, reading and writing are generally thought of as straightforward acts of communication, as basic skills to be learned and mastered, as universally "good" abilities. Our popular discourse about literacy, and especially our political discussions about education reform, generally focus on the need to foster these basic skills and rarely address the bewildering complexity of literacy. Moreover, all too often public discussions and press reports uncritically emphasize the urgency to "improve" literacy rates. The "literacy crisis," as reflected in standardized test scores thought to be too low, is represented as threatening the very heart of American culture and its political and economic systems. The now famous *Newsweek* article, "Why Johnny Can't Read," published in 1975, and the strenuous public reaction to it reflected this sense of crisis then, and that same sense runs through current debates about literacy and education. In his widely cited book, *Illiterate America*, Jonathan Kozol (1985) refers to another famous document in the recent history of literacy and literacy education in this country: "On April 26, 1983, pointing to the literacy crisis and to a collapse in standards at the secondary and the college levels, the National Commission on Excellence in Education warned: 'Our Nation is at risk'" (p. 6). Kozol's use of the term *the literacy crisis* is telling here; what is perhaps more telling is that in the public outcry that resulted from his book's publication, few critics or reviewers or columnists questioned the existence of such a crisis. It was taken as a given. More than a decade later, as Congress and President Bill Clinton helped push through the adoption of national education standards, including standards for literacy instruction, that sense of crisis remains. As I write this, the press in New York State is reporting on proposed new tougher standards for graduation from high schools in the state for 2001, invoking the same familiar language of crisis. Meanwhile, recent publications from the National Council of Teachers of English continue to play up that organization's role in the development of national standards for literacy education, again invoking the idea that literacy skills are at the heart of learning and are a primary means to individual empowerment. Clearly, our national and cultural belief in the importance of literacy—along with our worry about maintaining high standards of literacy—is deep.

Yet our collective understanding of literacy, which borders on the simplistic, can play out in what I find to be disturbing ways among even the most well-intentioned and well-trained educators. A recent experience illustrates my point. In 1995 I was invited to be part of a committee on the English language arts in a large suburban school district in upstate New York. The committee's charge was to identify and articulate specific standards for English instruction that would be consistent with the district's broader stated goals for its students. The committee also was charged with articulating these English language arts standards in a way that would enable teachers to construct curriculum based on those standards. The committee was composed of elementary, middle, and high school teachers from throughout the district; a few parent representatives; a few administrators and curriculum specialists; and me, the representative from higher education. In general, it was a rather encouraging exercise in which these teachers and parents and administrators worked together to try to specify just what their students should be able to do, in terms of literacy, by the time they completed their education in that school district. Yet the statements that began to emerge from our discussions resembled the rather vacuous platitudes that too often characterize professional discussions of literacy and mirrored, in my view, a disturbingly narrow and archaic view of what literacy is and what students should be taught in English classes. At one point during the process, which took place over the course of a school year, we were attempting to articulate specific characteristics of students under the heading of "effective communicators," which was one of the broad "graduation expectations" in the district's standards document. ("Students will be effective communicators," was the standard we were addressing; it's a good example of what I mean by the kind of vague platitudes that frequently emerge in such discussions.) The emerging list for this standard included similar vague statements about what students will be able to do, in terms of language skills, upon graduation from high school: They will "demonstrate an understanding of how language is used in a variety of contexts and situations," "employ language skills for literary response and expression," "apply knowledge of language conventions (spelling, punctuation, etc.) to convey ideas," and so on. Admittedly, it is no easy task to articulate such standards, and the statements the committee came up with were, for the most part, hard to argue with; moreover, given how these standards were to be used by teachers, it was important that they remain somewhat general to allow for flexibility in their implementation. But I was concerned that these statements were little more than superficial applications of standard educational jargon and that they amounted to vague descriptions of what these very earnest teachers already believed they were doing in their English classes. Most of them seemed convinced that in the course of completing traditional writing assignments (such as narrative writing or book reports), reading assignments (such as multicultural texts by writers like Chinua Achebe), and grammar exercises, those students were learning "how language is used in a variety of contexts and situations." In some general way, that may have been true. But my own sense was that what their students were really learning was how to do traditional school literacy activities in ways that were not very different from what Janet Emig described in her now-famous book, *The Composing Processes of Twelfth Graders* (1971), as "school-sponsored" writing (p. 3). At one meeting I voiced this concern and suggested that we include a statement to the effect that students should gain an understanding of how language, especially written language, *functions* in different rhetorical, cultural, and social contexts. My point was to highlight the idea that school-based writing and reading represent a particular kind of literacy that can differ in significant ways from the kinds of writing and reading students are likely to confront outside school in places like businesses, the courts, and so on; moreover, I was committed to the idea that these standards should encourage teachers to help students begin to gain a sense of the complexity of literacy, of its relation to specific contexts of use. The ensuing discussion—argument, really—revealed to me that literacy for most of the committee members meant school-sponsored writing and reading, which they saw largely as a straightforward matter of learning rule-governed ways of conveying meaning through text. And indeed, we. never actually discussed such thorny matters as "meaning" or "context"; rather, we referred to "varied" in-class writing activities such as business letters and to reading "diverse" texts. Literacy was easily reduced to conventional classroom tasks.

There are many ways to make sense of this incident. To be useful, any explanation would have to account for the complex political and institutional workings of such a committee in a public school district. It's also important to point out that including a single phrase such as "how language functions" in a formal bureaucratic document about language arts standards wouldn't likely have made any noticeable difference in what students and teachers actually did in their English classes in that school district. But I was struck at the time by the implicit conceptions of writing and reading that emerged from those discussions. The teachers in that group, all committed educators with long experience and rather sophisticated knowledge of the English language, seemed to share a strong functionalist belief in literacy as a set of skills, a belief influenced by what Knoblauch and Brannon (1993) call a "personal growth model" of literacy that places a premium on reading and writing as "self-actualization" activities (p. 21). Despite their many years of experience in teaching English and their considerable knowledge of language and literature, even these sophisticated educators seemed to adhere to a limited understanding of literacy. For them, language might be complex and even mysterious and beautiful, but ultimately written language is in their eyes a straightforward matter of communication governed by identifiable and rigid rules. To learn these rules is to learn "how language works"; to write correctly is to be able to write in any situation. For me, what was most dismaying about these discussions was that these educators seemed to share the same limited understanding of literacy that too often emerges in public discussions of literacy and education reform; indeed, I would argue that this kind of limited—and limiting—notion of literacy *characterizes* such discussions.

As many scholars have pointed out, these notions about literacy—and the attitudes and beliefs that govern literacy education—have long and complicated histories that relate to social, cultural, economic, demographic, and political developments as well as to educational trends and institutional pressures. Harvey Graff (1987), for example, has traced some of the ways in which literacy practices—and, not incidentally, literacy rates—can be associated with specific religious movements, such as Protestantism, at specific historical moments; he and Robert Arnove (1987) also have demonstrated that campaigns to improve literacy usually relate to "major transformations in social structure and belief systems" (p. 4) at particular points in time. Richard Ohmann (1976, 1985), among others, has linked conceptions and uses of literacy to the rise of corporate capitalism in the United States. Clearly, even simplistic notions about literacy have complicated histories. It is not my purpose here to trace these histories. But it is important to recognize, first, that literacy is so much more complex than it is often thought of in forums like the committee I have described above, where decisions about how children will be taught to read and write are made; and second, that beliefs about literacy will shape those decisions—whether those beliefs are simplistic or not.

LITERACY AND INDIVIDUALITY

With the backdrop of the experiences with literacy that I have described in this chapter—which are neither representative nor entirely unusual—I want to examine what I think is a key contradiction in how literacy seems to be understood in the ongoing debates about the "literacy crisis" and about education reform. At the outset, I want to reiterate what many scholars have already shown us about these debates: that they are new versions of old arguments about literacy and education. Our contemporary debates have their roots to some extent in the work of the now-famous Committee of Ten, a group of respected educators formed by the National Education Association in 1892 to recommend curriculum reforms for American schools in response to pressures on colleges associated with immigration and the rise of public education in the late nineteenth century—a story beyond the scope of this book. What is relevant for us here, though, is that the report of the Committee of Ten and the subsequent professional and public discussions about its recommendations set many of the terms of the debate about school reform and literacy education that we are engaged in today. As R. Baird Shuman (1990) has pointed out, the English curriculum, as recommended in that report, "aimed at preparing the university students who would pursue studies roughly equivalent today to the liberal arts curriculum" (p. 38). Such a curriculum rests on a set of assumptions about what constitutes desirable reading and writing skills—a set of assumptions that remains more or less intact among many contemporary educators, such as my colleagues on the language arts committee, and thus informs the way they think and talk about the academic study of English. And these assumptions, I would argue, relate to broader cultural beliefs about literacy and individuality. Here, then, is the key point I wish to emphasize in the following section: that our inability to address adequately the literacy needs of students is a function of a fundamental contradiction in prevailing conceptions of literacy that grows out of deeply held American beliefs about individuality and self-determination. In short, it is this: Although our culture still espouses a Romantic notion of the inspired Writer as a kind of iconic American individual, it also structures its literacy instruction—and indeed its formal educational system in general—around a limited conception of the individual student as a collection of individual abilities and potential. To state it somewhat more baldly, we valorize the Writer as a paragon of individual achievement, while we tend to denigrate the student writer as a flawed individual. I may be overstating matters a bit here, but I want to highlight this contradiction between *Writer* and *student writer*, because I believe it represents a significant obstacle in our often well-intentioned and intensive efforts to reform literacy education.

First, consider the conflicted idea of the Writer. In American culture, the idea of the Writer is deeply imbued with Romantic beliefs about individuality and truth. The Writer is a special, inspired individual who functions as a kind of conduit for personal and universal truth. Writing thus becomes an expression of this truth, something almost mystical. In his famous essay, "Tradition and the Individual Talent," originally published in 1919, T. S. Eliot (1985) described the special relationship of the writer, and specifically the poet, to literary tradition, arguing that

> the poet has, not a "personality" to express, but a particular medium, which is only a medium and not a personality, in which impressions and experiences combine in peculiar and unexpected ways. (p. 1206)

Eliot wanted to argue against "metaphysics and mysticism" in literary criticism and to "divert interest from the poet to the poetry" (p. 1208), but ironically he reinforced in his essay the exalted nature of the Writer, and the Romantic notion of poet as inspired mystic, that he sought to combat. Although Eliot cannot, of course, be seen as a spokesperson for contemporary visions of the poet or writer, I would argue that the strength of the Romantic conception of the Writer, against which he struggled, continues to drive popular conceptions of the Writer today and thus profoundly shapes current discussions of literacy in the public arena. Indeed, Writers continue to occupy in our culture the same sort of exalted status that worried Eliot. That status often is driven home for me whenever I hear a student or an acquaintance protest, "I am not a Writer." (My use of the capital "W" is intentional here.) In many cases, the speaker of this protest is an excellent student writer or an accomplished professional who routinely uses writing in his or her work and indeed whose success depends in large measure on his or her competence with written language. Nevertheless, the idea of Writer typically is equated not with competence in written language but with a special kind of inscrutable facility with words and an inspired access to ideas. This sense of the Writer is strong among educators as well. Nowhere is it more obvious than at the annual convention of the National Council of Teachers of English (NCTE), which has become in many respects a kind of celebration of professional (rather than student) writers. Each year the convention program boasts many special appearances by well-known Writers of both adult and children's literature, appearances that include book-signings, keynote addresses, and publishers' parties. I do not mean to criticize such practices as problematic (although I think there are grounds upon which one legitimately might do so), but I do want to point out the special hold that this idea of the Writer exerts on our cultural psyche—and on the imaginations of professional educators.[1]

At the same time, there is in our culture what David Bleich (1988) has described as a "deep monastic, monadic, and individualist urge to depersonalize and decontextualize language use" (p. 330). While the Writer enjoys special status as a kind of cultural icon, student writers are implicitly perceived (and sometimes explicitly defined) as collections of particular and often discreet writing skills—or lack thereof. Literacy thus becomes an "invariant set of skills to be learned" (Hourigan, 1994, p. 21) by all students in a formal educational system that is structured around standardization. These skills are catalogued and taught in ways that ignore or even deny context (a point I will pursue in Chapter 6), and the extent to which students have learned these skills is measured by standardized tests, almost all of which are inherently context-less.[2] The successful student writer, then, is one who has mastered these skills, which usually are defined as specific knowledge of rules and grammar and the ability to construct texts with specified formal features (such as coherence, focus, and organization). Implicit in this view of student writers and their writing is that each student is individually responsible for mastering the required generic skills. The student writer is thus understood as a kind of faceless individual who possesses (or does not possess) these required skills that are universally applicable rather than as a member of a language-using community or, perhaps more accurately, as a language user moving across the boundaries of various discourse communities. Even though in our professional discourse it is now taken as a given that all writing is context-bound and is inherently cultural and social, the focus of much literacy instruction and of standardized testing remains on the individual student writer, who must demonstrate discreet, specified writing and reading skills out of context—or, more accurately, within the context of school-based assessment. The infuriating paradox here is that students are assessed as *individual* writers, as individuals possessing certain "basic" literacy skills, yet those literacy skills are conceived and assessed in such a way as to allow for virtually no individuality or variance related to an individual student's experiences and background.

I want to emphasize that I am *not* arguing that all educators interested in or involved with literacy education consciously espouse the beliefs and assumptions about writers and writing that I have just described. Most committed teachers I know espouse beliefs about literacy that diverge widely from the narrow view I've described here. But I do wish to suggest that these beliefs about writing and individuality drive popular conceptions of literacy instruction and thus profoundly influence discussions of education reform. And I believe many well-intentioned educators remain unaware of the ways in which these cultural attitudes about writers and writing may undercut their own attempts to create effective pedagogies. I also want to assert that the *structure* of formal education in this country rests on this narrow view of writing and student writers. Jenny Cook-Gumperz (1986), an ethnographer of education whose ground-breaking studies of the language of schooling helped shed light on the social nature of literacy in formal education, emphasizes that formal literacy instruction is based on a descriptive view of literacy "as cognitive abilities which are promoted and assessed through schooling" (p. 14). According to Cook-Gumperz, "This . . . instrumental notion of literacy as a standardised set of basic cognitive skills is embedded in the selection and evaluation criteria that are central to schooling"; test results, she states, "form the principal basis of selection procedures in all modern bureaucracies. As a result of tests children's individual competencies are categorised" (p. 14). Cook-Gumperz goes on to show that this definition of literacy implicitly includes tacit knowledge about how to demonstrate these basic skills:

> The essential question for individuals is what they must do in order to demonstrate that they are "knowledgeable." . . . Schooling, therefore, as the teaching of literacy skills on which cognitive growth depends, is concerned not only with decoding skills for reading and encoding skills for writing, but also and perhaps more importantly with the uses of literacy in *communicating* knowledge. (p. 14, emphasis in original)

In the context of schooling, then, literacy is defined as a set of decoding and encoding skills and a means of demonstrating specified—and sanctioned—knowledge.

As Cook-Gumperz (1986) suggests, this view of literacy as a set of narrowly defined skills and ways of demonstrating them is built into the structure of schooling and thus unavoidably informs literacy instruction. Even teachers who openly oppose or resist such a narrow view of writing—and there are many—usually are faced with the challenge of preparing their students for standardized tests that grow out of—and reinforce—that view, for these tests are, as Cook-Gumperz points out, "the principal basis of selection" in schools. In addition, despite more progressive pedagogical methods such as portfolio assessment and collaborative learning that can work against this view and open up for students and teachers new ways of understanding writing as social and cultural, most teachers must still assign grades to *individual* students at the end of a course or a grading period, and their students by and large are still required to take large-scale statewide and national standardized assessments (such as the Regents exams in New York and the ISTEPs in Indiana). The very act of assessment, which rests on the idea of individual ability defined cognitively, reifies writing as the exclusive product of an individual possessing certain cognitive skills and formal knowledge.

The structure of formal education, centered as it is on narrowly defined skills and the standardized assessment of individual students, both grows out of and reinforces deeply held cultural beliefs regarding the nature of individual ability. Despite the civil rights movements of the 1960s and 1970s, which helped reveal inherent inequalities in American society and especially in American education, Americans for the most part seem to remain committed to long-held notions of individuality and self-reliance: You can do anything you want if you are given the opportunity and work hard enough. Formal education is the primary means by which individuals are given opportunities, and curricula seem structured in such a way as to enable those individuals to try to take advantage of those opportunities. In so many public discussions of education reform, the implicit goal seems to be to provide equal opportunity to all students; then it's up to the individual to make the most of that opportunity. These basic assumptions about individual responsibility are intimately tied to the ideology of capitalism, with its promise of economic opportunity for all who are willing to compete for it. This ideology is manifested in our culture through images of what C. H. Knoblauch (1991) has termed "The Good Life." According to Knoblauch, so pervasive is this vision of The Good Life among his students that "where The Good Life does not exist as social reality, it exists as an aspiration concretized through the manipulations of mass culture" (p. 14). Knoblauch describes his students as driven by this aspiration and committed to its underlying ideology of self-reliance. His students, mostly traditional college students in a mid-sized state university, he writes,

> believe that their prosperity is a function of natural merit matched with achievement, through hard work, in the competitive academic marketplace. . . . [They] accept the stories about freedom and self-actualization, fair play and altruism, progress and prosperity that their history books have composed to portray the American experience. (p. 13)

Knoblauch's characterization of his students' beliefs in individual ability and opportunity is echoed elsewhere in the professional literature (e.g., see Hourigan, 1994; Tinberg, 1991), and it rings true in my own experience. For me, one experience stands out as emblematic of the pervasive strength of my students' belief in individual opportunity and the promise of The Good Life.

In an advanced writing class I taught during a recent semester (in the same university where Knoblauch worked), a young woman named Hannah wrote a moving essay about a disturbing experience she had with her senior high school guidance counselor. In her essay, Hannah tells the story of how she worked as a waitress for a time after her high school graduation and eventually entered a local community college. After graduating from that community college, she enrolled in the university in the hope of earning a bachelor's degree. Hannah describes her high school years as "hardly perfect": "My parents had recently divorced, and my family had little money. I didn't have the time or the means to get involved in sports or any other extracurricular activities." As a result, she writes,

> I fit in with a group of kids who were viewed as undesirables. Most of my teachers didn't give me as much attention as they did other students who were more popular and well off. Still, I tried to get good grades because I wanted to go to college.

In her senior year, she met with her guidance counselor "to discuss my plans for the future. I was looking forward to it because I was excited about what the future might hold for me." Her counselor, however, had a different assessment of Hannah's prospects. She describes the scene, which I reproduce here in full to convey a sense of Hannah's understanding of her experience.

> I cheerfully had a seat in my counselor's office. My eyes glanced at all of the college catalogues and manuals as I waited for him to find my file.
> "Well, it won't be long now until graduation, Hannah."
> "Yep, I can't wait."
> "Have you given any thought to what you want to do?"
> "Well, I'm not sure but . . ."
> "Did you ever consider going to a vocational school? A career in horticulture may be just the thing for someone like you. I know you like to be creative," he interrupted.
> "What about college?" I questioned.
> He responded in a gentle manner with these words: "Given your circumstances, Hannah, college is probably not for you."
> I couldn't even speak. His words stung like a slap in the face. From that point on it seemed as if his words dissolved in

the air before they reached my ears. I left his office with a sheet of paper that neatly listed all of the programs the vocational school had to offer.

After the meeting I went to the girls' bathroom and cried. What did he mean college wasn't for me? Surely his assessment of me couldn't be based solely on my intelligence. My grades were average, and I had even made the honor roll a couple of times. I felt utterly confused. Then I started to think that maybe he was right. Maybe I didn't have what it took to succeed in college. All of my insecurities seemed to come alive that day. Suddenly, all of the excitement of planning for my future was completely destroyed, and my future seemed bleak.

What is striking to me about how Hannah represents her experience is the way she ultimately focuses exclusively on her own responsibility for her situation. In the opening paragraph of her essay she describes the powerful influence of what she calls "status" in her school: "Even the faculty seemed to put a great focus on status. It seemed as if among themselves they silently labeled and classified the students. It wasn't meant to be obvious, but there were subtle differences in the way students were treated." Initially, she seems to want to suggest that her status as a member of a group of "undesirables" played a role in her guidance counselor's assessment of her college prospects and that he judged her unfairly because of her association with this group. But eventually she shifts blame to herself, entertaining the possibility that the counselor was right and that perhaps she "didn't have what it takes to succeed in college." In doing so, she dismisses the social influences related to her status that seemed so important in the beginning of her essay. And indeed this shift to a focus on individual responsibility emerges more clearly in her essay's final two paragraphs:

After the incident in the guidance office, I didn't bring up the subject of college again. I graduated with a local diploma[3] and a lot of self doubt. I started working as a waitress, but after the first week I knew that there had to be something better out there for me. I eventually came to the conclusion that my guidance counselor didn't know everything. I realized I didn't have to respect his opinion of me just because he was an adult. With a lot of encouragement from my parents and friends, I looked into college on my own. I decided on a two-year community college, and I graduated with honors. I felt an indescribable amount of pride and a great sense of accomplishment.

I still work as a waitress, so I can afford to further my education. My goal is to become a teacher. Hopefully, when I do attain my goal, I will encourage my students to reach their fullest potential. I want to help them realize that feeling a sense of worth is far more important than anyone else's opinion of us. I hope to enable them to break through the rigid boundaries and limitations that are sometimes set upon us.

In these paragraphs, the guidance counselor's assessment of Hannah becomes an "opinion" about her individual abilities and prospects rather than a judgment relating to her "undesirable" social status. And her eventual graduation from a community college and entrance into a 4-year university are represented as the result of her own resolve and effort. As Hannah presents her experience here, the "rigid boundaries and limitations" that she confronts, as unfair as they might seem, can be overcome with hard work, determination, and self-reliance (and encouragement from family and friends).

When we discussed a draft of her essay in conference, Hannah and I talked about how her experience mirrored those of some of her classmates who had written about similar incidents. After reading her draft for the first time, I assumed Hannah was trying to explore in her essay the ways in which social status can shape—and limit—a student's opportunities in school. However, Hannah resisted that assumption. Ultimately, she insisted, it was her own effort that made the difference. Her mistake, she claimed, was in accepting the counselor's assessment of her prospects for college. Had she believed *in herself* at that time, she would have ignored the counselor's advice, as she eventually did, and applied to 4-year schools instead of the community college. In short, it was her own fault.

I don't want to push too far in drawing conclusions from my experiences with Hannah, nor do I wish to hold up her essay as representative of all students' attitudes about schooling and careers. But I think this experience underscores the depth of our cultural belief in individual opportunity and self-reliance. Her essay can serve as an example of how these beliefs can play out in a student's attempts to make sense of her experience through writing. What is perhaps more striking about this example, though, is how common it is: My students in two large state universities in the midwest, my students in a mid-sized state university in New England, and my students in a private New England high school generally shared Hannah's belief in individual opportunity and self-reliance. And as I'll demonstrate momentarily, so did my students in a medium-security prison.

A sad irony here is that Hannah never completed my writing course, dropping out of the course and out of school entirely with only 3 weeks left in the semester. Her economic circumstances and, I suspect, the strain of pursuing difficult academic studies while working as a waitress to support herself eventually forced her to leave school and abandon (at least for a time) her goal of earning a bachelor's degree. Her unshakeable faith in individual opportunity remains a source of hope for her: She *can* return to school if she wants to. Yet she still does not accept that her working-class status, which seems to have been an obstacle to her academic success in high school, continues to play some role in the educational opportunities that are available to her. But an even harsher irony for me lies in the idea that this same cultural belief in individual opportunity to which Hannah tenaciously adheres undergirds the educational system in which she has struggled and that has defined her (at least temporarily) as a failure. (The fact that I assigned grades to Hannah's work—no matter how progressive my methods of teaching and assessment might be—makes me a party to that systemic definition of failure. This kind of complicity by literacy educators is precisely what so worries Elspeth Stuckey, as I noted in Chapter 1.) Nevertheless, as her teacher I encouraged Hannah to work hard to try to write herself into the discourses of educational and economic success, even as I wanted to problematize those discourses. In doing so, despite my simultaneous efforts to complicate her sense of literacy and individuality, I reluctantly called upon those same beliefs in self and school that shape her sense of the world. In other words, I cannot entirely abandon these beliefs because they provide so strong a motivation for Hannah as she struggles to obtain that personal (although socially defined) success that she seeks (see Chapter 6).

A cultural belief in individual opportunity and self-reliance thus figures into our conceptions of literacy in complex ways. As I've already noted, school-based literacy instruction for the most part is structured around the idea of *individual* abilities and achievement. Such a structure seems commonsensical to students like Hannah, who harbor a deep belief in individual opportunity and self-reliance. Reading and writing are *individual* activities that reflect an *individual's* effort and ability. This view, as common as it is, represents an enormous obstacle to proponents of alternative perspectives that emphasize the social and cultural nature of writing and to class-related or race-related or gender-related analyses of differences in language use. I would argue that the widespread public condemnation of the Oakland, California, school board's decision to declare "ebonics" a separate language in the winter of 1997 was at least in part a function of the connection between our

popular conception of literacy and our culture's belief in individualism: to acknowledge ebonics as a separate language is to implicitly
question the idea that there is something that can be identified as standard English and that English speakers who speak and write a different version of English have failed in their individual efforts to learn
the "proper" language. Some critics of that decision characterized it as
another way to offer an excuse for students and schools who failed to
meet standards. And despite mountains of available evidence indicating that how individuals read and write is intimately connected to the
specific socioeconomic, cultural, ethnic, regional, and even religious
contexts within which those individuals learned to read and write (see
especially Heath, 1983; Street, 1984), the criticisms of the decisions to
recognize ebonics as a legitimate dialect were cast in terms of an understanding of literacy as a collection of portable skills possessed and dis-
played by individual students.

This understanding of literacy as individual ability relates as well
to our culture's long-standing belief in a "classless" society. Maureen
Hourigan (1994), in examining the complex relationships among race,
class, and gender, critiques Thomas Fox's *The Social Uses of Writing*
(1990), in which Fox describes his attempts to challenge students to
explore "how students' memberships in social groups influence their
language use in the classroom" and his efforts to employ "a pedagogy
that will work against [the] sense of exclusion that many working
class, black, and women students feel in education" (p. 90; quoted in
Hourigan, p. 44). Fox describes the difficulty he encountered in em-
ploying such a pedagogy, which Hourigan explains as Fox's failure to
account fully for social class in his pedagogy. She concludes that

> Fox's students resisted his pedagogy . . . because they did not want to
> acknowledge "the gross inequities between the upper class and them-
> selves." I suspect as well that Fox's students were trying to acquire the
> capital that would enable them to join the ranks at the top. For them,
> the best way to achieve this goal is to distinguish themselves as unique
> individuals. (p. 50)

In other words, Fox's students denied social class as a factor in their own
educational situations and embraced the ideology of individualism as a
way to maintain the myth of The Good Life, as Knoblauch (1991) defines it, and the belief that that life is a possibility for them. Literacy—
more specifically, school-sponsored literacy—thus becomes a means to
the goal of attaining that Good Life, a belief that I think Hannah held
firmly as well. Hourigan goes on to describe her own students' articula-

tion of their goals in a basic writing course at the University of Nevada at Las Vegas, which amount to acquiring "the skills needed to become successful in life" (p. 51). Like Knoblauch's students, Hourigan's are also driven by the desire for The Good Life, a desire that shapes their understanding of and participation in the literate activities of school. Clearly, Hourigan writes with a touch of dismay: "Our students marginalized by class ask a great deal of literacy" (p. 51). Indeed.

THE AMBIGUITY OF LITERACY

I walk across the prison yard as the evening sun begins to touch the tops of the trees that line the pasture beyond the high chain link and barbed-wire fences. The yard is a lively mass of blue-clad inmates talking in groups, milling about, playing basketball, lifting weights, smoking their after-dinner cigarettes. Dressed in a jacket and tie and carrying my briefcase, I rush past them and into a decrepit brick building on the far side of the yard, show my pass to the guard at the door, and descend two flights of stairs past huge barred windows to a dimly lit, dirty basement classroom. The room is crowded with the 26 inmates who have enrolled in the basic writing class I am teaching, which is part of a college-level equivalency program offered through a state university at prisons throughout Ohio. This makeshift classroom sits in a medium-security prison in the middle of the farm country of central Ohio, an area where African-American residents are as rare as hills that rise higher than a highway overpass. Yet of my 26 students, all but three are Black. They come to my prison classroom by way of convoluted yet common roads: poverty, drugs, violence, abandonment. They range in age from 18 to 55, and their offenses represent the spectrum of crimes described every day in the popular press: car theft, drug dealing, embezzlement, murder. Some are taking this class as part of a 2-year degree program that they hope they can use out in the world. Some are young and trying to get back on track. Others have been in the prison system for years and are just trying to find ways to make it meaningful. Many have completed GED programs while in prison; others were sent here soon after or while still finishing high school. But all of them share an abiding belief that this class represents an important step for them in their own lives. They all share a belief that literacy can improve their lives.

I am returning essays that they submitted the week before. Like students in my high school and university classes, they wait anxiously for their papers and turn quickly to the grade when I hand them back.

I always hate giving out grades, and today is no exception. But this time the grading was especially tricky for me. The writing of many of these men was far below the conventional standards of the high school and college courses I have taught. Some of it was almost unreadable, as basic and flawed in terms of the conventions of academic writing as any student writing I'd ever seen. In the 2 weeks before the deadline for the assignment, I had worked through drafts with each of the students to help them address some of the many serious writing problems that weakened those drafts. And they had worked diligently, assiduously, amid circumstances that made me ill with fear and anger. I could imagine no more distracting or difficult setting in which to try to write: hideously overcrowded bunkrooms housing three times more men than they were originally designed for; incessant noise; a complete absence of private space and time; woeful facilities that lacked even basic accoutrements much less adequate materials for writing and reading; a constant and insidious tension that grows out of the ever-present threat of physical violence. In such a setting these men had written their essays, revised them, and worked on improving them. And now I was being asked to evaluate that work, to say, "Here's how good—or bad— your writing is." These were men who had been told by their society that they were inadequate as citizens, that they had failed as individuals, and I was about to tell many of them that they were inadequate as writers, too. I shuffled papers uncomfortably on the desk at the front of the room while they read my comments.

In reading the essays those men submitted to me in that class, I could not divorce what they wrote from how they wrote it or from where they wrote it, because what they wrote was often about why they *couldn't* write—or read: stories of school failure, personal tragedy, dangerous yet sometimes inescapable decisions that they would regret for the rest of their lives, the horror of their incarceration. To read their work was to get a glimpse of the ways in which literacy is not about equality. It was to get a firsthand look at the implications of the kind of relationship Stuckey discusses between literacy instruction and economic inequities in our society. At the same time, a profound sense of possibility pervaded the writing of those men. They were trying hard to write their stories, to make their statements about the lives they'd led, in a way that would gain them access, they believed, to possibilities that had been denied them. In an end-of-semester self-evaluation, one of these men wrote that he now looked at writing in "a whole new light. . . . I know I am going to have to keep up the hard work, in order for me to succeed in college. I'm willing to do this also." Another wrote that my sister and brother-in-law in California have notice the change in my letters to the good. My sister and brother-inlaw wish, for me to tell you thank you from them, comming from them is a compliment being that he is a vice president of a computer company. And my sister is a medical doctor.

Others expressed similar gratitude and hopes for success in their next English class and beyond. These men were, in Adrienne Rich's words, writing as if their lives depended upon it.

In his autobiography, Malcolm X (1964/1992) tells the now-famous story of how he taught himself to read and write while serving time in prison. In the chapter titled "Saved," Malcolm X describes the frustration he felt in trying to communicate through letters with his mentor and teacher, Elijah Muhammad: "In the street, I had been the most articulate hustler out there—I had commanded attention when I said something. But now, trying to write simple English, I not only wasn't articulate, I wasn't even functional" (p. 197). He goes on to recount the methods by which he developed his writing abilities and learned to read works of history and philosophy. He concludes, "I knew right there in prison that reading had forever changed the course of my life. As I see it today, the ability to read awoke inside me some long dormant craving to be mentally alive" (p. 206). It also gave him access to "new vistas" on what it means to be Black, on what he describes as "the deafness, dumbness, and blindness that was afflicting the black race in America" (p. 206). In Malcolm X's story, literacy is about possibility and power, a means of writing a way into a society that had written him off and working toward changing that society. It is an entrance to worlds of knowledge that were closed off to him on the streets where he grew up and where he made his name as a hustler. And it is a means of constructing identity and claiming agency in a way that had been denied him.

For the men in the prison where I taught, literacy was all those things, too. But its limitations were also apparent. Writing was a way to tell their powerful and often disturbing stories, to claim a voice for themselves, to validate themselves, to gain status as students; it was a way for them to voice their concerns and ideas about the problems that had directly shaped their lives: drugs, injustice, racism, poverty. But their stories gave them only limited access to the very avenues of power that were partly responsible for their being there in the first place. Their lack of the kinds of literacy skills valued in that mainstream culture ultimately excluded them from participation in that culture except in marginal ways. How might they write themselves into a mainstream society whose structures seemed to work against them? How might they also write within and yet against that mainstream, as Malcolm X did, in order to attain the kind of political agency that theorists like Paulo Freire write about? Even as I struggled to teach some of these men about sentence boundaries, I worried that the lessons I offered them only reinforced the ways in which literacy continued to marginalize them. And despite the satisfaction I gained from helping them feel some measure of control over their use of written language, I sometimes was left with a feeling reminiscent of Stuckey's (1991) depressing question at the end of her book: "What to do? What to do?"

bell hooks's (1994) offers one way to address such questions. Invoking a line from Adrienne Rich's poem "The Burning of Paper Instead of Children," "This is the oppressor's language yet I need it to talk to you," hooks acknowledges that standard English, as the "oppressor's language," "has the potential to disempower those of us who are just learning to speak, who are just learning to claim language as a place where we make ourselves subject" (p. 167). But hooks also realizes "that this language would need to be possessed, taken, claimed as a space of resistance" by those already oppressed by that language (p. 168). The extreme circumstances experienced by the men in my prison class highlight this ambiguous nature of literacy and the complicated ways it can function in the lives of people as they try to make their ways in a complex, unequal, and often unjust society. I suspect that the messages those men received about literacy were as contradictory as the messages I received as a boy—perhaps more so. Their belief in the power of literacy, amid profoundly depressing circumstances that could be seen as giving the lie to that very belief, underscores the strength of that belief in our culture. It is ironic that those men clung so tightly to that belief, since literacy—or, more accurately, "mainstream" or "official" literacies, as defined by anthropologist James Collins (1993)—is implicated in the economic and political system that incarcerated them, the same system that many critics argue perpetuates the inequitable material conditions in which most of those men grew up and that limited their opportunities to avoid the lives that led them to prison.

In his study of the relationship between the problems in one college basic writing program and the broader public discourse about the crisis in American education, Collins (1993) refers to "a broad historical trend in American education to define literacy as a skill" and argues that "this skills definition is a displacement, an avoidance of the enduring social conflicts in which literacy—as symbolic practice—is unavoidably implicated" (p. 180). As Collins goes on to point out, there is by now a voluminous literature that documents the ways in which, "rather than a basic skill, literacy is an essential aspect of social order and disorder" (p. 180), and a review of the history of literacy and education starkly reveals the limitations of popular conceptions of literacy in helping us understanding this dynamic. Moreover, the history of literacy and education, especially in Western culture, underscores the complex relationships among local acts of reading and writing, such as those engaged in by the students in my prison class, and broader economic, cultural, political, and social forces. For educators and others interested in understanding literacy and its role in our lives, confronting the lessons of this history is crucial.

One revelation from this history is a trend over time toward the evolution of broad "official" literacies that emerged from conflicts among competing ethnic, religious, and political entities. Collins (1993) describes this trend in the West as the "extrication of language from daily exigencies and its refiguring as an essential, context-free symbol of 'large-scale' association," which Collins traces to "the religious promulgation of reading literacy" (p. 181) that grew out of the conflict between the Catholic Church and the emerging Protestant denominations in the sixteenth and seventeenth centuries. According to Collins, a close look at the history of official literacies in the West reveals that any such literacy "is dissociated from the myriad complexities of local practices with texts and linked to a regulated symbolic realm of state religion and, later, various nationalist projects" (p. 181). The controversy over ebonics, to which I referred earlier, can be seen as one recent high-profile example of the ways in which a local literacy represents a challenge to an official or mainstream literacy; it also demonstrates the power of that mainstream literacy. African-American leaders were as vociferous in their criticism of the Oakland School Board's decision to declare ebonics a language as were conservative critics who traditionally have opposed such reforms as bilingual education and similar efforts to give access to students from marginalized groups. Many, including such prominent public figures as Jesse Jackson, emphasized the need for African-American students from difficult economic circumstances to become proficient in standard English in order to compete successfully for good jobs. Assigning ebonics the status of a recognized language, they asserted, only hampered the efforts of those students to become part of the mainstream. On the surface, such an argument seems, once again, commonsensical. But its effect is to deny validity to a nonmainstream way of using language and to reify the mainstream literacy (in this case, associated for the most part with schooling) without attention to the complexities of both those literacies or the ways in which literacy can be exclusionary. It is revealing that in such discussions, no distinctions are made between the literacy of schooling (what many scholars call "academic literacy") and, say, the literacy of corporate capitalism or what sometimes is described in university catalogues as "business writing." Although a great deal of scholarship has demonstrated that these literacies differ in significant ways, in the public discourse about ebonics such distinctions are never made. Instead, ebonics is distinguished only from standard English and in fact is represented by some critics as a substandard form of English. Indeed, the same "language of exclusion" that characterizes basic writing in colleges as deficient rather than different (see Rose, 1985) emerged in the debates about ebonics. In this way, mainstream conceptions of literacy can function as a means of exclusion.

What is also obscured in such debates is what Collins describes as "the myriad complexities of local practices with texts" (p. 181). As the work of scholars like Shirley Brice Heath, Brian Street, and Sylvia Scribner and Michael Cole indicates, and as the writing of my prison students compellingly shows, people use literacy in all kinds of ways to negotiate the challenges of living in a complex world and to manage their daily lives. The letters to his sister referred to in the self-evaluation by one of my prison students are one example of how seemingly mundane acts of literacy figure prominently in people's lives. The many tales of legal manuevering told by those students reveal the ways in which those local and personal acts of writing and reading intersect with official literacies in contexts like the courts and parole hearings. Further, many of these men used writing, as Malcolm X did, to redirect their lives and engage in new ways of thinking about themselves and how they might confront their personal circumstances. These many (often unseen) local acts of writing and reading often draw on, resist, intersect with, and deviate from official literacies, yet they are no less vital to the lives of these men. To ignore them—and to ignore the fact that official literacies can marginalize as well as empower—is to perpetuate the kinds of oppressive literacy practices, and attitudes toward those practices, that Collins describes.

Harvey Graff (1987), in his impressive histories of literacy in the West, has documented many instances in which writing and reading served as means of social control. For example, Graff traces the convoluted development of literacy and schooling in the United States during the nineteenth century and concludes that

> one of the most common and important uses of literacy was in extending the moral bases of society. . . . Much reading was religious and moral

in origin, orientation and content. From the mid-1820's, religious groups published literally millions of copies of books, tracts, periodicals, and newspapers, and developed means of distributing them widely. Such publications were aimed at women, families, and youths; the field of children's publishing, in particular, was revolutionized. (p. 355)

Although Graff acknowledges the many ways in which literacy was a means of liberation and social progress for individuals and certain social groups during the nineteenth century, he also emphasizes that literacy's

potential for liberation was at best one use among many and perhaps not the dominant one. Literacy was also used for order, cultural hegemony, work preparation, assimilation and adaptation, and instillation of a pan-Protestant morality; in addition, it contributed to work and wealth. (p. 340)

Such a view of literacy stands in sharp contrast to the deep confidence in literacy as a "good," which I grew up with and which seemed to be shared by my colleagues on the language arts committee.

Much of Graff's (1987) analysis, however, focuses on the relationship of literacy to schooling, and especially to formal education. He demonstrates that there was wide agreement among progressive as well as conservative reformers about "the moral and civic goals" of education; as a result, "the use of schools for assimilation and sociocultural cohesion developed rapidly as a social goal in the early nineteenth century" (p. 341). According to Graff, this use of schooling was not altruistic for the majority of reformers and policy makers; rather, "the desire was to control the lower class, not to assist their advancement" (p. 342). As a result, "educational opportunities expanded greatly after 1784, emphasizing religion and morality, including through literacy" (p. 342). Less than 100 years later, as public education became widespread, most children were enrolled in schools. Graff writes:

The Western faith in and commitment to education as a requirement for cohesion, stability, and progress were being translated into practice; mass public education was created and spread for the systematic and controlled transmission of literacy and the values that accompanied it. (pp. 350–351)

It's important to note here that this "systematic and controlled transmission of literacy and the values that accompanied it" is not a straightforward matter of policy or practice but rather "a process of recreating cultural hegemony" (p. 264), and Graff is careful to define hegemony here as "the result of a complex and subtle process, conscious and unconscious, of control, in which the predominance of one class is established over others, by consent rather than by force" (p. 264). Graff draws on Antonio Gramsci's conception of hegemony to distinguish it from domination, which refers to overt coercion. Given this distinction, Graff argues that "literacy is not likely a technique for domination or coercion; for hegemony, however, it has proved a much more viable option and often a successful tool" (p. 12); he shows how "various reformers [since the Reformation] have sought through literacy and education to establish or maintain hegemony" (p. 12).

Graff's analysis of literacy as a means for establishing or maintaining hegemony helps illuminate one of the key points I have tried to make in this chapter, that the narrow definition of literacy as a set of basic skills is woefully inadequate for the task of understanding the many levels on which literacy functions in our daily lives. As Graff shows in his study:

> Although literacy as a skill was often important and highly valued, its moral bases have been historically more dominant. The inculcations of values, habits, norms, and attitudes to transform the masses, rather than skills alone per se, was the developing task of schooling and its legitimate theme. Literacy was to serve as an instrument of training in a close and mutually reinforcing relationship with morality. (p. 12)

Although Graff's study focuses on the history of literacy prior to the twentieth century, his analysis is applicable to our current situation with respect to school reform efforts and public and professional discussions of literacy. The "norming" function of literacy that Graff describes is largely unacknowledged in contemporary debates about literacy and schooling, except by a handful of scholars (like Graff) who are especially interested in understanding connections among schooling, literacy, and power. Indeed, the focus on literacy as basic skills serves in part to obscure this function of literacy, as I think the controversy about ebonics demonstrates.

Graff also helps us see that arguments that literacy by itself inevitably leads to individual or social progress are simplistic at best, notwithstanding the earnest hopes of students like Hannah or the men in my prison writing class. In examining literacy in the United States in the latter part of the nineteenth century, Graff writes that

> class, enthicity, gender, age, and race were the central elements in social divisions and opportunities for advancement. Literacy in and of itself was

insufficient to erase other elements that shaped the stratification of society and the structures of inequality; it did not prove liberating in that respect. . . . Literacy was not a guarantee of success or even escape from poverty. (p. 350)

Despite voluminous evidence to the contrary provided by studies such as Graff's, we as a culture continue to believe in what Graff (1979) has called "the literacy myth": the abiding belief that literacy leads to individual and social advancement. Clearly, the complex circumstances that Graff describes in his study of the development of literacy in various regions at various historical periods differ markedly from the conditions in which most of us live today, especially with respect to technology. Nevertheless, part of the humbling power of a study like Graff's lies in the way it reminds us that literacy continues to be poorly understood despite its complex and often crucial role in our social, cultural, economic, and political lives. Maureen Hourigan (1994), in her review of the literacy "crises" in the United States in the past 100 years, writes that

a comparison of the origins of literacy crises and campaigns of the last half of the nineteenth century with those of the last quarter of the twentieth century is instructive, for it reveals that similar social, political, and economic features underlie the crises and campaigns of both centuries. (pp. 2–3)

The language of the current debates all too often echoes the language of the earlier debates (see the first chapter of Mike Rose's *Lives on the Boundary* [1989] for a good overview of this point), although rarely do the debaters acknowledge the broken-record quality of their pontifications. Even more rarely do they acknowledge the role of factors such as race and class and gender in literacy development and educational achievement. Graff (1987) writes of literacy in nineteenth-century America:

Social ascription—in terms of class, ethnicity, gender, and race—has long remained an important characteristic of North American social stratification and its structures of inequality. Literacy did not overturn those relationships. (p. 351)

The same can be said of the United States in the late twentieth century. Yet high-profile participants in the public debates about literacy and schooling, including current and former public officials like William Bennett and Lynn Cheney, continue to speak of needed reforms as if class, ethnicity, gender, and race would disappear if only more "disadvantaged" students were taught "the basics." Similarly, public criticism of whole language programs, especially those in California, present the problem as simply a lack of instruction in the basics of the alphabet, as if all students came into school with the same implicit knowledge of literacy, the same experiences with literacy, the same language-using abilities, the same access to power. What's more dismaying is that the students and teachers I work with continue to embrace the same simplistic ideas about literacy and education, and even when their circumstances indicate otherwise, they believe, like Hannah, that their own hard work in school will enable them to overcome whatever obstacles might stand in their way. In many ways, Malcolm X and his story about learning to read in prison provide the quintessential American fable about literacy; my students in that prison classroom and those who enter my university classroom continue to try to write new versions of that fable.

WRITING AND READING, CONTRADICTION AND POSSIBILITY

And yet there is no denying that literacy did represent power and opportunity for Malcolm X; there is no denying that he did learn to read and write on his own. And there is no denying that Malcolm X's literacy learning affected millions of people. If Abby, the student I described in Chapter 1, needs evidence that literacy matters, she need look no further than Malcolm X.

On the day that I returned the first graded essays to the men in my prison class, this sense of possibility overshadowed the obvious disappointment and frustrations that many of those men exhibited as they read my comments and saw their grades. All of them had struggled with their essays in similar yet different ways. They all wrote within this same prison context, yet each wrote out of a different context—a context that, as I'll try to illuminate in the next chapter, represents a complex intersection of the social, cultural, and personal. The obvious similarities in the backgrounds of those students in terms of race and class and educational experience masked important differences: in the ways in which their inexperience with academic language played out in their prose; in the idiosyncratic ways they engaged that language, the specific texts they read, the ideas they encountered; in their unique responses to the specific challenges they faced; in the unique personal background and specific experiences that each brought to bear on his writing. These differences relate to the complex individual ways in which writers engage broader social and cultural discourses.

As their teacher I did not at the time have ready access to a way of understanding these differences. I understood their writing as problematic, as diverging from the conventions of mainstream, academic writing. Despite these important differences in the way these men wrote and in what their writing meant to them, I was able only to label them as other than competent mainstream writers struggling to gain access to the power of literacy. And although my pedagogical approaches were such that I did not label their writing as "wrong," I did consider it lacking in ways that I now believe were simplistic and perhaps counterproductive to the task of helping these men gain access to the discourses that affected their lives. Literacy educators in general, I think, often lack a way of talking about such differences except as deficiencies; similarly, we lack ways of talking about the possibilities of literacy without losing sight of the problems and complications associated with literacy—and the problems and complications associated with our ways of teaching writing and reading. Without these means of making sense of such differences and possibilities, we revert to conventional models. And this is precisely why the limited popular conceptions of literacy that I have described in this chapter are so troubling and potentially debilitating: To approach the writing of men like those in my prison class as a set of skills or as a means to personal growth, as is too often the case in our conventional pedagogies, is not only to oversimplify the writing of these men—its problems as well as its promise for them—but is also to ignore the complex connections between the specific literate acts of these individual men and the broader social, cultural, political, and economic contexts within which they write; it is to ignore the complexities and contradictions of literacy in general as those complexities and contradictions play out in the writing of these men.

The same is true of more conventional students like Hannah, who was not writing within the difficult circumstances of incarceration and whose literacy history was much more mainstream. Her essay about her experience with her high school guidance counselor looks quite acceptable according to prevailing notions of mainstream, academic writing. To judge it according to those notions alone is to leave in place the limited vision of literacy—and schooling—that informs her essay. Ultimately, such an approach also leaves her without the kind of "critical consciousness" that Freire (1970/1984) describes; it leaves her less able to engage in what Freire calls the "incessant struggle to regain . . . humanity" (p. 33). I'd amend Freire's phrase here and add that it also leaves her less able to engage in the struggle to *retain* her humanity. In short, as Hannah's teacher, I need ways of thinking about literacy—and about Hannah as a literate being—that enable me to understand her writing not only in terms of mainstream literacy but also in terms of her struggle to maintain control over her life.

If Malcolm X's story of learning to read is the quintessential American fable about literacy, then we can start the task of rethinking literacy by acknowledging that fable and the many contradictions about literacy that it obscures. Malcolm X's learning to read was indeed an achievement that empowered him in various ways. But how might we understand that achievement without ascribing it solely to individual perseverance and effort? How might we understand this "individual" achievement while at the same time confronting the ways in which literacy also contributed to Malcolm X's marginalized status as a Black man from a troubled urban environment? Our discourses about literacy and education leave us hard pressed to make these distinctions without oversimplifying literacy. Popular conceptions of literacy reduce Malcolm X to a reformed convict who overcame adversity and found success through individual initiative and hard work. On the other hand, it is hard to avoid the determinism that can result when we invoke current academic theories of literacy and language that focus on broad categories of race, class, and gender. Ultimately, Malcolm X, like the students in my prison class, like Hannah, too, engaged in specific acts of writing and reading within broader social, cultural, economic, and personal contexts. As a teacher of writing and reading, I need a way of understanding literacy that allows me to talk about the possibilities and problems that literacy represents for individual students. That's what I'll try to provide in the next chapter.

Chapter 3

Literacy, Discourse, and the Postmodern Subject

Individuals and Local Acts of Writing and Reading

Writing alone *is not an "agent of change"; its impact is determined by the manner in which human agency exploits it in a specific setting.*
—Harvey Graff, Legacies of Literacy

But the subject should not be entirely abandoned. It should be reconsidered, not to restore the theme of an originating subject, but to seize its functions, its intervention in discourse, and its system of dependencies.
—Michel Foucault, "What Is an Author?"

The jumbled hills of western Pennsylvania conceal countless streams twisting their inevitable way through ravines that curve back into each other in an endless confusion of hill and valley. Those rounded, tree-covered hills also conceal something else: subterranean veins of the shiny black rock that shaped the history of that region as completely as the streams shape its vistas. And if you drive one of the many roads that wind through those hills, you inevitably will pass remnants of the once-omnipresent (and omnipotent) coal-mining industry there: abandoned wooden buildings standing near dormant mine shafts; dirt and gravel roads that cut suddenly into thick brush toward some unseen corner of a defunct mining operation; huge piles of discarded slate and coal and dirt that local residents refer to as "boney piles." As I follow one of those circuitous roads in the spring of 1998 en route to Indiana, Pennsylvania, where I will be conducting a writing workshop, these reminders of the region's past periodically emerge around a bend or at the crest of a hill, and I am remembering my first visit to this part of the state 20 years earlier.

Then, coal mining was still a mainstay (although a declining one) of the economy in western Pennsylvania, especially in the rural highlands east of Pittsburgh. I was there to do research for an article on Pennsylvania coal mining, and I had come to talk to people who were still actively involved in mining long after the anthracite coal mines in northeastern Pennsylvania, where I grew up, had given way to oil after World War II. My guide on that visit was Greg, my college roommate, who grew up among these hills and who knew many people who worked in the few remaining active mines. Having grown up where the mining industry had all but disappeared by the time I was born, I had always looked upon coal mining as history: an intimate part of my past, but a distant part nonetheless. Both my grandfathers had been coal miners. Both, I knew, developed serious health problems (which eventually killed them) from "black lung," the deadly respiratory condition that resulted from years of breathing coal dust. And both told stories about their years in dank mineshafts, stories that struck my young ears like tales of ancient times, far removed from my own experience. In a nebulous kind of way, I was proud to be the grandson of coal miners, but that heritage always seemed just a bit out of reach: a tattered black-and-white photo of a mineshaft that no longer existed or of a young man who barely resembled the graying grandfather I knew. During my trip to western Pennsylvania, however, the people and places Greg introduced me to began to update those photos in my mind. With Greg as guide, that visit helped me touch a part of my own past.

A few weeks later, though, Greg's role in the creation of my article changed from guide to critic. Upon returning to campus, I began drafting the article itself, which was the culminating project for a class called "Article Writing" at Penn State University, where I was finishing my junior year. I worked hard on the article, and as I completed a revised version of the piece, I asked Greg to read it and comment on it. This kind of sharing was a practice that was never encouraged by my writing teachers in high school and college in the 1970s, but it was a practice in which my friends and I routinely engaged. For me, it was a tricky practice, since my sensitivity to criticism about my writing was excessive. I trusted few friends aside from Greg with my drafts-in-progress, and even then it was rarely a comfortable experience for me. In the case of my coal-mining article, my investment, both in terms of time and my commitment to the topic, had been substantial. But I had done good research and felt confident about the prose that I had crafted so carefully. Unknowingly, Greg smashed that confidence like a piece of coal on a boney pile. "I like it," he said after reading my manuscript. "It sounds just like a *Time* magazine article."

I am thinking about that moment as I drive through towns with odd but vaguely familiar names—Colver, Revloc (Colver spelled backwards), Nanty Glo—towns Greg introduced me to 20 years earlier. I remember how often Greg and I shared our issues of *Time* with each other during our years as college roommates, and I remember our discussions about writing. He patiently endured my youthful arrogance as I offered opinions about one writer or another, about this "good" book or that "lousy" novel. He knew how seriously I took writing and how seriously I took myself as a writer. Yet he couldn't know—nor could I—how intimately my sense of self was wrapped up in my writing; he couldn't know then the complicated connections between that article on coal mining and my sense of myself as a son, a grandson, a Polish American, a student, an aspiring professional. Those connections were deeply important, and perhaps they deepened the state of near despair that Greg's comment sent me into. I don't remember becoming upset or angry, but just a few days before the deadline for the article, I rewrote the piece. I rolled the proverbial blank page into my manual typewriter and began again. And I made sure that I didn't write another *Time* magazine article. It was a wholehearted revision of a kind that would have impressed even Donald Murray.

I am smiling as I remember all this from the vantage of 20 years of experience as a writer and teacher of writing. The names of the towns, the sight of vistas that I saw only once before, the setting sun sharply backlighting the treetops at the crest of every hill—these warm my memory of that article and of Greg. As I continue driving past more memories, I can see connections that were invisible to me—and to the teacher who graded that article—2 decades earlier, and I can point to that article, which a few months later became my first published work, as both a beginning and an end.

A day later I am leading a workshop on writing across the curriculum for a dozen college faculty. They are a diverse group, representing all manner of difference: gender, age, race, ethnicity, national origin, and teaching experience. Their disciplines represent diversity, too: Frank and Shirley and Sandra from criminology; Brooke and Chancey from sociology; Kiki, Rich, and Alev from English; Purba from biology; Gary from occupational health and safety; John from art history. The range of their teaching experience enriches our discussions about writing and learning. Inevitably, talk turns to student writers and the problems of motivation, uneven preparation, late or missing work, grading—the kinds of practical problems with which writing teachers are only too familiar. At one point, someone expresses frustration that students often squander opportunities for revision or ignore them altogether. Shirley, Gary, and a few others share stories of students whose revised work fell short of expectations or didn't appear at all, and we ponder the implications of these stories. How can we get students to see revision as an opportunity not just for improving a text but for deepening their engagement with the topic about which they're writing? Suggestions are offered. We talk about the difficulties students encounter in confronting the discourses of the academy and we discuss strategies. We talk, too, about the role of school-sponsored writing in students' lives.

Later, during a break, Chancey and I continue the conversation while pouring cups of coffee at a buffet table in the back of the room. He has been teaching sociology for more than 25 years, excuse enough to be a bit impatient with students, yet I am deeply impressed by his empathy with students and his unselfish interest in understanding better how he can address their needs. Later I will learn that he has been battling cancer, and I am even more impressed by the generous and self-effacing way he seems to approach his teaching. As he prepares his coffee, Chancey refers to a student whose story someone told earlier during our discussion about revision. It was a typical story of a student who revised a paper just enough, in the end, to earn a D or a C for an important writing assignment—the kind of story of apparent lack of motivation and unfulfilled potential that teachers often tell in frustrated tones. The teller meant to emphasize that simply providing opportunities for revision isn't enough to ensure good writing, that students sometimes will undermine our best intentions when we provide such opportunities. Chancey agrees but offers a different perspective. It's possible, he says, that the effort the student put into that revision was exactly appropriate for that student at that moment in his life. He points out that we talked a lot about the difficult life situations our students often must negotiate and the uncertain place that their academic work can have in such situations. Maybe, Chancey says, the student in this case simply had other problems to address; maybe a minimal revision was all that was called for. Maybe, given the student's circumstances at the time, the revision the student did was just what we should have expected—even if we, as teachers, consider it inadequate.

Chancey's disappearing white hair reveals his age, but his self-deprecating manner and his light-hearted and genuine way of talking hide the intensity in his commitment to his students and his empathetic sense of them as people in all their complexity. After so many years of teaching, he has agreed to attend this workshop, led by someone with a fraction of his experience, because he cares about helping his students write and learn, and because he understands how maddeningly complex that task can be. Why did that student write and revise as he did? Chancey reveals his sense that the answer to that question is as much about *who* that student is as it is about pedagogy or literacy skills. I think about the students I have worked with and wonder whether I have appreciated that complexity in them as Chancey seems to and whether as writing teachers we, collectively, attend to these complexities as we should. We understand the difficult and often esoteric discourses of our respective academic disciplines, and we know that those discourses represent both entry and obstacle for our students. Yet we seem to have trouble remembering that discourse isn't just language, that people construct it to construct themselves, and that such construction is tricky at best. I think especially of Steve, a junior at the high school where I taught in Vermont in the mid-1980s. Steve's father committed suicide when Steve was in grade school, an event that profoundly shaped much of his work as a writer in my class, especially one essay about his father that he resisted revising. I remember being disappointed with his revision, because it included such an incongruous happy ending to an otherwise unforgivingly sad story. But I now wonder whether it was exactly what I should have expected, exactly the right ending for Steve, exactly the ending he needed to write. So much of our students' writing, I offer to Chancey as our coffee break ends, grows out of circumstances of which we, as their teachers, are but a small part.

Later, after the workshop is finished and all of us teachers take new ideas back to our classrooms, I am driving east again, back over and between those jumbled hills, and thinking of Steve. I think, too, of that coal-mining article I wrote many years before. It was, after all, about much more than coal mining.

THE SPECIFICITY OF LITERACY

"Literacy," write psychologists Sylvia Scribner and Michael Cole (1981), "is not simply knowing how to read and write a particular script but applying this knowledge for specific purposes in specific contexts of use" (p. 236). In drawing conclusions from their landmark study, *The Psychology of Literacy*, Scribner and Cole state somewhat apologetically, "In this book we have made a seemingly relentless descent from the general to the specific" (p. 234). They began their ambitious study of literacy among the Vai people of Liberia, they say, "with grand and ancient speculations about the impact of literacy on history, on philosophy, and on the minds of individual human beings" (p. 234); they ended, however, "with details of experiments on mundane, everyday activities that would, under other circumstances, probably escape our notice or our interest" (p. 234). These "mundane, everyday activities" to which Scribner and Cole refer are acts of reading and writing common in Vai culture: writing letters to distant family members, studying and reciting the Koran, reading official documents from government agencies, and so on. Whereas Scribner and Cole began their study in hopes of demonstrating how literacy might lead to broad cognitive effects, they concluded that what mattered most about literacy lay in these everyday, mundane activities, in the ways in which individual persons used reading and writing "for specific purposes in specific contexts of use." They concluded, in other words, that what seemed to be most important in understanding literacy was understanding local acts of reading and writing.

The significance of these local acts of literacy, Scribner and Cole suggest, lies not so much in the thinking such acts might reflect, but in what those acts enable individuals to *do* in specific circumstances, in what those acts *mean* to those who engage in them. As such, literate acts may be far more complex and difficult to sort out than the cognitive effects associated with literacy that Scribner and Cole initially set out to explore. For to write is to construct the self, as postmodern theorists have helped us see, and that is no simple matter. And its complexity is multiplied by the infinite number of ways in which *individual* writers and readers can engage in specific acts of writing and reading. It seems trite to say that Greg likely would have written that article about coal mining differently than I did. But to ask *why* is to begin to point to the specificity of literacy as it plays out in actual instances of writing and reading: how literacy encompasses not only the specific circumstances of individual acts of writing and reading, but the identity of the writers and readers as well. As a community of educators—in rhetoric and composition, in English education, in literacy studies, in linguistics—we have only lately begun to examine the ways in which this uncertain but crucial relationship between the self and literacy shapes acts of writing and reading. My focus in this chapter is to tease out this connection as a way to illuminate the social and individual nature of literacy in order to help explain how particular student essays come to be.

In some ways, Scribner and Cole's (1981) "relentless descent from the general to the specific" (p. 234) describes a trend in literacy scholarship in the past few decades. Scholarly attention largely has turned away from theorizing about general connections between literacy and human cognition and turned toward attempts to understand the social and cultural functions of literacy in varied contexts (see, for example, Heath, 1983). For many scholars, interest in literacy now lies in what Brian Street (1984) calls "the social practices and conceptions of reading and writing" (p. 1). Accordingly, scholars and teachers interested in literacy pedagogy have turned their attention to the ways in which literacy relates to such factors as race, class, gender, and ethnicity. Pedagogy as that term currently is used by many scholars often seems to refer to critical pedagogies that focus the attention of teachers and students on the social and political significance of writing and reading rather than on the specific reading and writing skills that often are associated with literacy in popular discussions of education (as I noted in Chapter 2).

But in a puzzling sort of paradox, this "social turn," as some scholars have called it (e.g., see Trimbur, 1994), seems to have shifted our collective focus away from the kinds of local acts of writing and reading that Scribner and Cole described as central to the social functions of literacy in our lives—the specific acts of writing and reading that matter in our daily encounters with each other. As recently as the mid-1980s researchers like Linda Flower and John R. Hayes (1981, 1984) examined the decision-making and cognitive processes of individual writers as they completed specific writing tasks. As we became more aware of the social, cultural, and political complexities of literacy, however, such research came to be viewed by many as too narrowly focused on the individual writer and was critiqued as generalizing the cognitive aspects of writing in ways that ignored the broader social and cultural contexts of writing as well as the inherently political nature of literacy.[1] In short, as we began to understand individual writers and readers as manifestations of complex social and cultural factors relating to race, class, and gender, and to see their writing and reading as always situated within social and cultural contexts, we often seemed to ignore the specificity of the literate acts that those individual writers engage in; as we explore the inherently social and cultural nature of the individual, we seem to ignore the inherently individual nature of writing and reading.

Yet if we accept, as I do, the assumptions that writing and reading are social and cultural activities embedded in specific contexts, and that writing and reading cannot be adequately understood apart from those contexts, we still are left with questions about what individual writers and readers actually *do* as they engage in literate activities—questions about how to understand the writing of individual students in specific contexts. How might we explain not only students' texts but also the roles of those texts in the lives of those writers in a way that illuminates their individual acts of writing within the broader contexts that inevitably shaped those texts? If a cognitive perspective on writing generalizes about individuals to the exclusion of social and cultural factors, and if "expressivist" pedagogies ignore the ideological and political nature of a writer's work, as some critics have charged (see Jarratt, 1991), so too does much of our recent scholarship in writing and writing pedagogy seem to generalize about inherently complex factors such as race, class, and gender (three categories that are so routinely grouped together in the professional literature that they now constitute a kind of stock phrase, like "reading, writing, and 'rithmetic"). We now seem often to have lost sight of the individual writer, and in place of that writer we see categories: mainstream, marginalized, African-American, White, female, male, working class, and so on. As I noted in Chapter 1, we must, as Maureen Hourigan (1994) has argued, "consider the intersections of class, gender, and culture" (p. 75); more important, Hourigan reminds us that "these political categories must and do combine in almost every instance, but it is difficult to predict, in everyday life and in classroom situations, the self-presentation of gender, race, and class identities" (p. 73). It is precisely the writing and reading that occur in those everyday situations that constitute the most important sites of literate activity in our lives—and the most difficult to understand. In other words, what Hourigan calls "the *self-presentation* of gender, race, and class identities" may be much more important than the categories themselves in our efforts to understand the writing and reading our students do.

The influence of postmodern thinking, especially regarding conceptions of discourse and subjectivity, on our collective understanding of literacy has complicated matters further by obscuring the writer among the discourses to which that writer is subjected. In the introduction to their important volume, *Contending with Words: Composition and Rhetoric in a Postmodern Age*, Patricia Harkin and John Schilb (1991) embrace the postmodern assumption that "argument produces subjectivities, knowledge, and value" (p. 5). They address directly how this assumption has reshaped the way we understand writing and discourse, beginning with

> the realization that although language can be the weaponry of battles to make knowledge in a world where truth is absent, language is also the only tool we have for dealing with that situation. Language is a way of contending, in all senses of that word, with the processes through which discourse shapes human thought and social relations in a context of change and struggle. (p. 6)

Although I accept the assumption that we construct reality through language, I also worry about the often problematic ways in which such an assumption has transfomed our understanding of the student writer from *individual* into *subject* (in several senses of that term). In the same volume, John Clifford (1991) points out that poststructuralist thinking

> decenters writing as well as the self, seeing both not only as the effect of language patterns but as the result of multiple discourses already in place, already overdetermined by historical and social meanings in constant internal struggle. (p. 40)

In such a characterization, the self can become obscured and the possibility of its agency limited or even eliminated as we focus on "the multiple discourses already in place" and the constant struggles over meanings. For teachers of writing who must find ways to address the often conflicting needs and interests of a roomful of students representing a variety of races, ethnicities, backgrounds, experiences, and agendas all manifesting themselves in decidedly idiosyncratic ways, such a conception of writing and the writer can be disconcerting and even limiting. To see Hannah's essay, for example, as a reflection of broader discourses regarding school and work, individuality, and economic opportunity may be to overlook *her* engagement with those discourses and leave us unable to help her find useful ways of confronting those discourses through her own writing and reading. In this sense, an understanding of students as the "effects of language" and "the result of multiple discourses already in place" can be as totalizing as a cognitive perspective that describes those students and their writing in terms of writing skills and cognitive strategies. All but a few of the students in my prison classroom, for instance, were African-American men from urban settings, yet to understand them in terms of the broad categories of race or class and the discourses that "wrote" them as such is to leave me, as their teacher, no better able to address the profound differences in their ways of engaging those discourses and attempting to claim some measure of agency for themselves than if I had reduced their writing to cognitive "deficiencies." For me as teacher, then, the question becomes, How can postmodern ideas about discourse and subjectivity help me understand these differences among my students? How can they help me understand a student as writer and enable me to address her or his interests and needs in meaningful ways that are consistent with a social conception of literacy and a commitment to furthering Freire's project of possibility and empowerment? How is it possible to understand my students' writing—and to understand them as writing *subjects*—within those discourses "already in place" without losing sight of the individuals writing within those discourses?

In addition to the problem of maintaining some conception of the individual writer within a network of discourses, the contradictions that emerge from a closer examination of literacy practices of the kind I provided in Chapter 2—our conflicting and sometimes problematic beliefs about literacy and the complex ways in which literacy can both empower and oppress—further complicate our efforts to explain individual acts of writing and reading by students like Hannah or the men in my prison class. As their teacher, I need to find ways to understand and talk about literacy that allow me to keep these complications in view and yet enable me to address specific literate acts as *individual* acts. Accordingly, I want to construct a framework for understanding literacy that reflects a broad social and cultural view of literacy yet enables us to examine and understand local acts of reading and writing. A poststructuralist understanding of discourse can, I think, help provide such a framework, because it forces us to confront the ways in which discourse inevitably shapes specific acts of writing and reading; it forces us to recognize that context must be understood as something more complex than a set of factors relating to race, class, gender, and so on—that these are, in large measure, constructed through discourse rather than concrete, preexisting facts. But if such a framework is to help us construct ways of understanding literacy that lend themselves to developing the kind of Freirean pedagogies that can help promote social and individual transformation, it also must enable us to recognize that literacy is both potentially transformative in a broad social and political sense and empowering on a local, personal, individual level as well. Hannah is, after all, not just a young White woman, but a specific young White woman living in specific circumstances that shape her writing and reading in specific ways. Like Anne Herrington, who along with Marcia Curtis (in press) has carefully examined how students' writing grows out of varied and complex individual and social contexts, I am "trying to recognize the tension between individual and discourse." An adequate understanding of literacy requires accounting for this tension between individual writer and social context, between discourses that shape individual agency and the individuals who claim agency within discourse.

In the remainder of this chapter I want to propose a framework for understanding literacy that helps account for that tension and how it figures into the specific acts of writing and reading of our students. My purpose in proposing such a framework is to illuminate local acts of writing and reading in ways that might help us construct pedagogies that promote a critical literacy of the kind Freire describes.[2]

UNDERSTANDING THE WRITER IN WRITTEN DISCOURSE

On the first day of class, when I walked into that dingy prison classroom, its inadequate dirty windows obscuring a late-afternoon sun and a tense silence almost overcoming the constant drone of noise from the prison yard full of men, I confronted something I had not before and have rarely since confronted: the prospect of being in the racial minority. Of the 24 or 25 students who attended class on that first day, all but three or four were African-American. I quickly learned that most of these men had come from cities—Cleveland, Cincinnati, Canton—and the stories they shared with me about their difficult lives in those cites were disturbingly similar. Most of them described less-than-stellar efforts in school; some were dropouts. Most came from difficult circumstances in which the pressure to participate in illegal activities was great. The only obvious difference among them was age: the majority were young, in their 20s and even their teens, while some were middle-aged and a few were older, approaching 60. Otherwise, these men seemed easily categorized: They were poor, urban, African-American men.

But of course they were so much more than that. In thinking about how they came to be there, I have always been struck by the tension between the larger factors that seemed beyond their control—the difficult conditions into which many of them were born; the limiting economic realities for which they were not responsible; an often inadequate educational system they did not create; institutionalized racism that they could not often combat—and the sometimes startling differences in the personal paths that brought them to that classroom. Mr. James was a hustler from Cincinnati who had been involved in illegal gambling activities for all of his adult life, a good part of which he had spent in prison. One of the "perks" of his becoming older (he was at least 50) while in the state prison system was that he had been transferred from tougher prisons to the medium-security facility where I was teaching. After so many years in that system, he had decided to earn a 2-year degree, and found himself underprepared for college-level writing. He had a grandfatherly air about him, with a disarmingly gentle manner, and he interacted easily with the much younger men in the class.

One of those younger men was Mr. Smith, an 18-year-old from Canton, where he had been arrested for automobile theft and sentenced to 4 years. At the time of his arrest, his father was incarcerated, and he and his brother lived with their mother in a neighborhood where most of the kids their age made money selling drugs. His introduction to the drug trade, he told me, was a seemingly casual offer of expensive athletic shoes in return for delivering a package of drugs. Mr. Smith had a 2-year-old daughter, and he seemed intensely committed to earning an early release on parole and supporting her as his father had not done for him.

Mr. Jarrel lived in a suburban section of Cleveland, where he was working his way through college. One day he arrived home early to find a friend robbing his apartment, apparently in need of drug money. A fight broke out, during which his friend pulled a knife. Both men were seriously hurt in the altercation, and Mr. Jarrel was still recovering in the hospital when he was charged with felonious assault and attempted murder. In the months leading up to his trial, he lost his job, had to quit school, and was forced to move back home with his mother. To me, he always seemed angry yet genuinely befuddled by the fact that he could go from self-supporting college student to convicted felon in little more than the time it took to surprise an intruder in his home.

"Poor, urban, African-American male" as a category seems woefully inadequate for describing the important differences among these men and the way those differences might influence what and how they wrote. "Inmate" isn't much better.

Nor is the category of "basic writer," which is how the university that ran the college-equivalency program in the prison described these men: They had all been assigned to Basic Writing, a remedial course intended to prepare them for the required first-year composition course. In many ways, their weaknesses as writers—their inability to write effective conventional academic prose—were similar: insufficiently developed ideas; poorly organized essays; problematic and often confusing syntax; abundant surface errors. Versions of these problems emerged in the writing of all the men in that class. Many of these problems could perhaps be explained by the men's lack of experience with the conventions of academic writing and inadequate writing instruction in schools they attended (or very little instruction of any kind, in the cases of the men who had dropped out of school). Indeed, scholarship on basic writers suggests that these kinds of writing problems could be linked to differences between mainstream discourse of the kind valued in schools and the cultural backgrounds these men brought to their writing. In one intriguing study, Glynda Hull and Mike Rose (1989) examined the writing of a student, Tanya, in an urban community college in the context of her past school experiences, her ideas about literacy, and her own plans for her future after school. Their analysis reveals that some of the specific textual errors in students' writing can be traced to the students' misunderstanding of certain rules of conventional academic writing as well as to language practices in the students' home community that differ from those expected in school. We have other compelling evidence that reveals the daunting complexity of this relationship between literacy and sociocultural context (e.g., Heath, 1983; Scribner & Cole, 1981; Street, 1984).

At the same time, a close look at the writing of these men reveals the error in trying to understand them as all falling into a single category—for instance, "basic writer" or "urban, African-American male." The differences that can emerge in the way individual writers engage in specific (similar) acts of writing suggest that we must look beyond the obvious contextual factors for some insight into why these writers made the choices they made to produce their texts. And indeed, the idea of choice here, which implies agency, is crucial, as I will try to show momentarily.

Consider, for example, two essays written by students in my prison class, Mr. Green and Mr. Jarrel. Both were African-American men who grew up in urban environments in the midwest; both were in their late 20s or early 30s. Both had spent several years behind bars. Their assignment was to identify and discuss a social problem that concerned them; their essays were to be more or less conventional academic analytic essays of a kind they learned about in class.

ADD IT UP. AMERICA OWES THE BLACK MAN
BY MR. GREEN

America owes the black man something. We don't want you to dole it out in walfare checks. If you give us what you owe us, we'll take it from there. But will America do that? We don't

know. But, America detained thousands of Japanese American's
in concentration camps (during World War II), confiscated their
property, and now congress says that America treated the
Japanese Americans wrongly; and, have okayed several billions
of dollars to be paid to the Japanese in reparations. The Germans reconize the evil that they did to the Jews, and right now
they are paying reparations to Israel. East Germany wanted to
unite with West Germany, and in order to do so, they repented
and stated thier intentions to pay Israel reparations. "We ask the
Jews of the world to forgive us," the East German parliament
said in a formal statement. We ask the people of Israel to forgive
us for the hypocrisy and hostility of official East Germany
policy toward Israel, and for the persecution and degradation of
Jewis citizens, also after 1945, in our country. "We declare our
willingness to contribute as much as possible to the healing of
mental and physical sufferings of survivors and to provide just
compensation for the material losses."

That's a wonderful thing done by the East Germans. Now
let's rewrite this a little bit and let's put it in the hands of
America. Wouldn't it be wonderful if America said, "We ask the
Blacks of the world to forgive us? We ask the Black people of
America to forgive us for our hypocrisy and the hostility of
official United States policy toward Black people. And for the
persecution and degradation of Black people even after 1863
when we called them citizens and said they were free. "And we
(the government of America), "decline our willingness to
contribute as much as possible to the healing of mental and
physical sufering of any survivors and to provide just compensation for material losses."

Now let's add up what they owe us. Do you have your
computers ready? Let's start in Africa. The late W. E. B. DuBois
said that we have lost 50 to 100 million Black lives. The Jews
lost six (6) million lives in the Holocaust. I know that's a lot of
live's, but they are being paid for their losses. And six (6) million white lives do not compare with one hundred million Black
lives. For the Bible says, "A life for a life." So what is one (1)
Black life worth? Three hundred years of working from "cain't
see morning" to "cain't see night," for no pay. Three hundred
years working millions of slaves for nothing. ADD IT UP! ADD IT UP!
ADD IT UP!

The killing of our mothers and fathers aftermating them
like animals. Then taking the chldren and naming us after

them, stripping us of our language, our God, our religion, our minds. ADD IT UP! ADD IT UP! Theink about it? The destruction of our families.

Black folk fought in the Revolutionary War that made America free from England, yet we're not free. ADD IT UP! We fought in the War of 1812. ADD IT UP! We fought in the Civil War 400,000 Blacks on the side of the North and South, some fighting wo preserve the Old South, others fighting to preserve the Union. After the Union was preserved, we had no Union, but thousands of Black lives were lost in that war. ADD IT UP! . . .

I really feel the white's of today are innocent of what their Great grandfathers did, but they are in a great position because of what their fathers did and Blacks are in a hell of a position because of what their fathers did. So if you, the whites of today, want to escape what is justly due then they've got to do justice by the Black man. They must do the right thing.

What is the right thing? You add it up white folks, you gonna have to give us the country. ADD IT UP, white man. The whole thing belongs to the oppressed, if you add it up. But we don't want the whole thing, just give us some of it and let us build for ourselves. Since you don't want us, don't keep us here and kill us. Let us go and let us build a new place in the name of God. But you don't have to give us anything. We'll leave it up to God to decide. He'll take from whom he pleases. I'm just trying to save your life. God will take an eye for an eye, a tooth for a tooth and a life for a life. ADD IT UP! ADD IT UP!

You have about 150 million white people on earth. ADD IT UP! A life for a, life, then God is justified in killing everything that refuses to submit as he killed Pharoah and his people, as he destroyed Babylon, and Sodom and Gomorrah. And he warned you that it was water the first time, but fire the next time. You better add it up. ADD IT UP! ADD IT UP! ADD IT UP!

ILLITERACY IN PRISON
BY MR. JARREL

It's evening time in the prison, all the inmates are locked in there proper dorms. Mine in particular is dorm 3.

The halls are crowded especially by the phones. As I walked does the hall someone stops me, a well groomed young adult about twenty-two or twenty-three. He saids to me, "Could you dial this number for me, I forgot my glasses." He hands me a paper with a number on it. I dial the number for him, He says, "thanks."

Later on that evening while resting on my buink another inmate comes up to me. We talk a few minutes. He ask was I in college. I said, "Yes." Then we make small conversations, then he saids "I'm no good at filling out these commisary slips, could you help me?" I agreed, but all the while I was trying to show him, I notice I was doing all the writing and adding of the price list. He would say, "do they have cigaretttes?" "What kind?" "How much?" "I only have this much to spend." "How many can I get with this much?" After all these questions I knew something was not right with the picture I was in. I just blew the whole thing off.

Until one day a man about middle thirties came to me and asked me to write a letter to his wife, without thinking I asked him, why did he ask me. He said another inmate told him I could read. I responded by saying, "Can't everybody?" He told me I would be surprised of how many people in the institution couldn't read or write. So I helped the man. The next day I went to Ms. Jones, the case managers office to inquired about this problem in the institution. She told me they were starting a new project at the prison it's a tutoing program which you have to take some classes learning the Laubach way of tutoring. I was very interested and asked if I could enroll. She said, "Yes." "We need all the help we can get."

A few months later I received a pass instructing me to go to the school building. When I reached the school there was a very small, rosy cheek, lady with a big smile on her face. She introduced herself as Mrs. Benton, she explain that illiteracy was a big problem in the world. This made me very concern and curious about illiteracy, so I was very eger to learn as well as help in everyway possible.

In class I learned that illiteracy is the number one problem for economic downfall. Twenty-seven million American adults are functionally illiterate. 40% are in prison, most prisoners that were out in society and was functionally illiterated earned less than 42% that a person who graduated from high school. This adds up to billions of dollars in lost revenues and yet still it takes more billions to support welfare recipients, which occur due to lack of education. The basic point in research was that most illiterated people in society did crimes to get money because they either never took the time to learn to read or write or force to quit school because of problems.

Today there training individuals to read and write in the institutions hoping this would prevent a prisoner from return-ing. Most inmates who can't read or write are scared to come forward with there problem but the small percent that do will learn the basic skills of writing and reading and mathmatics, to help them go on and be able to enter G.E.D. classes, these classes will enable people to understand how to fill out job applications because they'll be able to read it and most impor-tant they'll be able to read and write there loved ones.

This is a start to help illiterate inmates, I felt a good one. I went and told everybody I could reach in my dorm in hopes they would understand the problem.

The gentleman that had approached me before are making an effort. I explain to them this is a start, you won't learn over night and you might not ever make as much money as you did with the crimes dealing with money, but you won't end up back in the prison system or away from the people you love. I told to get there GED and then go to college and make the best of a bad situation like were in now and the only way to beat the system is by there way. Knowledge, and when you all learn this pre-cious gift knowledge go back in society and teach someone you might know that can't read or write, teach them first the Laubach way to begin with and then tell them to go for all they can, like Mr. Laubach says, "each one teach one."

I present these essays here primarily to illustrate the strikingly dif-ferent ways in which these two men approached this conventional academic writing assignment and to underscore the limitations of in-voking broad categories of race, class, gender, and so on in trying to understand student writing. To what extent can the writing of these men—and the obvious differences in that writing—be attributed to sociocultural factors such as race and class, which so often are cited in current discussions of literacy? Mr. Green and Mr. Jarrel were the same in quite obvious ways: their race, gender, socioeconomic background, prior school experiences, and current living conditions. Yet each ne-gotiated this task in a very different way. I should point out here that such similarities and differences were perhaps more pronounced in my prison class than in my more conventional classes in the universities and the private high school where I have taught. But in any setting, reading such student writing prompts the question, How did this *spe-*

cific piece of writing come to be? How did *this* writer construct *this* text and why does it look the way it does? Why, for instance, does Mr. Green adopt such an openly polemical voice in his essay, while Mr. Jarrel constructs a much more conventional, moderate tone? What explains the different choices in language that these men made or the very different rhetorical strategies they employed?

To account for such differences is to raise a set of questions concerning the crucial concepts of *self, individual*, and *subjectivity*—problematic concepts made more so in a postmodern age that has called into question traditional ways of understanding them.

THE POSTSTRUCTURALIST CHALLENGE TO THE WRITER

How to understand the self or the subject is an old problem, "caught up," as Paul Smith (1988) puts it, "in the set of philosphical terms and problems which are familiar from Descartes, Locke, Hume, Hegel, Heidegger, Sartre, and many others" (p. xxvii). But in the past 2 decades the problem has taken on a special urgency for teachers and scholars interested in understanding literacy, largely as a result of developments associated with poststructuralist theories of language, discourse, and epistemology as well as broader developments in what has come to be called "postmodern" thought.[3] The influence of these theoretical movements on our collective understanding of the subject is crucial to understanding the literate acts of individual writers and readers.

In 1969, French theorist Michel Foucault, in an essay called "What Is an Author" (Foucault, 1977), argued that the term *author*, or what he calls an *author-function*, "does not refer, purely and simply, to an actual individual" (pp. 130–131); rather, an *author* is a *subject* that must be understood "as a complex and variable function of discourse" (p. 138). Such a view of *author* seems counterintuitive to those whose conception of author is so deeply imbued with the Romantic ideal of the inspired writer and so inextricably linked to American cultural beliefs in individualism and self-determination (as I pointed out in Chapter 2). I remember being struck by something the editor of a children's book I wrote said in response to my comment about the collaborative nature of that book. The book was really the result of a whole series of collaborations, I suggested to the editor, between myself and the illustrator, the several editors who worked on it, even my children, for whom I originally wrote it—so much so that it seemed inaccurate to place only my name on the cover as author. The story itself was profoundly shaped by the reactions of my children to early versions of it, which I read to them at bedtime; it changed further after the editor suggested revisions to the version I had submitted to her, and then again after the illustrator created early versions of the drawings that would accompany the text. In recounting this process to the editor, I noted that the story that was going to press was very different from the one I'd written originally; moreover, it was not my story at all but one written by these many other people. But it was *your* idea, the editor replied; without that idea, she insisted, there would have been no book. Her sense of the special nature of individual authorship and of the status of the author reflects the deeply held and widespread cultural beliefs about writers and individual authorship that I examined in Chapter 2 (see also Yagelski, 1994a). And those beliefs, as Foucault and others have shown, rest on a modernist conception of the individual—the *subject*—as autonomous and stable.

As John Clifford (1991) points out, this modernist conception of the subject has long been the foundation for understanding writing and the writer, especially in English studies: "For the traditional humanist, the writer has always been seen as a creative individual, the locus of significance, the originator of meaning, an autonomous being, aware of ends and means, of authorial intentions and motivations" (p. 39). Within this traditional conception of the writer, to understand writing means ultimately understanding a particular writer's particular motives; the text is thus a reflection of those motives, of that writer's individual consciousness. As Clifford points out, however, this notion of writing was profoundly challenged by structuralist linguists like Claude Levi-Strauss. Structuralists posited that writers do not simply express their unique ideas or their individual consciousness; rather, their writing reflects linguistic and cultural codes that in turn reflect broader universal patterns in specific textual forms, such as myths and folktales. Thus, as Clifford sums up this argument, "writing does not directly express an individual's ideas; it transmits universal codes" (p. 40). According to this structuralist view, the writer is not the free and autonomous meaning maker as in a modernist view, but is instead always working within these universal codes. The writer negotiates meaning through these codes, but she or he cannot determine that meaning alone. Inevitably, then, a writer becomes a kind of vehicle for those codes, and his or her text is a specific manifestation of those codes; the writer's individual and unique ideas are always a function of these codes.

Poststructuralists pushed this reconceptualization of the writer further. Theorists such as Foucault and Jacques Derrida called into question the very idea of intentional meaning itself in writing. For them, meaning resides solely in the discourse. In other words, it is not the writer who determines what a text or an utterance means, but the discourse within which that text or utterance is made that does so. For Foucault (1977), an *author* is not even essential for texts to function within discourse. The author, he writes,

> is undoubtedly only one of the possible specifications of the subject and, considering past historical transformations, it appears that the form, the complexity, and even the existence of this function are far from immutable. We can easily imagine a culture where discourse could circulate without any need for an author. (1977, p. 138)

Indeed, Foucault demonstrates that discourses in contemporary Western society sometimes do function without *authors*. In examining the cultural role of an author's name, Foucault asserts that

> in our culture, the name of an author is a variable that accompanies only certain texts to the exclusion of others: a private letter may have a signatory, but it does not have an author; a contract can have an underwriter, but not an author; and similarly, an anonymous poster attached to a wall may have a writer, but he cannot be an author. In this sense, the function of an author is to characterize the existence, circulation, and operation of certain discourses within a society. (p. 124)

The focus of a poststructuralist analysis of writing is thus not on the writer at all but on the discourses of which any writing is inevitably a part. According to this view, my children's book, for instance, is not the product of my unique consciousness (a concept itself questioned by poststructuralist theory) nor is its "meaning" a reflection of my individual intentions. Instead, that text is a product of existing discourses within which the book's meanings are determined: the discourses of children's literature, popular discourses surrounding children and literacy, the discourses of narrative and story, and the broader cultural discourses related to the subject matter of the book involving such issues as gender roles and social and economic practices (e.g., the children's book deals in part with commerce and with specific occupations like farmer or doctor). As writer, I construct a text by drawing on those discourses, which in turn shape the potential meanings of that text, regardless of any authorial intent on my part (which, in any case, would be defined as a function of discourse as well). Indeed, the very topics I addressed in the book already exist within those discourses.

From a poststructuralist perspective, then, the writer or author does not function as an autonomous creator making specific and intended meanings in a text. In fact, Foucault (1977) takes pains to make a distinction between "author" and the actual person identified as the author of a specific text. That "author's name," he argues, "characterizes a particular manner of existence of discourse. . . . Its status and its manner of reception are regulated by the culture in which it circulates" (p. 123). For Foucault, the focus of our attention in any effort to understand writing thus should be on the writing itself and not on the author, except to the extent that the author functions as a manifestation of discourses. The essential act of any writing, Foucault argues, "is not the exalted emotions related to the act of composition or the insertion of a subject into language. Rather, it is primarily concerned with creating an opening where the writing subject endlessly disappears" (p. 116). What is important, according to Foucault, is how the discourse works, not how writers write. "In short," he concludes, "the subject (and its substitutes) must be stripped of its creative role and analyzed as a complex and variable function of discourse" (p. 138). Clifford (1991) sums up this poststructuralist perspective on writing and the writer in this way:

> Poststructuralism, then, decenters writing as well as the self, seeing both as not only the effect of language patterns but as the *result* of multiple discourses already in place, already overdetermined by the historial and social meanings in constant internal struggle. (p. 40, emphasis added)

Despite its broad acceptance in recent decades among scholars, such a perspective can seem extreme, for it runs counter to deeply held cultural beliefs about writers and literacy. My experiences in working with teachers suggest that many English teachers find this perspective threatening, because it seems to call into question the entire project of teaching individual students to write or read, on which their professional existence depends. Moreover, for many of these teachers, the pressing need to deal with a room full of students defined within institutionalized education (and within our culture generally) as "individuals" makes poststructuralist thinking about writing and writers seem useless. At some point, these teachers must confront those piles of essays submitted to them by individual students, each of whom is to be understood and (not incidentally) assessed as an individual. In such a context, the idea that the writer disappears in discourse seems only slightly less silly than using a Scantron machine to grade all those essays.

I am overstating matters a bit here, but I don't want to trivialize the practical pressures that attend the teaching of writing nor do I want to lose sight of the power of our cultural beliefs in literacy as an expression of individual ideas and skills. At the same time, the poststructuralist critique of the modernist view of the writer as an autonomous subject can help complicate our understanding of the writer in what I believe are productive ways; it can help teachers find useful new ways to understand their students as writers and to rethink their conventional approaches to reading their students' writing. In addition, it can challenge what I see as counterproductive notions of the writer that continue to inhibit substantive reform of teaching methods that do not serve students' needs. Despite problems with a poststructuralist understanding of writing and the writer, which I will address momentarily, poststructuralist thought on writing, and specifically on the writer as subject, can, I think, deepen our understanding of what it means to write so that we might better explain local acts of writing and reading.

The question raised by the poststructuralist critique of the author for many literacy educators is something like this: If the writer is not autonomous, who is doing the writing? In other words, if the writer is "written" by preexisting discourses, if both writing and the writer are, to quote John Clifford (1991) again, "the result of multiple discourses already in place" (p. 40), how are we to understand the writer—that is, a specific person writing—and his or her act of creating a text? How are we to understand, for instance, the men in my prison class if not as individual writers whose decisions as writers gave rise to the specific texts they created and whose texts can have real consequences for them in terms of the conditions of their lives? How are we to make sense of the two essays presented earlier in this chapter by Mr. Green and Mr. Jarrel, which seem to reflect two individual writers and the specific ideas they wished to convey in their writing? How should we characterize Hannah's essay, presented in Chapter 2, if not as *her* narrative of *her* school experiences? After all, isn't she describing experiences that *she* had in school, experiences that were uniquely hers? One step toward answering such questions is to examine more carefully what it means to understand a subject as a "result of multiple discourses"; a second crucial step is to distinguish between the subject and agency.

UNDERSTANDING THE WRITER AS SUBJECT

When a writer writes, she or he never begins from scratch, to use a cliché, because the broader discourses that Clifford (1991) describes as "already in place" shape—and even determine to an extent—what that writer can and will write. For instance, in writing my children's book, I adopted a genre with conventions regarding style, structure, and content that I did not create but that already exist within our culture. Those conventions shaped my text and influenced the decisions I made about what that text would look like. Moreover, in writing about a particular subject matter—in this case, how a community is inherently connected through its commerce and its social relations—I was drawing on the broader social, economic, historical, and cultural discourses that have shaped my (and our collective) understanding of that subject matter. Those discourses, to a great extent, determined what I might say about those matters—not because there are explicit rules governing what I could write about those subjects, but because what I knew about those subjects and what I believed about them resulted from my engagement with these broader discourses. Further, *how* I wrote about those matters reflects other, more complex discourses about economics and gender and community. In other words, my assumptions about such things as gender roles and commerce grow out of my engagement with the broader discourses about those issues; my words reflect those discourses even as they might resist or question them. And we can say the same kinds of things about my coal-mining article, although we would be referring to other discourses perhaps, with different kinds of conventions and assumptions.

Similarly, the men in my prison class, in writing about their lives for the assignments I gave them, wrote within such broader discourses as well. For example, Mr. Green's angry indictment of white America did not arise solely from his unique experience as a Black man in a predominantly White culture; his words reflect broader discourses about race and race relations, history, economic opportunity, and religion in our culture. Moreover, in writing his essay, he draws upon social codes and narrative structures that already exist. For instance, his repetition throughout his essay of the phrase "Add it up!" can be seen as his use of a rhetorical technique common in the oratory of Black preachers, to which Mr. Green would have been exposed as someone growing up in a Black community. Many of his arguments, too, are common arguments in the literature on "Black consciousness" that he was reading at the time. In addition, his words reflect academic discourses: conventions of language use that grow out of his prior school experiences and his experiences in my class. All these inevitably shape what he writes.

Clearly, the discourses to which a specific writer writing a specific text is subjected are many and complex, often overlapping and conflicting. But understanding that text is not a matter of simply identifying specific discourses as they influence a writer. While it may be true, for instance, that Mr. Green's narrative was influenced directly by Black

religious oratory or by a widely known text such as James Baldwin's
The Fire Next Time (to which he seems to refer in his concluding paragraph), it is an oversimplification to posit a cause-and-effect relationship between his text and those other texts and discourses. That is
because his very ideas, his conception of himself as a man and as a Black
man, are bound up in his interactions with a variety of discourses regarding race in America: public policy discussions, Black histories, religious teachings, popular press reports, literature, and so on. All these
shape how he understands these matters in complex ways about which
he may be largely unaware but that he has internalized over time
through his ongoing engagement with these discourses. In this sense,
these discourses can be seen as both internal and external. Thus, it is
more productive to think of Mr. Green, the writer of his narrative, as
reflecting these various discourses at the same time that he is writing
within them. James Berlin (1996) sums it up this way: "The subject is
the point of intersection and influence of various conflicted discourses—discourses about class, race, gender, ethnicity, sexual orientation, age, religion, and the like" (p. 78).

At the same time, Mr. Green does make decisions about his text;
he uses language in specific ways that at some level *he* determines—
ways that differ from, say, Mr. Jarrel's language use and tone. He finds
a particular way into the discourses that are "already in place," even as
those discourses shape his text. As Berlin puts it,

> Of equal importance, the subject in turn acts upon these discourses. The
> individual is the location of a variety of significations, but it is also an
> agent of change, not simply an unwitting product of external discursive
> and material forces. The subject negotiates and resists codes rather than
> simply accommodating them. (pp. 78–79)

And here the crucial distinction between *subject* and *agency* comes into
play.

Despite the usefulness of poststructuralist analyses in helping us
see the complicated ways in which the subject is not autonomous, is
not free of or separate from discourse, a view of the subject as solely a
product of discourse approaches determinism. In other words, if the
subject is never free of discourse, if it is always a product of discourse,
then discourse must always determine how the subject is constituted
and what it can say or write. A subject conceived in this way cannot
"act" on its own; it has no agency except that which is assigned to it
by a particular discourse that constitutes it. Thus, Mr. Green can write
only what is determined by the discourses that constitute his subjec-

tivity. If so, what possibility exists that he also can, as Berlin writes, "act upon those discourses," that he can resist or shape them? This question describes a central problem for those who would apply postmodern thought to their understanding of literacy.

Theorist Paul Smith (1988) has addressed this problem directly by arguing that "ideological discourses are *not* unstintingly effective in identifying their appropriate 'subject,' but that manners of resistance can be glimpsed as soon as the 'subject' is no longer theorized as an abstract . . . entity" (pp. xxx–xxxi). For Smith, then, a crucial step in conceptualizing the subject is in understanding that subject as something more than a theoretical abstraction: "[C]urrent conceptions of the 'subject'," he argues, "have tended to produce a purely *theoretical* 'subject,' removed almost entirely from the political and ethical realities in which human agents actually live" (p. xxix, emphasis in original). (It is this "purely theoretical subject" that, in my experience, teachers resist.) Smith is concerned with the ways in which an individual subject can *act* within the very discourses that shape that same subject. To put it more concretely, a writer like Mr. Green is indeed constituted by discourses already in place, but he somehow lives and *acts* within those discourses in ways that differ from others around him who are subjected to those same discourses and who are, like him, constituted by those discourses; he is, to use Smith's term, a "human agent." The question now becomes, How can we understand Mr. Green's *agency* as a function of discourse but yet not wholly determined by discourse? How does the *subject* act within the discourses that constitute it? And how do we understand the different ways in which different subjects act? How do we understand the many different ways in which the men in my prison classroom acted within similar discourses about race, class, law, gender, religion, and so on?

For Smith, part of the answer is to acknowledge, first, that the "'subject' is constituted heterogeneously and is continually changing" (p. 156). Although "the agent is never *only* an active force, but also an actor for the ideological script" of these broader discourses, that agent is not unified, and those discourses are not consistent. Thus there is "always a contradiction in the 'subject'" (p. 156, emphasis in original). This contradiction opens a space for agency. In other words, the subject can act because of the contradictions inherent in its own constitution, which reflect contradictions in the discourses that constitute it; it can resist those discourses because they are never consistent and unified. For Smith, this space for resistance is best seen as a "*process*, or a tension which is the product of its [the subject's] having been called upon to adopt multifarious subject-positions" (p. 157, emphasis in original). That is, as the subject engages these discourses, the inherently contradictory and competing nature of the discourses prevents the subject from constituting itself as unified and consistent; its constitution is therefore unstable and shifting within and among the various discourses that constitute it. To put it another way, Mr. Green is constituted in various ways by various discourses—discourses of race, class, gender, law, morality, corrections, education, and so on. He is never "the same" Mr. Green in all instances. He is sometimes a man, sometimes a Black man, sometimes an inmate, sometimes a student, sometimes various combinations of these, depending on the situation he is in and on the discourses at play in that situation. Imagine, for example, the "subject" he becomes at a parole board hearing as opposed to the "subject" he is as a student in my class or as a member of his community church or as a resident in his own neighborhood. At a parole board hearing, he is understood—constructed—as an inmate seeking to change his status within an institutional system of corrections; as such, certain assumptions about him govern how he is understood as a person—as a *subject*—within that system, assumptions that are reflected in the discourses of corrections and law that function in that setting. Thus, his *subjectivity* is determined in large part by those assumptions about his "subject-position" (as a convicted criminal, an inmate) within those discourses. His racial identity may not figure into that discourse in the way it would, say, in his church or neighborhood or in school; his beliefs as a man, as a Black man, as a son, a father, or a spouse may have no place in that setting or may be understood in very specific ways in that setting (for example, his identity as a father of a small child may be understood as a positive factor in a decision to grant him parole, although that role of father would be understood and valued differently in his church or neighborhood). There's much, much more to say about the way he might be constructed as a subject in this setting, but the point is that he is a particular kind of subject in that setting— one that may contrast sharply with the kind of subject he becomes in my classroom or in his neighborhood or in his church. As a result of the different discourses that come into play in those different situations, his subject-positions in those situations overlap in certain ways and may contradict each other in other ways. Thus, Mr. Green as subject is always "constituted heterogeneously and is continually changing."

Smith argues that this kind of "contradictory constitution [of the subject's] is given over to the articulation of needs and self-interest" (p. 157). Invoking *self-interest* is the crucial move in our efforts to answer our previous questions about agency, about how a subject acts. For within a specific setting—a parole hearing or a college class—Mr. Green does make decisions about what he says and writes, about how he participates in the discourses functioning in that setting, even as his subject-position is determined in part by the discourses already in place. For Smith, understanding those decisions—those acts—requires understanding self-interest. Smith conceives of self-interest as partly conscious—that is, partly a function of decisions and motives of which the subject is aware; but Smith understands self-interest also "as being continually crossed by unconscious components—desire, memory, repressions, anxieties, and so on." Self-interest is thus "best considered as an ultimately unfixable process whose meaning is not unproblematically available" (p. 157). That is, one can never determine precisely a subject's self-interest, since that self-interest is continually in process. "However," Smith continues, "the actions that arise from such a process are themselves significant in the simple sense that they must enter the world of signification: they achieve and exhibit their meaning primarily there" (p. 157). In other words, while we can never entirely pin down one's self-interest precisely, the subject's self-interest as an ongoing process is manifested in its actions, which are expressed through signs, including the sign system of language. Mr. Green's self-interest is available to us partially through his actions, which are manifested partially in his words, written and oral.

The next step is clear: Each subject, while inevitably constituted by discourses already in place, reflects a unique, though continually changing and circumscribed, self-interest. And that unique self-interest is, as Smith puts it, "bound up with—indeed, in part built up by—a singular history . . . [or] self-narrative" (p. 158). At the same time, that subject's actions "are also equally engagements or interventions in everyone else's history, and have real effects there; these two histories are mediated in a dialectical process as the 'subject' negotiates its self-interest in relation not only to itself, but to the world" (p. 158). According to Smith, self-interest is thus "unavoidably a negotiation," one that is social; it can never be seen exclusively as the product of a subject's self-narrative, nor "is it useful to think of that self-narrative as mere noise in the processes of social negotiation: the 'subject's' history informs, dialectically, the social process and is therefore a crucial pressure upon it" (p. 158). Ultimately, then, self-interest is "the product of the 'subject's' heterogeneous constitution and the 'subject's' experience" (p. 158). To understand the subject adequately, and to understand *agency* as well, requires "a recognition of both the specificity of any 'subject's' history and also of the necessary negotiation with other 'subjects'" (p. 158), all of which, of course, takes place within discourse.

Such a view of the subject enables us to begin to understand the complex ways in which Mr. Green and Mr. Jarrel and their classmates— and indeed writers in general—claim agency both within and against the discourses that shape their own subjectivities. Mr. Jarrel, for example, appropriates some of the language of the Laubach literacy movement and writes within several discourses—public discourses relating to literacy and education, popular discourses of self-help, cultural discourses of individualism and opportunity—to argue for a literacy program designed to help nonliterate inmates; he also adopts a form (first-person narrative) whose use is shaped to an extent by those discourses. (Think, for instance, of Malcolm X's story of learning to read in prison or W. E. B. DuBois's similar narrative.) These discourses shape the position he takes and the voice of possibility that he constructs. Indeed, his own understanding of the issues he is addressing is inevitably shaped by his engagement with these various discourses. Further, Mr. Jarrel's own experiences with literacy and with nonliterate persons shape his beliefs and affect how he understands these issues. These experiences are part of the self-interest out of which Mr. Jarrel acts—in this case, out of which he constructs his argument for the literacy program. This self-interest represents a unique configuration of his experiences and other factors that help explain why Mr. Jarrel might approach a particular writing task differently than Mr. Green, who draws on and negotiates among different discourses in different ways (a function of his own unique self-interest) than Mr. Jarrel does.

In this admittedly partial account of texts such as Mr. Jarrel's and Mr. Green's, we can recognize the possibility for agency not simply as a vehicle for *resistance*—a term that has become virtually synonymous in the professional literature with a kind of left-wing political opposition to "dominant" discourses—but also as a means to begin to understand their texts and the differences between them. If we understand agency in the way Smith conceptualizes it—as both enabled and limited by discourse, as a process of negotiation within and among discourses mediated by an individual's self-interest—then we must conceive of literacy not simply as a social and cultural activity, but as an inevitably *local* act manifested in specific statements and specific texts, as a set of social and cultural practices that play out in myriad ways in the individual acts of writing and reading completed by individual writers and readers; literacy is thus a function of discourse, but at the same time it is a product of individual agents working within and sometimes against discourses—a manifestation, that is, of a writer's circumscribed and situated agency.

Conceiving of literacy and agency in these ways may illuminate not only the struggles student writers often face in writing and reading for their courses but also the ways in which those struggles reflect the local decisions those writers make in constructing their texts—and their participation in the discourses of school and society—decisions that often are hidden from us as we think about students and writing in more conventional ways. It enables us to recognize the crucial differences in the ways in which students experience and engage in reading and writing activities within broader academic and cultural discourses. Each of our students, as a function of his or her *self-interest*, participates in these discourses differently, and their respective texts manifest these differences. Thus, their decisions—about the assertions they make in a specific assignment for the class, about how they position themselves in that assignment, about the sort of texts they write— reflect their agency. It is in this sense that literacy is inevitably local.

INDIVIDUAL AGENCY AND LOCAL LITERACIES

To argue for a conception of literacy as local and individual is not to deny the social, but to try to understand the ways in which the social plays out in specific acts of writing and reading. It is part of the effort to try to explain how individual texts come to be and what they mean to individual writers and readers working within complex, inherently social contexts and discourses. It is to examine how a text like Mr. Green's essay grows out of his own negotiation of the same discourses that constitute him as a subject; how it is a product of his own self-interest, which helps determine the decisions he makes as a writer as he constructs his text. It helps us to specify what it means to say that Mr. Green's text is a negotiation among powerful and often conflicting discourses mediated by Mr. Green's self-interest, which itself is shaped by those discourses of Black consciousness, religious oratory, and racial politics. This mediation reflects his self-interest that grows out of his deeply felt identity as an African American (itself constructed in part through discourse) and his sense of membership in a racially defined community. (And it is in this process of mediation, I would argue, that some of the "problems" we might identify in his essay emerge.) The postmodern framework I have sketched out in this chapter thus reveals Mr. Green's essay as much more than an angry personal diatribe or an argument for racial justice or perhaps an attempt to make an emotional yet appropriate academic argument—all of which are valid ways to understand his text. Instead, this framework understands his essay as a construction of a specific writer writing within existing discourses; it shows this text to be a manifestation of a particular writer's complex and even uncertain subjectivity. And while it encourages us to remember that this specific text and this particular writer exist only within a complex and extensive set of social networks formed largely through discourse, it foregrounds that writer's *agency* within those discourses. Ultimately, this framework is about understanding those individual student writers who sit before the writing teacher and who represent a myriad of ways to engage the broader discourses that shape their lives.

I would argue that such a framework works against the limited conceptions of literacy that I described in the previous chapter. Those conceptions of literacy do indeed focus on the individual but they do so in a way that largely ignores the complex and problematic nature of the individual as subject and the uncertain ways in which the individual writer writes within and against existing discourses. The framework I am proposing here encourages teachers to approach their students' texts as social acts within a network of discourses, but not at the expense of denying or ignoring the deeply personal nature of those texts as meaning-making acts within those discourses. It helps explain why Mr. Green's essay can differ so dramatically from Mr. Jarrel's, without resorting to an oversimplified conception of the writer as a collection of specific cognitive skills (or "deficiencies") or presenting that writer's intentionality as autonomous and unproblematic.

As I try to understand the specific moves Mr. Green and Mr. Jarrel made as writers of their texts, I find myself moving between the general level of discourse and the more specific level of their individual decisions about their texts. On one level, I am interested in understanding how Mr. Green's approach to his subject matter, for instance, reflects his engagement with the broader discourses that seem to come into play in his essay—the legal and political and social and religious discourses I have already mentioned. I want to try to understand his text as working both within and against those discourses, drawing, for example, on religious oratory and legal rhetoric in ways that inform his stance toward his subject matter and shape his argument. I want to see his essay as *his* attempt to engage those discourses and the issues and ideas that circulate among them. And some of the "problems" I see in his text emerge at this level and can be seen as difficulties related to his efforts (which he may be largely unaware of) to negotiate these discourses. On another level, like any teacher of writing, I need to understand specific textual moves he has made in order to address other difficulties or problems in his essay. I wonder, for example, why Mr. Green sometimes shifts between the third person and the second person in referring to White people in his essay in a way that can be distracting or even confusing. To what extent do these shifts grow out of his attempt to negotiate among several discourses—political, religious, academic, racial—each of which might position readers of his essay as well as Mr. Green himself somewhat differently? Might these shifts indicate ways in which the subject-positions available to Mr. Green differ within each of these discourses? And to what extent might these shifts represent his difficulty with the specific conventions of academic prose (which would value a consistent point of view and perhaps discourage the use of the second person)? His use of the second person (*You* white people) can be seen as perhaps his drawing on the conventions of religious oratory, in which the listeners would be addressed directly in a sermon with the kind of moral tone Mr. Green adopts here. At the same time, the second person would be less common, even unacceptable, in conventional academic prose and in the broader legal and political discourses that he seems to invoke earlier in his essay (where he refers to the German war reparations for Jews). Is Mr. Green even conscious of these issues as he writes? Does he consider such matters as he tries to address the requirements of the rhetorical task? How does he understand this "problem" of shifting point of view?

Such questions point to the local ways in which broader discourses play out in a specific text and in the moment-to-moment decisions a writer makes as he or she creates that text. Typically, such local decisions have been approached by teachers and by some scholars, notably Linda Flower, as *cognitive* issues, and such a cognitive understanding of literacy, so deeply embedded in our schools, remains an appealing way for many teachers to explain the specific problems in their students' writing and reading, even as a social conception of writing seems to have become the generally accepted view among scholars. The framework I am proposing in this chapter challenges the idea that the kinds of decisions I have been referring to in discussing Mr. Green's essay are manifestations of a writer's cognitive processes, even if, as Flower (1994) has argued, "cognition is embedded within and shaped by the social contexts and emotional realities" (p. 89). At the same time, the framework I have outlined here retains a focus on individual writers struggling to make meaning in complex but specific rhetorical situations, a focus that has driven Flower's work. What I find valuable in Flower's efforts to explain student writing from within her "social cognitive" framework is her unwavering focus on individual writers negotiating complex social contexts and her insistence that such a focus can lead to valuable insights into why our students write as they do. She worries, as I do, that proponents of what she calls "social construction theory" or overtly "social" Marxist or cultural studies perspectives base their strong claims about what writers do on ideological assumptions that are not always acknowledged *as* ideological. For example, she refers to Patricia Bizzell's (1989) claim that the difficulties Bizzell's women students have in writing effective academic arguments probably result from "the effect on them of the cultural assumptions concerning feminine compliance and modesty" (p. 485). While Flower agrees with the notion that ideology is "a powerful force in our lives" and thus accepts the possibility that women may indeed be socialized in the way Bizzell suggests, she questions the way in which Bizzell's suspicion about the effects of ideology—a decidedly common suspicion in current scholarship in literacy—on her women students is "elevated to an assertion." In short, Flower argues that approaching student writing from a social perspective that totalizes them (in this case, as women imbued with an ideology that teaches them to be compliant and modest in a sexist world) may be completely ineffectual in helping us understand the specific texts of specific students and in helping us help them negotiate those "marginalizing" discourses that shape their thinking and writing; it may leave us unable to help them write the kinds of academic arguments that they apparently are learning to write in Bizzell's class. I would add here that such a perspective also does not account for the kinds of contradictions in discourses (which reflect complex and often conflicting ideologies) that Smith refers to nor does it do justice to the complexities of the identities the individual women in Bizzell's class manifest. Like Mr. Green and Mr. Jarrel, the women in Bizzell's class are much more than simply compliant females constructed as such by broader discourses.

Flower thus insists on the "specificity" of literacy, on the local nature of acts of writing and reading. Local, for Flower, means something slightly different from what it means to researchers like Shirley Brice Heath (1983), who examined the nature of literacy practices in two communities and described differences in those practices and their value to the people who lived there. Heath concludes from her study that literacy could be understood only, as Scribner and Cole (1981) put it, "in specific contexts of use" (p. 236)—that is, as local. For Flower, by contrast, "local" refers to the way in which an individual writer cognitively negotiates a specific rhetorical situation. I would argue that Flower ultimately gives too little weight to the ways in which broader discourses shape that writer's cognition and thus influence the decisions that result from that writer's cognitive strategies; for her, the real work of writing gets done "inside" the writer's mind. I find that the distinction she implies between "mind" and "social context" is too hard and fast, as some cognitive psychologists have suggested (e.g., Rogoff, 1990). Nevertheless, I want to retain part of the sense of "local" that Flower implicitly works with here and thus offer a multilayered conception of local as referring to a specific act of writing and reading within a specific social and rhetorical context as well as to an individual writer's *specific and unique* negotiation of that context and the broader discourses that inform it. Such a conception of local rests on Paul Smith's notions of the contingent *subject* and its unique yet circumscribed *self-interest* in a way that enables us to keep those broader discourses in view while focusing on the individual writer's specific decisions as he or she constructs a text within a specific social and rhetorical situation.

Such a sense of the local in an act of writing or reading also enables us to account for the deeply personal significance that literate acts often hold for our students as they struggle to construct viable selves and claim agency within the discourses that shape their writing and reading. As the essays by Hannah, Mr. Green, and Mr. Jarrel suggest, that personal significance is not separate from the rhetorical and social contexts within which these students wrote but is itself a function of the discourses they seek to enter (and sometimes resist). This same sense of a contingent and socially mediated personal significance runs through Hull and Rose's (1989) case study of Tanya, to which I referred earlier, as well as through the portraits of the four students in the study by Curtis and Herrington (in press), to which I also referred earlier. In that study we see students engaging in, and sometimes resisting, discourses associated with school, with American culture, with certain professions and academic fields. But we also see the personal nature of those engagements and resistances: how they are mediated by the unique self-interest of each writer. Like Hannah and Mr. Green and Mr. Jarrel, the students Curtis and Herrington describe write in ways that are inevitably local even as their writing can occur only within broader contexts and discourses. It is that "local-ness" that teachers ultimately must confront in working with their students. And it is no simple matter to do so.

As I struggle to articulate the framework for a "local literacy" that I have tried to sketch out in this chapter, I am visited by images that remind me of the limitations of theoretical concepts—such as *subjectivity* or *self-interest* or *agency*—in helping us confront the complexity of the "local-ness" and the "human-ness" of writing and reading.

As he hands me the revised version of his essay, "Add It Up," Mr. Green wears a slight smile that displays something between pride and defiance. This essay carries precious meaning for him, and for a moment he reminds me of the many (mostly White) high school and college students who have handed in the papers I asked them to write. Their faces revealed nervous satisfaction, uncertainty, effort, investment. They trusted me with their ideas and their words. Mr. Green does, too, and in that way he is just like them. Then he turns around and walks back to his seat, and I see the bars on the window behind him and realize that the meanings his essay carries are many: contingent and complex and uncertain.

On another day, the students are working individually on an editing exercise intended to help them identify errors in an essay I have already returned to them. I am moving from desk to desk in our prison classroom, answering questions, helping with specific misspellings or punctuation and syntax errors, and I walk past Mr. Smith's desk. He is hunched over his paper, concentrating mightily, correcting the errors in his essay. As I pass him, he looks up, smiling, and says, "This is fun." It is a comment that strikes me as incongruous, an exclamation point where there should be a question mark, a whisper instead of a shriek. How can grammar be fun for someone who has been deemed "remedial" and told throughout his school years that his knowledge of standard English is "substandard"? This young man is sitting in a prison, locked away from his daughter and his home, correcting errors in his writing—and having fun. It occurs to me that he is expressing the simple joy of being able to manipulate written language in order to say something he has to say, the satisfaction of getting it right. But more than that: He also is feeling the subtle excitement that accompanies the realization that writing can represent a kind of power, a realization that he can make his voice heard in an academic setting in a way that gains him credibility and standing within that setting. He *can* do it right. I, too, have experienced that kind of joy—often—and I smile back. But I have never had to write as a Black man in prison, and I have never had to prove to a teacher of a remedial writing class that I can do it right. And I wonder whether my joy is really like his. For the power of literacy does not necessarily refer to the same thing for him that it does for me.

The "local-ness" of literacy can be insufferably complicated.

Chapter 4

Writing Roles for Ourselves

Local Literacies and Students' Lives

I write because I feel politically committed, because I would like to convince other people, without lying to them, that what I dream about and what I speak about and what causes me to struggle are worth *writing about. . . . That is, when we write, we cannot ignore our condition as historical beings. We cannot ignore that we are beings inserted into the social structures in which we participate as objects and subjects.*
—*Paulo Freire,* Letters to Christina

The self is completely autonomous, yet exists only in resonance with all other selves.
—*Robert Aitken,* The Mind of Clover

On a muggy Ohio summer afternoon I am validated. Four university professors stamp *approved* on my dissertation. Their approval comes at the end of the traditional 2-hour oral dissertation defense, held in a spare but neat English Department conference room, in which they questioned, wondered, argued, pushed, tested, grilled, chatted, laughed, invited, listened, disagreed, and finally agreed. My dissertation is accepted, and so am I.

Eli Goldblatt (1995) has written that "writing is central to the institutional existence of a university." "Take away the buildings," he goes on, "and you have a university in search of a home; take away the writing and a university is unimaginable" (p. 30). Take away my dissertation and I do not exist in that university in the same way I do as a result of that document's approval by my dissertation committee; take away that dissertation, and "I" disappear.

During the oral defense, this question of my "academic identity" is addressed directly. A significant portion of the 2-hour session, maybe

30 minutes or so, is devoted to discussion of a postscript I added to my dissertation. In that postscript, which I titled "On the Context of Writing This Dissertation," I described the trouble I had writing the dissertation: not the expected trouble of crafting a coherent argument or presenting data effectively or structuring the chapters logically; rather, I described my struggle "to maintain what I hoped to be a genuine voice in the writing while conforming to the conventions of an academic dissertation in the field of English—a form seemingly designed to snuff out the writer's voice" (1991, p. 329). Years later, that statement will strike me as simplistic and even naive, a reflection of my adherence to the Romantic conception of the writer (which I critiqued in Chapter 2). But during my oral defense, I cannot see it. And all four members of my committee are surprised by my complaints about "losing" my voice as I wrote the dissertation. One of them confides that she found my dissertation very readable and my voice engaging; she wonders what I found so troublesome about the writing. Others question me about my conception of "voice" (and only much later will I come to see how uncomplicated and problematic my conception of voice was at the time). My dissertation director, who is co-author of a well-known book on collaborative writing, challenges me on this point. You have argued throughout the dissertation that writing is inherently social, she says, so why do you want to hold onto the notion that *your own* writing is not? Why do you insist on valorizing *your* voice as a personal matter rather than something that is socially defined? I know she is right, but in answer to her questions I can only stumble about the familiar terrain of the Romantic writer. Despite my self-proclaimed adherence to a social view of writing, I am unable to think of *my* dissertation as social, as part of the professional discourses that shaped it.

My committee members knew, of course, how central that dissertation was to my professional life. They knew, too, how difficult it can be to write such a document. But they couldn't know at the time the extent to which my difficulties in writing that text went beyond the kinds of problems I discussed with them in the many meetings we had during the year-and-a-half leading up to that oral defense. They couldn't know that my frustration was not just a matter of learning to write academic prose of the kind expected in a dissertation. For I never confided to them that as I was writing that draft, I lamented the passing of the "writer" I once was—a freelance writer whose sense of self was a function of the newspaper and magazine articles I wrote, about whom my father's auto mechanic said, after reading one of my magazine articles, "You're a good *writer*." I worried that I was no longer that same good writer as I became the apprentice researcher/scholar/academic who authored not magazine articles but a dissertation. I felt my writerly voice becoming fainter with each page I wrote, even as I gained confidence in my ability to participate in the academic conversations that I was hoping to enter through the act of writing that dissertation. At the same time, as I worked through successive drafts of each chapter, I tried to ignore the gnawing suspicion that what I had to say in the dissertation was irrelevant and trite, that I had no business playing the role of scholar, that I knew no more about the importance of writing and reading than I had known all those years before as I whiled away summer afternoons reading in my bedroom or wrote magazine articles read by an appreciative auto mechanic. I imagined an audience of scholars dismissing my work as trivial; I imagined the elders in my family dismissing the "50-cent words" I was using.

Writers—student writers as well as professional writers—often confess to such doubts about their writing. Like all teachers, I have vivid memories of the anxiety with which students hesitantly have handed me essays about important matters in their lives, essays that they believed revealed all their flaws as writers—and as people. Such doubts have been explained in various ways in the professional literature, from "writing apprehension," an almost clinical malady that some researchers (e.g., Rose, 1985) have linked to the cognitive challenges of academic writing, to a lack of familiarity with academic discourse (see Bartholomae, 1985). My own difficulties in writing my dissertation suggest, I think, that such difficulties must be understood within the context of the multiple, shifting, overlapping, often conflicting discourses that are in place in any rhetorical situation: in my case, the disciplinary discourses of composition studies and empirical educational research; the professional discourses of graduate education and scholarly inquiry in the humanities and social sciences; the broader public discourses of education and that I discussed in Chapter 2. But the difficulties I experienced as dissertation writer—like those of Hannah, whose text is reproduced in Chapter 2—also point to the deeply *personal* nature of that decidedly social document. For whatever else it was, that dissertation was my attempt to construct myself within the university and within the broader disciplines I sought to enter as an academic; it is a construction of my *identity*—several identities, actually—just as Hannah's essay about coming to college was an assertion of her own sense of self-worth as a student and a person. In the postscript to my dissertation, I muse about the influence of my own background on my study: the fact that I am White, male, middle class, Polish, raised and schooled a Catholic, and so on. And I complain that somehow these aspects of the "I" who wrote that dissertation are lost in "the conventions governing academic dissertations" (p. 332). Like Abby, the student I describe in Chapter 1, I did not want to be made irrelevant by "the discourse." I was struggling to maintain some sense of self against a world of discourse that seemed to want to erase or re-define that self. At the same time, as I would eventually come to under-stand, it was only within discourse that I could construct that self that I so worried about losing.

In many ways, my struggle to construct an academic identity in my dissertation was far more straightforward than the struggles of stu-dents like Hannah or Mr. Green to construct themselves in the texts they write. In my case, despite the complexities of the rhetorical situ-ation, the task was rather clear, the purposes more or less overt and widely understood, and the discourses invoked relatively well-defined. But as we saw in the cases of Hannah and Mr. Green, the seemingly straightforward task of writing an academic essay for a college or high school class can be enormously complex and uncertain. To sort out the discourses that come into play in Mr. Green's essay, for example, is no simple matter—either for him or for me as his teacher. To con-sider the ways in which Mr. Green might effectively enter those dis-courses and construct a role for himself within them, as I began to do in Chapter 3, is trickier still. But it is essential, I think, to try to tease out the ways in which student writers can do so, keeping in view the contradictions and possibilities that literacy represents for them as they do. In other words, if literacy is participation in discourse, and if that participation is inescapably local, as I have been arguing, then literacy is inevitably about the complex and uncertain task of constructing a self or selves that can enter specific discourses in order to *act* in spe-cific situations for specific purposes—academic or otherwise.

As we saw in Chapter 3, that self is a complex, sometimes con-flicted, even uncertain entity, a multifaceted and contingent *subject*, one that arises from unique configurations of factors that Paul Smith (1988) has defined as the subject's *self-interest*. My dissertation was in the end an effort to construct a multifarious self. It was an attempt to claim a space for myself within the complex professional discourses I sought to participate in and to act within those discourses in a way that had real consequences in my life and the lives of others. And that effort to construct an academic identity was complicated by the fact that my "self" encompasses other identities that are ostensibly distinct from my academic identity: son, father, husband, brother, neighbor. Ultimately, that text, even though it was read by only a few people, and fewer still who were not academics (including my family), helped define my "nonacademic self" as much as it helped define my academic identity.

For students, this task of writing oneself through and into and (as we'll see momentarily) *against* discourses that are often conflicting, unfamiliar, and even "invisible" to them can be just as challenging but no less significant. As their teacher, I am interested in understanding better how their texts came to be so that I might be able to help them claim agency for themselves and ultimately develop the kind of critical literacy that Paulo Freire (1970/1984) describes, a literacy based on the notion that writing and reading are part of the ongoing struggle to become "fully human." And I believe to do so is to understand, to the extent that I can, how their specific texts represent local acts of self-construction, attempts to write themselves into the broader discourses that shape their lives. And so, drawing on the conception of *local literacy* that I laid out in Chapter 3, and keeping in view the contradictions and possibilities of literacy that I explored in Chapter 2, I want to look more closely at the writing of some of the students I have come to know, as a way to begin to understand their writing more fully as acts of self-construction in discourse.

CELINA

On the first day of class, I wend my way from my office through the network of tunnels and corridors that lie beneath the uptown campus of the State University of New York at Albany. I am on my way to the TV-studio-converted-to-computer-lab that will be my classroom for the semester. The *Peterson's Guide to Colleges and Universities* describes the campus tunnel system at SUNY–Albany as a practical and convenient way for students to avoid the sharp winter cold that usually arrives in upstate New York in early November and lingers through March. But the dim passages, with their partially painted cinder block walls and exposed pipes and ducts, feel dungeon-like to me. And the classroom they lead me to isn't much better. On three sides hang dark reddish, heavy curtains, obscuring the walls from the floor to the high ceiling, dingy reminders that this room was not originally intended for a writing class. Six or seven rows have been made from folding tables pushed together, end to end. Three dozen outdated DEC computers are spaced along these tables, with bunches of multicolored cables hanging down from the back of each computer, exposed, like sloppy remnants of threadbare bunting. A small desk with a newer computer, a portable blackboard, and an overhead projector stand at the front of the room. I walk to that desk, turn on the computer, and begin to pull papers from my bag as the students arrive.

The class is English 303Z, a nonfiction writing workshop that is part of the English Department's new undergraduate writing sequence. It has never before been offered at SUNY–Albany, and I am happy to have the opportunity to teach it. During the previous semester, when course schedules were being finalized, I requested that the class be scheduled in a computer lab. This converted TV studio was the only available facility. In some ways, the physical space made available to the class is a metaphor for the place of writing within the SUNY–Albany curriculum: The value of writing instruction of the kind offered in the course is questioned by many faculty, and unlike most larger state universities, SUNY–Albany has no required first-year writing course. But like the students in my prison writing class, the dozen or so students who signed up for this course harbor few doubts about the value of writing.

They reflect the diversity about which we talk so much in our professional discussions: White men and women of "traditional" college age, most from "the City" or "the Island," as they refer to New York City and Long Island; several students of color; a few older "nontraditional" students. But their diversity challenges these ready categories. Gary, for instance, who will graduate at the end of the semester, immigrated with his parents from Haiti to New York City when he was in sixth or seventh grade. His bilingual background and difficulties with English qualified him for ESL programs in the public school he attended. To describe him as a person of color or as an ESL student is to obscure the complex background he brings to his writing class, where he will describe in one essay the experience of being treated unfairly and with obvious bias by an African-American teacher who, he says, disliked Haitians. Larry is a 25-year-old White man from a rural area north of Albany who found his way to SUNY after taking courses at several community colleges. Like Gary, he will graduate at the end of the semester; like Gary, his command of academic English is tenuous at best. Unlike Gary, he is White and middle class. Celina, an African-American woman in her mid-20s, is a single mother who works full-time as a supervisor in an insurance company and attends school nearly full-time as well. She is from a nearby city that is both urban and suburban, where she lives in a predominantly White neighborhood and attended a predominantly White public high school. Sophia, a White woman in her 30s, is also a single mother. She has been raising her three children in "the projects" (as she calls her urban neighborhood) of a nearby city after her abusive husband left her. She is able to attend school full-time through public assistance, whose rules prevent her from earning extra money. Jennifer is a White woman who seems in every way a "traditional" undergraduate. Around mid-semester she will stop attending classes and eventually take an "incomplete" for the course in order to have a baby, which she will raise on her own. There are a few others whose backgrounds are also more diverse than the categories of "White woman" or "African-American man" suggest.

By this point in the semester, when the dust from registration, financial aid, and drop/add procedures finally has begun to settle, only nine students remain in the course—well short of the 15-student limit for these new writing workshop courses. A few minutes after today's class begins, they are spread out in the dim makeshift computer classroom, each at his or her favorite seat. The many empty chairs and tables, the blank curtain-covered walls, and the high ceiling make their small number seem even smaller. Today, we will discuss Celina's draft of her essay for the second formal writing assignment of the semester. For that second assignment, I have asked the students "to draw on your own experiences to explore an issue or problem in education that might interest the rest of us and help us better understand education." Their first assignment was a narrative of a "significant experience in education" in which they were asked to tell the story of that experience in a way that might reveal something about education, about learning, about school. This second assignment, I have told them, is not a narrative; its purpose is to explore more broadly an issue or problem in education that grew out of the narrative they wrote for the first assignment. Celina's response to this assignment startles me. She is a quiet, almost serene woman whose soft eyes are always observant, engaged. She has not been the most active participant in our classroom discussions, but when she does speak, her insight emerges. There is a calm confidence about her that seems anomalous in light of how constantly hectic her life outside the classroom is. She is also confident as a writer, although up to this point in the semester she has not taken what I would consider to be any obvious risks in her work. Her first essay was the story of her mother's experience in returning to school as a middle-aged single mother who moved from the rural southern town where she grew up to Albany, New York. It is a touching story, but after reading the revised version, I did not think that Celina quite did justice to it. She wasn't entirely satisfied with the piece either, but she seemed to want to play it safe. So I am not quite ready for the approach she takes in her second essay.

Be Who We Been

*Everyone in the room realized that our decision in favor of Black English
had doomed our writings, even as the distinctive reality of our Black lives
always has doomed our efforts to "be who we been" in this country.*
                                                                    —June Jordan

Langston Hughes, June Jordan, Franz Fanon, Malcolm X, all of
dem wrote about Black English. So it aint nothin new. But white
people keep it out the schools and out the books so black people
only learn what white call standard English. Black people been
pushed out they own culture and pushed into white culture.
White people set up a whole system to hold Black people down.
Where black people live, where they go to school, what they
watch on t.v, where they work, what they buy at the store,
where they work, what they learn in school, how they talk,
white people try to control all a that. And they been doin it
since forever in this country.

Slavery, then segregation and Jim Crow, then now when
white people in newspapers and t.v. talkin about racism is gone
which is a lie, but now they tryin to take away anything that
help black people. For the whole time, they been working on
black people to make black people think like white people
think. White peoople own just about everything and they
decide what is good or bad and then everything they do got a
part of how they think in it. Like they think black people is
criminals and they harass, arrest and put mostly black people in
jail. They think white people is better workers, smarter and
more reliable than black people and they discriminate. and hire
white people instead a black people. And white people got the
best jobs and make the most money. Then they take they
money and buy the best houses and move into the best neighborhoods and send they kids to the best schools. Meantime,
black people aint hardly got no money and live in the worst
places and got to live where people tryin to survive legally or
illegally and they kids go to the worst schools.

All a this been buildin up year after year since slavery one
way or another and black people been tryin to get out a they
situation. Black people see everywhere, in everything, what
white people do and what they got, how they different. Everything they see tells dem that white people and all the things
white people got is so much better than what they got. Then

they start tryin to imitate white people and what they got. White people want black people to do that. They want them to think like that. That way wont nothin really change. White people will be on top and black people will think they need to be at the top and be like white people. Or they think the only way to get to the top is be like white people. White people been sayin black people is inferior since they ships was at Africa shore. Black people is savages, they been sayin, that need to be civilized. They claim to be civilizing black people with every-thing they do and that they the most civilized. They put they "civilized" in everything so that nobody wont think no other way: Europe got the most refined, "civilized" cities; the greatest leaders in history was white; the American dream is bein blue eyed, blonde headed, livin in the suburbs—mommy, daddy and 2.5 kids; our founding fathers made this country great; classical music is civilized, rap aint; standard English is English, Black English aint.

Black people took in all a the ideas white people put out in society. They believed it. They aint the only ones. A whole lotta people get worked on by ideology. But black people usually the biggest victim because everything they do gets suppressed, pushed out. That how they language get kept out a schools and school books. And it aint but a few novels and things that wrote in Black English period. A language a whole group a people got shut out and almost got took away. White people say that standard English the correct English. How come it is? They American English aint the same as England English. Its they own English. Black English aint the same as standard English. Its black peoples own English.

Black English grew out a combination of all kinds of African languages mixing up since from slavery time and the standard English mixing up with it too. Black English done changed some since way back like other languages. Black English got rules and follow a pattern. Thats why people that talk Black English under-stand each other even if they never met or never even lived in the same place. Black English do got dialects so some words or things people from a different area dont understand.

Black English aint no harder than standard English to learn. Aint nothin wrong with Black English that it aint considered part a "correct" English except that the white people and ideology got everybody thinking that its only one right lan-guage and that the one they put into everything. But its like

this, why cant we have more than one right language? Why we
got to talk only one way? Why that one way gotta be standard
English? Why aint it Black English? What make standard English better that Black English cant do the same thing?

White people keep they way a thinkin in everything including language and they set things up so that nobody dont even
hardly recognize whats happening. Everybody just be thinking
that one thing is good or better than something else, like
standard English is better than Black English, and everybody
start trying to write and talk and read in standard English. Black
people trying to change how they communicate so it could be
like the standard English. So they can get some of the power
that white people got and so that they can be like them. Black
people tying to change the way they communicate so it could
be like the standard English. When they block out they language, they block out they history, they culture. They think like
the standard English tell you to think. They pick up the values
that all in standard English and they pick up the culture that
makes standard English and sustain it. Standard English push all
a the blackness out and try to stop black people from being who
we been.

If I am surprised by this essay, I shouldn't be surprised by the discussion it provokes during our class workshop. Sophia, never one to
hesitate to offer her view, says that Celina's unconventional approach
in the essay is right on target. Celina, she says, needs to use "Black
English" to make her point. A few others agree. But there is some uneasiness as well. Larry, who has struggled to write effectively in academic forms, worries about standards. Celina's point is important, he
says, and her approach is interesting, but allowing such writing in academic settings inevitably would weaken standards. That comment, of
course, leads to much discussion about language conventions and race
and education. It is a sometimes-intense discussion, although never
hostile, and I consider it productive, for it raises issues about literacy
that I want my students to consider carefully. It is the kind of discussion that can begin to challenge the myths about literacy, such as I
examined in Chapter 2, that many of them espouse.

Despite the intensity of the discussion, Celina is her usual calm,
measured self. In truth, the discussion was really not about Celina's
draft but about the larger issues her essay was intended to raise about
language and power and race relations. And she seems pleased by that
(as am I). But what is hidden from her classmates as they engage her

text are the many other meanings that it carries for her. In other circumstances, such as a larger class in which I would have fewer one-on-one interactions with the students, those meanings, and the struggles her text represents for her as a writer and as a person, would be hidden from me as well.

Later, in my office, Celina and I discuss her draft as she considers revising it for the required mid-semester portfolio. She confesses to having had trouble with the language in the original draft, and she is unsure about some of the revisions suggested by her classmates. In an email message she sent to me prior to our meeting, she tried to describe her uncertainties.

> I used as a basis for the technical aspect of writing and constructing the language the rules June Jordan listed in her book. I tried to follow the rule that says use direct language, which is why I repeatedly list white people in my piece. I also used the rule which says that if it dont sound like it came out of somebody's mouth, it aint right. I fear that in focusing on getting the language right, I missed focusing on the direction and content of the paper . . . I am still struggling to let go of my standard English in favor of Black English so there are some problems with consistency of language.

Celina's sophisticated sense of how language works is evident in this message. She is able to articulate the complexities of language use in a much savvier way than most undergraduates I have worked with. We talk again about her concerns and about her goals for the piece (some of which have already been realized, given the discussion the draft provoked during our in-class workshop). But I am not much help. My suggestions focus on matters of style and tone and how these will affect her readers, and I confess to her my worry that her use of Black English, as she calls it, will undercut her implicit argument about language and community and power. Some readers, I suggest, especially white readers, might dismiss her essay as too simplistic and focus on the intentional "errors" in the essay, thus missing the compelling argument about language and race that drives the piece. (Larry's reaction during the workshop is an example of the kind of concern I am expressing.) I suggest that she try to incorporate elements of conventional academic argument into her piece without changing the Black English style; that is, she might try to make reference to some of the other readings we have done as a way to bolster her position. Or she can try to use multiple voices, weaving together "Black English" with "standard" academic prose. In other words, I am advising her to retain her argument but to make it something a little closer to a conventional academic argumentative essay. She is unsure. She knows what she wants to say in her piece, but my suggestions seem unsatisfactory, as if I can't quite see the real issue.

Struggling to Construct a Self Within Discourse

In some ways, Celina's difficulties with this essay are straightforward and not entirely surprising given the challenges such an essay presents to a student writer. We can think of those challenges in terms of the *voice* she is trying to construct, the *style* she uses to help construct that voice, and the expectations of her intended audience (in this case, her classmates and myself)—all of which are conventional and valid "writerly" concerns. We might also address the nature of *argument* in academic writing (for despite its unconventional nature, her essay is still an academic piece): how it functions in a context such as her writing class and in the institutional setting of the university; the conventions governing academic argument; and so on. To an extent, these issues did come up in the workshop, and I addressed them as well in my conference with Celina.

But although these concerns represent valid ways of thinking and talking about this essay, they don't enable us to address adequately the way in which this essay functions within the context of the broader academic and cultural discourses that seem to be at play in this piece of writing; nor do they allow us to gain insight into the more personal significance of this essay for Celina: how this essay represents her ongoing effort to confront those discourses and find voice within and against them, how the essay reflects her struggle to claim agency for herself in an academic context. If we begin to examine Celina's essay in terms of this struggle to participate in discourse and to construct a self that can act within discourses that inevitably shape that self, other issues come more clearly into view, and we may gain some insight into her text that can be hidden when we focus on those more conventional issues I focused on in my meeting with her; we may see better what this essay "means."

First, consider the overt and even self-conscious way that Celina's essay draws on several rather well-defined discourses. Three emerge as central to her essay: (1) the specific discourse of "Black English," which relates to other discourses about language and race; (2) the broader cultural discourse surrounding race relations in contemporary American society; (3) and the more or less conventional academic discourses implicit in her writing, to which she refers in her email comment. Obviously, the distinctions I am making here among these discourses are artificial, since these discourses overlap and cannot be separated so easily from each other. And that is part of the point here: For although we try to define these discourses separately in order to illuminate Celina's writing, the larger cultural discourses about language and race relations overlap with, inform, and at the same time conflict with the discourses of academic writing, linguistics, and language theory such that distinctions blur. Thus, how we talk about, in the popular media, and understand, say, ebonics as an issue of language use cannot be separated from popular conceptions and ways of talking about race relations or from educational discussions about teaching writing and reading or from academic discussions about representations of race and language, and so on. The controversy surrounding ebonics in Oakland, California, in 1997 revealed the complex ways in which these various discourses intermingle in public and professional discussions. Similarly, Celina's attempt to make an academic argument about language use by consciously adopting a nonacademic style cannot be seen as situated entirely within a distinct and specific academic discourse. *Discourse* is simply too messy to allow for such clean distinctions and definitions. Instead, Celina's essay can be seen as situated at the shifting intersections of these various discourses that somehow encompass issues of language and race.

It's important to keep in mind that these discourses are not static nor are they monolithic. As Paul Smith (1988) points out, discourses not only contradict each other, but they contain inherent contradictions within themselves. For example, professional discussions about literacy education often focus on the importance of valuing a student's own language even when that language is unconventional (as articulated, for example, in the well-known NCTE document *Students' Right to Their Own Language*); at the same time, specific standards of language use are reaffirmed and also valued (as in the standards movement supported by NCTE in the late 1990s). In addition, popular discussions of literacy education often focus on the importance of setting rigorous standards for writing and reading performance in schools in ways that clash with how standards for literacy are understood in professional educational discussions. So ways of thinking and talking about specific issues can vary and diverge both within and among discourses.

Furthermore, since we confront and construct our worlds through language, discourse inevitably shapes not just how we use language but how we think about and understand our worlds. In this case,

Celina does not merely draw on specific *styles* or conventions of language use associated with specific discourses as if she is selecting a font style in her word processing program; she conceptualizes the issues about which she writes within and through those same discourses. So the discourses—of academic argument, of race relations, of language use, and so on—upon which she draws and within which she writes shape both her language and her understanding of these matters as well. And she, in turn, *acts* upon those discourses through her writing. Further, Celina's sense of herself—as a student, as a woman, as an African American—is also a function of these same discourses. Each of those discourses makes available to her specific "subject-positions" at the same time that it limits the subject-positions that are available to her. Celina is positioned differently within these different discourses. Her *identity* is thus not a direct effect of discourse, but it also cannot be separated from discourse.

In short, if we see Celina's essay as an act of self-construction in discourse, the complexity of that act begins to emerge in ways that can be obscured by our more conventional emphases on matters of academic style and convention.

At this point it's also important to distinguish here between the very useful arguments of scholars like David Bartholomae and Patricia Bizzell about the role of *academic discourse* in student writing and the kind of analysis of writing as participation in discourse that I am trying to conduct here. For scholars like Bartholomae and Bizzell, the primary assumption is that when students engage in academic reading and writing activities, they are in effect being asked to enter a discourse community with which they are largely unfamiliar and to which they do not necessarily already belong. As Bartholomae (1985) puts it, they are, in effect, learning

> to speak our language, to speak as we do, to try on the peculiar ways of knowing, selecting, evaluating, reporting, concluding, and arguing that define the discourse of our community. Or perhaps I should say the *various* discourses of our community, since it is in the nature of a liberal arts education that a student, after the first year or two, must learn to try on a variety of voices and interpretive schemes—to write, for example, as a literary critic one day and as an experimental psychologist the next; to work within fields where rules governing the presentation of examples or the development of an argument are both distinct and, even to a professional, mysterious. (pp. 134–135, emphasis in original)

These students are, Bartholomae says, "trying to write their way into a new community" (p. 156).

This perspective provides a powerful way to explain some of the difficulties students have with school-sponsored writing as they try to master the conventions of this "new language" and acquire unfamiliar ways of knowing that characterize academic discourse. We can make sense of many of the "problems" we saw in Mr. Green's and Mr. Jarrel's essays in Chapter 3, for instance, by thinking of their essays as attempts to use the conventions of academic writing with which they are not entirely familiar or comfortable. We can gain insight into Celina's essay in the same way. For instance, her struggle to make a coherent argument throughout her essay may arise in part from her lack of experience in constructing conventional academic arguments. But I wish to extend the analysis beyond a focus on discourse itself to the role of the student writer within discourse. Bartholomae's focus on language convention and specific ways of knowing that are associated with academic discourse, I think, tends to obscure the complexity of that discourse—really, *discourses*, as Bartholomae himself points out; moreover, it does not give us sufficient means by which to examine how those discourses figure into how students understand and construct themselves as writers and thinkers and persons, nor does it enable us to see the conflicted relationship between academic discourses and the other discourses that are in place in a situation such as this. For there is more, I think, to Celina's essay than her struggle to negotiate a rather tricky rhetorical situation and to make an ambitious although unconventional academic argument. It is not just an attempt to enter an unfamiliar academic discourse community but also part of her effort to construct a self that can claim agency within as well as outside that community and its discourses.

Self-Interest and the Complexity of Self-Construction

Celina provided some insight into all this when she discussed this essay in her portfolio. I had asked the students to include a self-evaluation in which they discussed their first two essays for the course. The second essay to which Celina refers below is the essay on Black English (reproduced above); the first is the narrative about her mother that I referred to earlier. Here, in part, is what she wrote about her work on that second essay:

> The best of the two essays is the second essay. While I was struggling somewhat to work out the piece, I think I accomplished much more of what I wanted to than with the first piece. The second essay is also a more objective piece meaning it is not specifically about me and I am much more comfortable to

write about subjects that are not too personal or that are specifically about me or my family. The second essay was as much an exercise of constructing the right tone and the right language and the right message as it was about the "implications" of the piece. Questions came up, from within and from others, about who I am writing this for; to whom is this message addressed, what audience. Also what is the best way to structure the piece? Should it be written completely in Black English? . . . Anyway, I finally concluded that I will use strictly Black English, with the exception of one part, and there is an explicit reason why I use standard English there. The paper is a "political" piece, I decided, and that the message has to be made "all the way live", there can be no "half steppin" here. So the second essay worked on a lot more than just my technical writing skills— putting a well written essay together and making my point. The whole question of well written was at stake here and I was not so sure that I could make it work. I was determined, but not sure. I had to play out, or talk out, the essay over and over again in my head, to myself out loud, to my friends, to my peers, to teachers, to my co-workers. Everyone's opinion could be categorized by race. The White people that I talked to said—mix the language. It was too "simple" sounding and too easy to "dismiss". It was never going to be considered "acceptable". The Black people that I talked to said—don't give up anything. If you are going to make the statement say it, and say it right.

It seems clear that this essay was about more than just "putting a well written essay together and making my point," as Celina puts it. She obviously invested a great deal of herself in this essay, and perhaps the more so since she was one of only two students of color in the class for which she was writing this piece. Celina was making her case about the validity of "Black English" to her White classmates but also to a broader imagined (and perhaps real) audience of White readers. But she makes it plain that she also was writing for Black readers, almost as if to assert that she is not "half steppin" in a way that could be seen as repudiating her home dialect and her race. She is, in other words, not just making an academic argument; she is writing also to construct an identity that encompasses the successful student in a mainstream academic institution as well as the African-American woman who grew up in a suburban community and in predominantly Black urban communities in Albany, Detroit, New York City, and Chicago, where her extended family lived. It is an identity that encompasses a home language that differs from mainstream academic language but is deeply important in her daily life. Constructing that identity is more than a matter of becoming familiar with the conventions of academic discourse; it is a matter of negotiating among various complicated, overlapping discourses and claiming agency for herself within and against them.

That self-construction is mediated by Celina's complex *self-interest*. She claims in her self-evaluation that she is much more comfortable writing "about subjects that are not too personal or that are specifically about me or my family." And while that revelation may seem to explain some of the decisions she made in her second essay, it also implicitly reflects the complex personal aspects that came into play as she wrote that essay. Her first essay, which told the story of her mother's struggle to raise her children and return to school to earn a nursing degree, revealed the power of her desire to validate and give voice to her mother as single Black mother. But it also represented her attempt to define herself as a Black woman, one who, like her mother, is also a single parent returning to school. In that first essay, she described her mother's struggle to overcome a difficult past characterized by segregated schools and a relocation from the southern state where she was born to New York, where eventually she succeeded, on her own, as a returning student. Although Celina never refers overtly to this part of her personal life in her essay on Black English, the experiences she describes in the first essay and her sense of herself as the daughter of a determined Black woman nevertheless seem to energize that second essay. In other words, given what we know of Celina as a person—a woman of color, a single parent, the daughter of a single mother who achieves academic and professional success—her second essay becomes more than an attempt to enter the discourses about language use and race relations; it becomes another part of her effort to construct her complex identity within those discourses.

I want to emphasize at this point that I am not referring specifically to *personal* writing here. Much debate in composition studies and English education has focused on the relative merits—and dangers—of assigning personal narrative essays in English or composition classes.[1] The terms of that debate, in my view, largely ignore the fact that to some extent *all* writing is "personal" and that genres such as personal narrative are not always as clearly defined as they may seem. In my English 303Z class, I assigned a personal narrative for the first assignment primarily as a vehicle for exploration of the issues concerning literacy and education that I wanted to encourage students to confront;

only secondarily was I interested in allowing students opportunities to explore personal narrative as a genre. But whether they were writing something that might be called "personal narrative" or "academic argument," their complicated *self-interest* came into play as they made the countless decisions about subject matter and language and style that writers must make as they construct their texts. What I am suggesting here is that to understand Celina's writing adequately—both her narrative about her mother and her argument about Black English— I must try to take that self-interest into account as best I can and understand her essay not only as shaped by that self-interest but also as a statement about herself. And in doing so I can gain insight into how her essay came to be—and the significance it might carry for her. With that insight, perhaps I can find ways to help her make that essay work better for her own purposes as well as for the purposes of the course for which she is writing.

This effort to account for a student writer's self-interest goes beyond the traditional effort on the part of teachers to understand something of their students' life situations in order to work more effectively with students. Good writing teachers, I think, always approach their students' work with a measure of empathy and understanding. But I am suggesting something more here: that in completing her academic writing assignments for my writing course, Celina is not simply negotiating the complexities of academic discourses but is also engaging in acts of self-construction through writing; her writing is thus about who she is and can be within specific circumstances as much as about what she wants to say. Her texts become a kind of "shared territory," as Margaret Himley (1991) puts it, "in which persons *compose* and express their individuation within, through, and against culture" (p. 5, emphasis added).

Over the course of the semester—and subsequent semesters—I learned more about Celina and came to appreciate more fully the significance of her essay on Black English to her. I learned, for example, that as one of the few African-American students in her mostly White public school, she felt a need to adopt several more or less public social roles that were available to her within these communities and within the discourses in place in those communities. One of those roles was the "good Black student" who spoke and acted "properly"—that is, who spoke and acted "White." Another was the "Black student" who interacted easily with the few other African-American students in the school—that is, who could act "Black" in ways that were acceptable both to her African-American friends and to the mostly White student body and faculty. Another still was the "Black girl" who lived in a predominantly White neighborhood—that is, who could act "Black" in ways that were acceptable and appropriate in that community. And still another was "Black daughter/cousin/niece/mother" who could speak and act in ways that were appropriate in an African-American community as well. All these roles involved different language practices. And these language practices not only were vehicles by which Celina adopted roles for herself, but were also reflections of these roles—social markers, as it were. For Celina, awareness of the ways in which these roles often conflicted with each other began to emerge as she moved from high school to college. She initially attended Howard University, an historically Black college where she was asked to be "Black" in ways that differed from her home and high school community. That experience brought into relief some of her difficulties in adopting those various "Black" roles in her high school and home community. Of course, Howard was a place that gave rise to other roles for her as well: African-American scholar, African-American woman academic. At Howard, too, she encountered new discourses of the academy within which these roles were defined.

As her writing teacher, I did not necessarily have to know all this in order to help Celina become a more proficient academic writer. But knowing some of her background not only illuminated for me the struggles she faced in writing an essay like the one about Black English but also began to reveal the ways in which that essay related to her sense of self and her effort to construct an identity and claim agency for herself within and outside the university. Clearly, it was in *my* interest as her teacher to understand something about how her self-interest—which was a function of these varied and complex experiences and roles—played out in her writing. Such an understanding can help me avoid approaching her essay as a straightforward response to a conventional academic writing assignment, which would oversimplify matters in ways that would not, I believe, serve Celina's needs as writer and person. Certainly, some of the difficulties she experienced in writing her essay about Black English arose from the intellectual challenge of constructing a complex academic argument about language and power; similarly, some arose from her attempt to work within and against the conventions of academic writing. Just as certainly, her essay was much more than an academic exercise. It was part of her struggle to write herself into the discourses—academic and cultural—about race and language; it was an effort to construct herself as a young African-American woman within and through—and against—those discourses.

bell hooks (1989) has written eloquently about the tricky ground that she traversed as an African-American woman trying to find a voice within the sometimes exclusionary discourses of the academy. She describes a struggle, much like Celina's, to construct an identity within the academy that enables her to gain access to the privileges of the academy without erasing or repudiating her race and gender and class background. It is no easy task to construct such an identity, and hooks refers to the obstacles to doing so within the academy and to her need to do so in the face of such obstacles: "I want to speak about these contradictions [between home and school] because sorting through them, seeking resolution and reconciliation has been important to me both as it affects my development as a writer, my effort to be fully self-realized, and my longing to remain close to the family and community that provided the groundwork for much of my thinking, writing, and being" (p. 75). Hooks insists that giving voice to this struggle to construct an identity sometimes means working explicitly against the language conventions of the academic world: "[T]he use of a language and style of presentation that alienates most folks who are not academically trained reinforces the notion that the academic world is separate from real life, that everyday world where we constantly adjust our language and behavior to meet diverse needs" (p. 78). Accordingly, she argues for a language that works against insularity, against a situation in which "academics and/or intellectuals can only speak to one another" (p. 78). For hooks, this effort involves more than writing and speaking plainly in ways that nonacademics can easily understand. It is about power: "What is true is that we make choices, that we choose our audiences, that we choose voices to hear and voices to silence" (p. 78).

In some ways, Celina's essay about Black English represents a concrete example of the kind of struggle that hooks describes and reinforces hooks's insistence that other, nonacademic discourses be brought into academic conversations. To do so is to validate the racial and gendered and class-based identity that hooks wants to preserve as she carves out a space for herself in the discourses of the academy. But hooks's characterization of academic language practices and her description of her efforts to remain true to her family and community seem to mask some of the complexities of the challenges facing a student writer like Celina. For Celina, there is no straightforward dichotomy between her "home" language and the language of the academy. Discourse, as I've already noted, is messier than that. And although Celina's essay about Black English might suggest that the problem is a relatively simple matter of making allowances within the academy—and in society more generally—for "alternative" or nonmainstream ways of speaking and writing, her own experience as an African American negotiating among several discourse communities indicates that the issue is more complicated, for just as academic discourse is not mono-lithic, neither is Black English. Further, hooks (1989) suggests that the central struggle is to maintain some sense of her "real" identity as a Black, working-class woman within a setting whose language and lan-guage practices work against such an identity. But as I suggested in Chapter 3, "identity" is always conflicted and necessarily constructed within discourse, such that Celina's identity outside academe is as complex and circumscribed as is her identity on campus. Her experi-ence thus underscores this complex relationship among language, lit-eracy, and identity: She adopts different roles in different settings and constructs slightly different identities—or has different identities con-structed for her—through discourse in those different settings. She is always "Black," but "Black" might mean different things in, say, her home community, her high school English classroom, and her high school cafeteria; it means something different at Howard University and at SUNY–Albany. And her engagement in specific acts of reading and writing—and speaking—in these different settings reflects those varied and sometimes conflicting identities. In short, the effort to con-struct a self that can claim some agency in a specific situation—aca-demic or otherwise—is never so simple a matter as overtly resisting discourse conventions or writing (or speaking) in one's "true" language.

I am arguing here that this effort to construct such a self is always part of the writing and reading that students do, that we all do, even when those acts of writing and reading seem to be relatively straight-forward efforts to complete a conventional academic task. Celina's final essay of the semester in English 303Z, for instance, was ostensibly a conventional research paper that grew out of the previous writing and reading assignments in the course. Celina chose as her topic the movement to establish African-American immersion schools, all-Black primary and secondary schools whose curricula emphasize African-American culture. But a look at the opening passage of her paper, which she titled "It Takes a Whole Village to Raise a Child: The Need for African-American Immersion Schools in the Post-Integration Era," in-dicates that this apparently conventional paper is as much a part of her ongoing effort to construct herself and claim agency for herself as her essay on Black English was. Her attempt to write herself into the various discourses that are in place with respect to these complex issues seems clear in the context of her previous writing.

> I was not yet born when the U.S. Supreme Court unanimously agreed that the doctrine of "separate but equal" was inherently unequal and ordered the desegregation of schools, but I do

know that decision has greatly impacted my life. I was raised in the suburbs and I have lived a fairly comfortable life. I have never wanted for food or clothes or shelter, nor front or back-yard in which to play, nor toys or activities to occupy my time, nor a room of my own. And I am blessed with a family full of my best friends. As a child I liked to play kick ball, tennis, ride bikes and go swimming. . . .

Living a comfortable life in the suburbs and attending well funded schools that provided me the opportunity to get the education and develop the talents and skills that are highly valued in the larger society was part of the legacy of desegrega-tion. I have been well versed in the norms and culture of White mainstream society.

Perhaps the flip side of my experience is the Black students in inner city schools, the children who languish in schools and in environments that have blocked their opportunities to survive, let alone flourish. Some four decades after the Brown v. Board of Education decision, Blacks are still disproportionately affected by poverty, crime, violence, poor living and working conditions, under and unemployment, undereducation and miseducation. Black children in inner city schools are more likely than their White counterparts to be truant, suspended or expelled or drop out of high school. Traditional schooling has been largely unsuccessful in meeting the needs of African American students even in this post-integration era. A quote from one frustrated student at a poor, inner city school in East St. Louis sums up the sad state of today's poor urban schools: "We have a school in East St. Louis named for Dr. King. . . . The school is full of sewer water and the doors are locked with chains. Every student in that school is black. It's like a terrible joke on history" (Qtd in Kozol 35).

Too many African American children have not benefited from the social and (personal) rewards that desegregation promised. Consider this:

- Homicide is the leading cause of death for Black males ages 15–24 (Wright 14). . . .
- The gap between Black and White unemployment rates grew in the 1980s and for the most part, the difference has always been *at least double* (Marger 322).
- Black college graduates have jobless rates much higher than White college graduates (Marger 322).

- White high school drop outs have a lower jobless rate than college educated Blacks (Marger 321). . . .

    In the mid 1980s educators, public administrators, journalists, parents and scholars began seriously rethinking schools and education in an effort to address the failures of schools for Black children in the inner city. As a result, African American immersion schools (AAIS) emerged.

As a writing teacher, I see in this text a student writer who has mastered many of the most important conventions of academic writing and who has developed the ability to successfully complete a specialized if conventional academic task. That ability in itself, as scholars like Patricia Bizzell (1989) and Lisa Delpit (1995) have provocatively argued, represents a measure of power for Celina. It is a means for claiming agency by entering the conversations of academe and society and giving voice to her ideas and concerns. This is no small achievement for any student. And yet these few paragraphs of Celina's research paper also reveal that this piece of writing is anything but conventional, that it grows out of—and is part of—her effort to construct a self, to write herself into the discourses that shape her life. In that sense, the achievement this paper represented for her was even greater.

LARRY

Later in that same semester, I am sitting in our basement classroom with Larry. Class has finished for the day, but Larry and I remain to work on a draft of an essay he is writing. Sophia is there, too, having stayed after class to ask me a question about an assignment. So is Gary, who is having some of the same problems Larry is having—except that Gary's difficulties result largely from what ESL scholars call "second language interference." The four of us sit together at one of the rows in the center of the room, and our physical closeness makes the room feel even emptier than it normally feels. Larry is a bit frustrated with his draft, and he is asking me about some of the comments I have written on it. After reading it a day or two earlier, I asked him to speak to me directly, because the draft contained so many problems that worried me so late in the semester. Some are problems that I expect to see in student writing even at this stage: lack of focus, underdeveloped ideas, weak organization—troublesome but relatively straightforward "technical" writing problems that teachers routinely address in student writing. But some are problems that I don't expect to see very much in an advanced writing workshop, especially in the draft of a student who will graduate in a few weeks: sentence fragments and run-on sentences that indicate to me a lack of control of some basic conventions of written English; and larger difficulties with the development of ideas, which indicate difficulty in sustaining a coherent, extended argument in an academic essay. These problems appeared periodically in Larry's writing earlier in the semester, and we discussed them in conference. But his latest essay seems to have even more of these problems. I am worried, and I tell him so.

Despite the seriousness of the writing problems I want to discuss with Larry, the atmosphere in that almost-empty classroom is relaxed. And that's no surprise, since by now Larry has established himself as something of the class cut-up. He likes to throw out one-liners in an unthreatening kind of way that endears him to most of his classmates, who appreciate the way he helps lighten the atmosphere in that dingy classroom. In turn Larry seems to relish the subtle jokes that I sometimes return at his expense.

"Wait a minute!" he interrupted as I demonstrated a computer technique during a recent class. His interjection provoked smiles and a few chuckles from his classmates, who are by now well acquainted with his computer foibles. "I'm stuck!" The slight smile, barely visible in the dim light, betrayed his enjoyment of the attention he receives whenever he gets "stuck."

"Yes, Larry," I replied, with feigned frustration, enjoying the game myself. "Did you turn the computer *on*?" The laughs from his classmates broadened his own smile.

Maybe this unthreatening clowning endears Larry to me, too, for despite the serious problems in his writing and my growing sense of my inability to help him address those problems, I enjoy working with him. Now, away from the stage that the class meetings provide him, we are still trading jokes as we focus on an especially troublesome passage in his draft.

"Do you see what's wrong with this sentence?" I ask him, pointing to a fragment in the passage that I had underlined.

"Yeah, it's too short," he says after a pause. And perhaps because we have been joking, Sophia and Gary chuckle. But it's no joke. That's his answer, and I am stunned.

"Larry!" I say, emphasizing my astonishment. "Too short?!"

"Yeah." But of course now he knows he is wrong.

"Look," I say, "'Go!' is a complete, grammatically correct sentence, and it contains a single word. Length has nothing to do with it."

"Really?" He says sheepishly, and although he is still smiling, he betrays concern of his own. He really didn't know that.

This impromptu lesson continues for another 45 or 50 minutes, during which I explain, with occasional help from Sophia, some of the other errors in his draft and learn more about his understanding of these errors—or lack of it. I realize that I should have had this conversation with Larry much earlier in the semester. In my commitment to help my students engage "theory" and explore the complexities of language in ways that Celina tries to do in her essay on Black English, I have overlooked serious problems in this one seemingly ordinary student that prevent him from engaging these complex issues of language in ways that I designed the class to facilitate. I am upset with myself and shocked by Larry's good-natured response to our session, even as the seriousness of his writing problems begins to come clear to him.

"You know," he says as we pack up our books and I begin to shut down the computers, "no one has ever pointed this stuff out to me, except one guy." He goes on to explain that among the several writing teachers he had at two community colleges he attended before coming to SUNY–Albany the previous semester, only one—an older, experienced faculty member at a nearby 2-year college—had spent any class time on what Larry calls "grammar."

"He was hard," Larry says, "but he made us do corrections. Other than that guy, no one paid any attention to my grammar."

I ask him how he did in these other writing classes, and he tells me he generally earned Bs. And when I ask him about other courses— not writing courses—he tells me the same thing. I am incredulous. He is struggling to maintain a C in my course, and that grade is largely a result of the fact that my grading scheme in the course rewards participation and completion of drafts.

"I always knew my grammar was bad, but it never really mattered much," he says.

But it's clear that he knows it does matter—not the "grammar" as such but what it reflects about his abilities as a writer: that he hasn't learned how to write in ways that the academy values, despite earning Bs in his courses. It seems to me that Larry's devil-may-care, class cut-up personality, whatever else it might say about him, masks the seriousness with which he approaches his academic writing and hides his deep worry that he isn't ready to be the successful citizen that he came to college to be. For Larry, literacy is a means to becoming that person, and as he prepares to graduate from college, he senses that literacy has become an obstacle rather than a vehicle to that goal.

Writing Competence and Writing a Competent Self

I share this story about Larry as a kind of counterbalance to my earlier story about Celina. Celina's struggles to negotiate among various discourse communities circumscribed by the tricky factors of race, gender, and class underscore my point about the complex connections between literacy and identity. In some ways, Celina's racial identity makes it easier to see those connections as she confronts the ways of writing and reading and speaking valued in the academic world. By contrast, Larry, on the surface, seems to be "mainstream" as that term tends to be used in professional discussions about literacy and education: He is White, male, ostensibly middle class. Yet it's clear that Larry's struggles as a writer—and the significance of those struggles in his life—involve more than his apparently "mainstream" identity. In that sense, he and Celina are engaged in the same complex struggle to write themselves into their world, although their struggles play out in very different ways.

For Larry, that struggle seemed to grow out of an ongoing effort—which he tends to characterize largely as unsuccessful—to establish himself as a competent person in school and in school-related venues such as sports. I won't offer a pseudo-psychological analysis to show the relationship between Larry's apparently conscious effort to set himself up as class clown and his sense of self-esteem, but in his writing Larry consistently dealt with issues of competence and self-esteem. (See Tobin, 1993, for a provocative discussion about the inherent "psychological" transaction that Tobin sees at the center of teaching writing.) In response to the first assignment for my class, a narrative about a significant school-related experience (the assignment for which Celina wrote about her mother), Larry wrote about the unfair and almost abusive treatment he received at the hands of his high school track coach, Mr. Farmer. Larry seems to have had some ability as a runner, but his essay includes relatively little discussion of the sport itself; rather, the essay focuses on how his coach viewed and treated him as a person. It raises issues of self-esteem that Larry would return to throughout the semester. In the following excerpt, the second paragraph of his first essay, those issues begin to emerge:

In most schools (from what I've heard) the class clown was placed on a voting list and the winner ended up on a Superlatives page, in the year book. I was a nominee but never a winner by any stretch of the imagination. During my junior year, I remember having a track coach by the name of Mr. Farmer.

Don't be fooled by the name though, he wasn't one for agricul-
ture. He never bred plantlife, nor did he breed any decent
runners, shotputters or discus throwers. He could run his feet as
well as his mouth, however, he seemed to always be searching
for "the right words" and never found them. I remember Mr.
Farmer as being tall, slender and very aerodynamic (ie. he lacked
hair). I also remember him as my Chemistry teacher. I lacked in
the fundementals in the math and science venues, as a matter
of fact I still do. Whenever I recieved a sub-par grade on a test or
a quiz I would use humor to raise my self esteem. I can't think
of many teachers who appreciate the class clown and I can tell
you Mr. Farmer (again not a real Farmer . . . no overalls) was one
who didn't. Not on the track and not in chemistry class. I
suppose it would be safe for me to say I enjoyed the two seasons
I ran track, and if cohearsed I could utter the words "I liked
chemistry", but as for Mr. Farmer there was little to like.

Some of the kinds of "grammar" problems that would so concern me
later in the semester appear in this passage (for example, spelling and
punctuation errors, run-ons), along with a lack of cohesion as Larry
offers a somewhat random description of his former teacher. But what
struck me—and pleased me—at the time as I looked over this first effort to write in my class is Larry's ability to engage me as a reader with
his strong voice and his knack for turning a phrase. In addition, Larry
displays an eye for detail and a sense of how to use detail effectively in
his description of his teacher, and his wit suggests a sharp mind as well.
Perhaps it was these qualities that led his other writing teachers—and
me—to overlook some of the serious problems Larry had in his academic
writing. But whatever the case, I was not troubled by those problems in
this first essay; instead, I saw potential here. As a narrative, Larry's essay
worked fairly well, in my estimation, and he raised what I thought were
important issues about the authority of teachers, issues to be explored
as we continued with the sequence of writing assignments.

But perhaps because I enjoyed the pleasant jokester that he was in
class, I also overlooked the anger in Larry's voice in this first essay—
anger that would characterize all his writing for the course. I discussed
with him the issues of self-esteem as they emerged in his descriptions
of the relationships between students and teachers and coaches, and I
saw Larry trying to confront these issues in productive ways that would
fit in well with my goals in that course. But I didn't hear his anger that
I now see as growing out of his frustration—even years after the experiences about which he was writing—to be the person he wanted to

be. And that frustration, I now think, was two-pronged: frustration that he was never able to be the successful athlete and student—and person—that he wished to be, and frustration that was unable to write about his experiences in ways that are considered "successful" in an academic setting. Like my students in the prison writing class, Larry was implicitly told he was a failure as a person and explicitly told he was a failure as a student. No wonder he was angry.

At the time I neglected to see his writing—and his difficulties with his writing—as a function of his ongoing struggle to construct a self that could be deemed "successful" in academe and outside it. Rather, like Bizzell and Bartholomae and others who have helped us understand the difficulties students encounter when they enter academic discourse communities, I saw the problems in Larry's essays as a result of his inexperience with academic writing and his lack of understanding and control of the conventions of academic discourse. I still think such a perspective was valid in helping me make sense of some of what I was seeing in Larry's writing. But it wasn't the whole picture.

For the second assignment, which asked students to discuss an issue that emerged from their first essay, Larry focused directly on the matter of self-esteem, and although this assignment called for a more measured academic voice, Larry's anger is loud. The following passage is the second paragraph of his second essay:

> We know what happens when someone tries and fails . . . that person may be considered to be a loser. And there often is no place on a team for the loser who tries. When high school competition is in question one must first look at the process in which the children are selected. There are the "try" -outs, which oddly enough in some schools is the only encouragement for trying. The children try to get on the team. I can remember being the last one picked in gym class to play basketball because I couldn't make a basket if the hoop was the size of a manhole and the ball was a tennis ball. I was the last one picked and everyone knew who not to pass to. It was my teammates judgment, their assessment of my playing ability, that sidelined me. I might've had a bad day the first time I played; nevertheless, I was judged. The verdict was in and I was found guilty of being a poor player. This is how kids are judged outside of gym class in a more organized setting. All of the children are expected to perform as well as they can under an extreme amount of pressure. They're all lined up and they're judged. They're judged by the coach and they're judged by their peers. Behaviors toward

the kids that don't make the team change and the behaviors within the those kids change. They may feel below average and subhuman. The "nanny, nanny, nah, nah" effect takes place at times. The "I made the team and you didn't" breeds foul words and foul feelings. The child in essence can be placed upon a crucifix for their entire world to see. The children can feel embarrassed, beaten and hopeless. The coach can avoid such things by explaining that everyone has done well, however, only so many positions are available, and there are too many children who want them.

This second assignment did not call for a narrative, yet it seems that Larry is telling the same story of mistreatment and low self-esteem that he told in the narrative he wrote for the first assignment. He was to have discussed an issue or problem, but he quickly returns to *his* issue, *his* problem. And his essay becomes another effort to confront that problem and reclaim some sense of self-worth—very much as Hannah's essay, which I discussed in Chapter 2, was about her belief in herself as a student who *can* succeed. He continues to try to construct a viable self within a set of discourses that define him as marginal.

For the third essay assignment, students were asked to read their classmates' narratives from the first assignment and write what I called a "reflective analysis" in which they were to identify a key theme or problem that emerged from those essays and try to explain it. Even in the context of this assignment, which asked Larry to focus on other students' essays directly, the same issues of self-esteem and mistreatment—and the same angry voice—are evident. In this case, Larry chose to discuss Celina's essay about her mother and Gary's essay about his experiences in New York City schools as a recent immigrant from Haiti. Interestingly, Larry, the White, middle-class male, chose to discuss the essays written by the only two Black students in the class. Yet he really doesn't deal with issues of race as much as he deals with the same issues of self-worth that he himself confronted in his overwhelmingly White, rural high school. Here are extended excerpts from the essay (which was untitled):

What is education? What exactly does it entail? What are the job descriptions and obligations of the people who work within this system? Everyone has their own answers to these questions and their own definition of education. However, just like snowflakes there are never two that are exactly alike. In a blizzard of possible narrations, two students draw upon their experiences to paint a picture of education for us. Unfortunately, the only colors used are that of black and white. Racism and ignorance are proving to be immortal creatures that continue to plague our society.

Gary and Celina both had discussed the issue of racism within the education system. Gary is in his twenty's and he hails from Haiti. His first white teacher also happened to be his first white contact in the United States. Her name was Mrs. Findley and she held the African American and the Hatian american students in low esteem. Then a very young Gary had an experience with her he will never soon forget.

It was apparent to Gary and other students that Mrs. Findley held something against her minority students. There was one day in particular that Gary recalls and his writing makes this scene vivid and proves to be an effective tool. Mrs. Findley used to wait until the last five minutes of class to post the homework assignment on the board. This may not seem problematic to those of us who are native to this country. However, Gary's native language isn't english and it took additional time to record the assignment to his notebook. As he copied the assignment down Mrs. Findley grew more and more impatient. On his way out of class he was grabbed by her and shoved into the wall. She was scolding him for taking too much time to copy the assignments. Instead of posting the assignments earlier she took her frustrations out on young Gary. He remembers crying, but he doesn't say how long he cried for. Perhaps from time to time he sheds a few tears while recalling Mrs. Findley. The fact is our teachers within the education system are trusted with the children to teach the information and to make sure they are protected within the time spent on campus. Gary wasn't being protected, if anything he became in danger while within reach of Mrs. Findleys grasp. It would appear that our trust as well as our minority students are being violated in todays schools. . . .

These are the years that are crucial to a childs develpment. This experience has scarred him for life. What business of the teacher is it to humliate a child? Would Mrs. Findley have trated a white student with the same disrespect? Perhaps, perhaps not, it is Gary's opinion that she would not have. Can we afford racial conflicts in our schools? Can we afford to take the words of our children over that of a teacher? I ask you, can we afford not to?

Celina tells of her mother's experiences in a segregated mississippi grade school. This story had taken place twenty years before Gary's experience with Mrs. Findley. The teachers in Celina's mother's school were poorly trained and unusually young. The black kids stayed with black kids and the white stayed with the white. The black children were forced to use books of yesterdays past. They were horribly outdated and decrepit. Celina's mother wasn't forced to sit in the back of the bus. As a matter of fact she wasn't allowed on the bus at all. This was a priveledge reserved for the white children exclusively. Celina's mother remembers throwing rocks at the bus while it sped past filled with white children laughing at her.

It obviously was the opinion within the school board that it was okay that these children use inadequate facilities and tools to learn with. Gary and Celina's mother do not concur. . . .

What can we do? We can listen to our chilren with patient ears. We can create an environment within schools that are appropriate to learn within. it is obvious that over the years between the youth of a woman in her fourties and the youth of a man in his twenties that this society hasn't hardly evolved at all. After twenty years, segregation is still actively encouraged. However, it isn't a physical segregation it is emotional and we should be ashamed.

It's worth noting here that the "grammar" problems that seemed to concern Larry later in the semester were largely absent from the passage taken from his second essay (above) but reappear in this third essay with a vengeance. I'd suggest that one reason for this is the difficulty Larry had in constructing and sustaining a conventional academic argument—a task he struggled with throughout the rest of the semester. But what strikes me about this essay is the way in which it continues—implicitly—to tell Larry's story of mistreatment and low self-esteem, and in that sense it can be seen as part of his ongoing struggle to construct through his writing a sense of identity that reclaims that self-esteem as a competent young White man about to leave college and enter the workaday world.

Self-Interest and Self-Worth

Larry's struggle, as personal as it clearly is, nevertheless must be understood within the context of the ways in which he is positioned by the discourses he is confronting as he engages in these acts of writing and reading: He is a "novice" within the discourses of academic writing and education reform, as those discourses are manifested in the reading and writing assignments I gave to the class and more broadly in the discussions within the popular media about education; he is a "student" in those same discourses; he is a "student athlete" within the broader discourses in our culture surrounding competitive sports and interscholastic athletics; he is a "male athlete" and a "young man" defined in specific ways within those same discourses and within other cultural discourses about gender. In short, like Mr. Green, whom I discussed in Chapter 3, Larry is positioned variously within all these discourses, and these various subject-positions shape his struggle to construct an identity that allows him some sense of self-worth. In other words, how Larry understands himself and these various circumstances that he describes (competing on a high school track team, for instance) is partly a function of these various, sometimes conflicting discourses that shape his sense of what it means to be a student, an athlete, a man, and a writer. What is striking to me is that in each case Larry seems somehow compromised and relatively powerless. He has rather marginal competence as a student writer, for example, and if we take him at his word, he seems not to have been successful as either a "student athlete" or a "young man" in high school. Yet the various discourses that position him in these roles inevitably shape his own sense of self. It's an insidious kind of catch-22, in which he can adopt only roles that are available to him—that are constructed for him within these broader discourses—yet in adopting those roles, he is constructed as something less than competent.

In the previous chapter I argued that literacy must always be understood as "local" in the sense that each writer and reader engages the discourses in place in a specific situation in decidedly personal ways; I invoked the concept of *self-interest* to help explain this dynamic between the broad, inherently social and cultural discourses that we all encounter as we read and write and the idiosyncratic and unique individual writer and reader who is constructed through specific literate acts. Larry cannot escape those discourses that assign certain subject-positions to him, but he confronts those roles—and adopts or resists them—in ways that are mediated by his self-interest. If we could identify key aspects of that self-interest, we undoubtedly would include his prior experiences with teachers and coaches like Mr. Farmer; for Celina, we would focus on her experiences as a young African-American woman moving among several different community and institutional contexts, each of which values her race and language in different ways, and we would likely include her relationship with her mother, and so on. For each student, these specific elements that can be said to be part of his or her self-interest are different. Yet the task facing each student is fundamentally similar: to write (and read) a way into those discourses and claim space for himself or herself. And my task, as their teacher, is to help them understand the complexities of written language and develop some measure of competence with it so that they might find viable—and satisfying—ways to write themselves into those discourses. That is a task that goes well beyond helping such students acquire some mastery over the conventions of writing in specific contexts.

In working with Larry I did not appreciate this. Although at the time I supported the arguments Larry tried to make in his essays and empathized with his sense of indignity and injustice, I did not understand the extent to which Larry's writing in my class was all really about the same set of difficult and complex and personally troubling issues as he tried to write himself into discourses that defined him in complex and troubling ways. I am confident that I helped Larry become a better writer by helping him work through drafts of these essays in order to address the obvious "technical" problems of focus and organization and the frustrating grammatical mistakes; I am confident that I helped him understand better some of the conventions of academic writing and enabled him to make some small progress toward learning to use those conventions in sustaining academic arguments or analyses. And I think I helped him gain insight into the social and cultural nature of written discourse. But I'm not sure I helped Larry make any progress in his real project that semester: to construct an identity through his writing that would enable him to claim a sense of agency—one that encompasses a sense of confidence and self-worth—within the discourses of academe and of our culture more generally; to become fully human, in Freire's sense of that term. The decisions Larry made about what and how he wrote in my class that semester were, I would argue, much more intimately a function of this project than they were of his inexperience with academic discourse or the intellectual challenges of the writing and reading tasks I was asking him to complete. In other words, I might have better understood those decisions—and the difficulties he had in his writing—had I been able to see his writing in terms of his effort to construct a viable self in his academic work.

As I write this chapter nearly 2 years after that semester ended, Larry's self-evaluation, which I assigned as part of the required course portfolio, seems to underscore my inability, as his teacher, to appreciate his struggle to construct that self. In that self-evaluation, Larry refers to the writing problems that frustrated him all semester: sentence structure, focus, organization—which he calls "the basic structure of writing." He establishes the sober tone of that brief document in the very first line: "I have struggled all of this semester. I have struggled with sub-topics, and I have struggled with commas. As well as having an over-all struggle with computers." I'm sure he did not intend the irony in that last sentence fragment. And then, without a hint of the humor that was so much a part of his classroom presence, he concedes that he did learn something as a result of his struggle with computer technology, the use of which he resisted all semester: "By the way I used computer applications like you showed me to reorganize my paper. Don't feel like a total failure. I learned how to do that from you." He encourages me not to feel like a failure, yet he implies that he does. Again.

His self-evaluation was thus one more part of the larger, inter-related set of texts through which he struggled to define himself as something other than a failure. In my obsession to help him under-stand writing as discourse, I didn't see it. I didn't see that his individual struggle to confront discourse was, for him, not about the discourse itself but about his place within it.

PERSONAL AGENCY AND POLITICAL EXISTENCE

The day's mail brings, unexpectedly, an anonymous flyer, which begins,

NEIGHBORS, WE MUST BE VIGILANT!
Do we really need or want a high density housing area just west of Green Meadows?
Is there room for 230 houses on only 77 acres? . . .
To those living in Green Meadows, what happens to your water pressure and sewage?
What does the future hold?

I am one of the "neighbors" to whom this document is addressed, one of "those living in Green Meadows," a subdivision some 2 miles outside of West Lafayette, Indiana, where Purdue University, my employer, is located. As I walk from the roadside mailbox back up the driveway to our house, I skim the flyer, then I read it again, more carefully. I am aware of plans for expanding this subdivision, a modest neighborhood of some

150 homes that has existed for nearly 50 years, but the numbers—230 new houses, 77 acres—are new to me. And they concern me. My wife, Cheryl, and I chose to live in this neighborhood for a variety of reasons, but we were especially attracted to the quiet, settled character of the subdivision, which suggested that we would not have to deal with rapid new construction of the kind we witnessed near our previous home in Ohio. Our choice was perhaps shaped mostly by the fact that this was our first house (we previously had rented), and we wanted it to be just the right place for our two school-aged boys and for us. The flyer's tone of warning brings back all these considerations at once, a rush of thoughts that intensifies my reading. "WE MUST BE VIGILANT!"

If self-interest, as I have been using that term, uniquely shaped how Larry and Celina wrote their essays for my composition class, it just as surely shaped how I read that flyer. I read that text not only as a new homeowner, but as a husband, a father, a parent of schoolchildren, a taxpayer, a mortgage holder, a voter, a neighbor. Each of those roles—those subject-positions—is circumscribed by various discourses—economic, political, cultural, social. But those roles are mediated in terms of my self-interest—which encompasses my prior experiences as, say, a voter and taxpayer and renter and son of homeowners as well as my knowledge of matters like taxes and zoning and drainage. Those experiences and that knowledge, along with my broader beliefs about such things as development and private property (beliefs that are themselves a function of discourse) and my "skills" and experience as a reader (a literate person)—all these mediated my engagement with this text and thus shaped the way I made meaning of it. More important, my effort to make meaning of this text—to determine its meaning *for me*—represented an act that reflected a measure of agency on my part. That is, the meaning of this flyer was a function of the significance of that text, as I understood it, given the circumstances I have described. That meaning will change from reader to reader—as a function of each reader's circumstances and self-interest—and thus is always *local*.

But that's not the whole story. For literacy represents power only within broader economic, political, social, cultural, and institutional contexts within which it is assigned value. As Deborah Brandt (1998) reminds us, "Literacy, like land, is a valued commodity in this economy, a key resource in gaining profit and edge" (p. 169). In this sense, the flyer by itself is just a text; what I might *do* with it—beyond my act of "decoding" it—and what I *can* do with it within these broader contexts and within this particular situation make all the difference. I can, for example, throw it in the trash can, in which case the act of reading it

amounts to little more than decoding the words and does not necessarily represent the kind of potential empowerment that I have associated with literacy. Or I can show it to a neighbor and use it as a way to
engage that neighbor in a discussion, which may include our collective decision making about some further act. That act may include
attending one of the meetings to which the flyer refers, or it may include voting for or against the unnamed county commissioner in the
next election, or it may mean making phone calls to "let everyone know
that this area needs to remain as low-density and non-commercial,"
as the flyer suggests, or it may mean writing a letter to the county planning commission or to the local newspaper expressing opposition to
the development. Any such act would be influenced by my prior act of
reading that flyer, and in that sense my reading of it may represent
the kind of Freirean empowerment that I believe literacy can be. As an
experienced writer and reader who possesses a general understanding
of matters that are important in this instance (mortgages, taxes, etc.),
then, I do have some measure of potential power, circumscribed though
that power ultimately may be.

Ideally, I want my students to acquire such power, too; I want literacy to represent a means of action in whatever situations they may
confront that matter in their lives as much as the subdivision development mattered in mine. Student loan documents, rental agreements,
employee tax forms, leases—such texts might intersect their lives in significant ways as the flyer intersected mine. How they read those texts—
how they *can* read them—may determine what kind of action is possible
for them in those situations. And in this sense, the kind of self-construction that I have described Celina and Larry engaging in through their
academic writing must be seen, eventually, within the broader contexts
of their literate lives outside the classroom. In other words, literacy represents an ultimately limited kind of empowerment for them if it is only
about how they construct themselves in their academic papers. If those
acts of self-construction cannot be extended beyond the classroom, to
intersect with others in social and political and economic contexts, then
their writing and reading, as important as they may be in helping them
construct a sense of self, will not become a significant means by which
they can act as citizens and voters, by which their self-construction can
become meaningful in a social and political sense. Thus, literacy can represent empowerment for Celina and Larry only to the extent that they
can use it to negotiate the challenges they face in their lives outside the
classroom. Their self-construction in writing may always be local, but it
will not always be school-sponsored (see Chapter 6).

Elspeth Stuckey (1991) offers the depressing insight that literacy is "an economic and social regulation" (p. 19). The truth of her statement is evident—for me, at least—at a meeting I attend some months after the flyer appeared in my mailbox. The meeting has to do with the sale of some land adjacent to the subdivision that is owned by the corporate entity that operates the Green Meadows water system. As I sit on one of a few dozen folding chairs arranged in hasty rows in the brightly painted basement of a church a few blocks from my home, I try to understand the status of this entity—a nonprofit, nongovernmental corporation that has controlled the water system since its construction 45 or so years earlier. The three vaguely familiar 50-ish men sitting at the table in the front of the room politely answer questions posed by their neighbors. Everyone knows everyone else here. The friendly, air-conditioned atmosphere makes it easy to forget the oppressive summer heat outside and the seriousness of the matter at hand. Large placards with blueprints and information about the sale stand at either side of the table, and as they talk, the men distribute several handouts with more information—including statistics about tax assessments and land values—to the dozen or so of us sitting in front of them. Each attendee is asked to sign a list that is circulating among the rows. I imagine that this list will serve as documentation for the number of attendees that will be noted in the official minutes of the meeting. Little concern is expressed about the fact that this sale almost certainly will result in development of the land, which lies across a county road that forms the southern border of the subdivision and which is now a patchwork of open meadows and small woodlots where the neighborhood kids regularly play. Cheryl and I and our sons live directly across from that land, and we like the rural feel it gives to the neighborhood. I try to match the figures and maps on the handouts with that pleasant image of the meadows and woodlots and kids in my mind. And I listen to the casual talk of legal statutes and tax assessments and mortgage arrangements as I sit there.

Two years later we will sell that house and move to another state. By then, both subdivision developments—the one described in the flyer and the one discussed at the church basement meeting—are completed, or nearly so. A great deal of writing will have shaped that work, most of it invisible or inaccessible to the residents of the neighborhood. Dozens more homes will become part of the subdivision. Its settled character that so appealed to us when we bought the house will be changed. As we leave, we will carry with us dozens of complicated legal documents relating to the sale of our house and the purchase of another—documents that reflect a bewildering complexity of discourses that assign us roles, that shape the meanings we make of them, that change the landscape of our lives.

I do not know what kinds of documents Celina and Larry will read and write as they confront important situations in their lives as students and citizens and voters and employees and tenants and property owners. But I know they will.

Chapter 5

Technology, Subjectivity, and Local Literacies

Technology, along with the issues that surrround its use in reading- and writing-intensive classrooms, both physically and intellectually disrupts the ways in which we make meaning—the ways in which we communicate. Computers change the ways in which we read, construct, and interpret texts. In doing so, technology forces us to rethink what it means to be human.

—Cynthia L. Selfe and Susan Hilligoss,
Literacy and Computers

It seems to me to be fundamental for us today, whether we be mechanics or physicists, pedagogues or stonemasons, cabinetmakers or biologists, to adopt a critical, vigilant, scrutinizing attitude toward technology, without either demonizing it or "divinizing" it.

—Paulo Freire, A Pedagogy of Hope

In the eleventh week of the semester, Sammy posts the following message to the email list I have set up for a graduate course I am teaching at SUNY–Albany called "Literacy, Technology, and English Studies"[1]:

From: Sammy
To: English 725
Subject: late
hello all. my commentary is going to be late, but i would like to share some things with you as to why.

on the one hand such sharing is a demand i suppose, and considering the medium and the context, an imposition. i have read __imagologies__ once already, but i do want to, am reading it again, getting new hits i hadn't gotten before. the last few days have been dizzying to say the least: i've driven six hundred

miles in two days this past thursday/friday, four hundred of
which in one day, i've assumed a major medical responsibility
and twenty years of ghosts that should be raging have been
more or less quiet, something that has given cause to others
close to me to be alarmed. everyone wants to know how i am
feeling about the recent turn of events and are somewhat
disgusted/surprised by my insistance of not feeling anything
particular . . .

it began with a phone call. my lover picked up the phone,
listened and the first thing she had said into the receiver was,
what's wrong? she then turned to me and handed me the
receiver. hello? it was my mother, she asked me how i was.
what's wrong? i asked, she asked me again how i was. what's
wrong? what happened? my mother's voice broke. something
about my father and a hospital. my father. what, what? what
happened? your father suffered an aneurism. an aneurism burst,
he's in the hospital. Sammy, Sammy, your father. where?
atlantic city.

i stopped. atlantic city? my parents live . . . 150 miles from
atlantic city. it was a wednesday, my father has an autobody
shop in long island, my father wakes five am in the morning
and comes home seven at night six days a week. it was four in
in the afternoon, what was my father doing in atlantic city? i
asked, are we we talking about mike, my father? my father is/n't
mike. mike is/n't my father. he's my stepfather, but i don't like
the sound of it, especially in english, a step down, etc. he's my
"ba", my "baba", an ethnic version of daddy. came in my life at
fifteen and weathered through my rebellion until my early
twenties. he's my lighthouse, my rock, he's everything that i
want to value: human and imperfect and strong and sensible
and funny and bull-headed. who were we talking about?

Sammy, your father. your real father.

i don't know if i told you any of this before: my father, my real
father was a bastard. he drank and gambled and womanized. it
isn't enough to leave it at that. he lived off my mother's earn-
ings, played out his own. when my mother would question his
whereabouts as he would go out at two in the morning, he
would beat her into such a state that she couldn't pick me up

out of the crib to feed. he beat the strength out of her. even that isn't enough. i remember two things, two memories distinctly. one: the time he beat my mother as she came out of the shower, ripped the phone out of the wall when she threatened to call the police, and threw me off his back when he set in to beat her again. two: the time i went to take his cold cup of coffee off the dresser by the bed he was sleeping in, and there was a fly in his coffee and he awoke and he touched my face.

i think i was four, or maybe i think that because he left soon after. i remember other things, but even before he left us, he never was really much around. the police did show up, only after he had left, and they were looking for him for questioning. once, at the old house in queens that we had lost because my mother could barely support herself and i let alone a mortgage. another time they had called, seven years later, when we had moved to an apartment three blocks away, asking about his whereabouts. the point is, we never had the number changed, he could have found us whenever he wanted. he never came back, not even to sign the divorce papers.

alot of my life has been spent with these memories: of beatings and alcohol and of what became of my father . . .

now, on the phone, my mother telling me it was him, my father. i was relieved it wasn't my father. my father father, mike, with the smile and the nerdy laugh and the thinning hair and the stomach problems and the mustache. but it was my father, my real father. i was relieved and confused. i asked where he was, how she found out. we had broken all ties with my father's side of the family (as he had done twenty years ago) when my mother married mike and we moved. it wasn't just her decision, it was mine as well. . . .

she felt that we both had to go see him. i wanted to go alone. it mattered i think the most to me at one time and there was no need. she was angry, crying, insistant. i will be there for you, you're not going to do this on your own. i got off the phone with her, searched the web for hospitals near or around atlantic city. i called one, he was there. they asked who was i? his son. we've been looking for you, they said, but couldn't tell me anything more because i was after all just a voice on the phone.

i found out the address and hit the web again. found a map engine and got directions on how to go from albany. i looked up my father's only living relative in the states, my uncle, and called him. i hadn't spoken to the man in over a decade since he had disowned me for attending his daughter's 'illicit' marriage. i had been twelve at the time. he couldn't talk, mid sentence would give the phone to his german wife who spoke better greek than i did, to cry. she mentioned alcoholism and lung, kidney, and heart failure. they asked for my number. i gave it. how tragic to re-establish contact over this kind of news, she said. . .

i hung up and called my mother. i told her to be ready by the next morning, i was coming down to pick her up. i hung up and asked my lover if she could come, she agreed. if i was to see him, i would go as i am, not as i was. i am not alone, not now, and i think four years ago i realized, not ever . . . when we got there, my mother was asking secretaries about my father's condition. they couldn't answer her, after all, they didn't know who were yet. my mother was nervous about this monster ruining our lives. she couldn't sit. a social worker who had my father's case came to talk to us. she asked for my id. we made sure not to mention where my mother lived now and her new surname. there had been police involved in my father's life previously and the circumstances of his arrival to the hospital were curious, i didn't want any of the business my father was mixed up to show up at our door. i showed the social worker a photograph i had taken with me from my parents house. she looked at it. she said it didn't look like him or any of the id's they found on him. there were many. . .

when he had gotten out of the surgery to remove blood from his stomach, we were allowed to see him. . . we went in and indeed he was a monster the way we become monsters when our bodies fail and doctors intervene. . . his hands were re-strained because even heavily sedated, he would pull his iv out and, because of new surgical procedures that leave your wounds unstitched, they were afraid he might tear out one of his organs. i stared. his hair line receded almost to the back of his head, his mouth was agape. a tube ran from an opening in his throat, he had lost some teeth, particularly from the front and left side of his mouth, along with some weight. i walked to the other side of his bed. i pulled out the photograph i showed to the social worker, it was from my christening. i stared. the eyelashes, the nose and ears matched. his frame was the same, the way the meat hung around his mouth. he looked more like my college id when i was drunk and drugged than he did the photograph in my hands. i looked at his hands, at his face. he still had sideburns. his breath was ragged, silent but forceful. i asked my mother and my partner to leave the room. i leaned over him. i said maybe five words. my partner says that when while we were there his breathing had become more haggard, nervous, it seemed as if he was trembling. i just remembered how the ekg machine skipped a beat when i said goodbye.

as some of you know, i've recently changed my number. against my parents advice, i've taken responsibility for whatever medical procedures to be done on him. i've asked for all of my contact information to be withheld from everyone, including him, if he pulls through. i'm tempted, and i think this is the hardest part to write, to place a DNR request on his chart. DNR stands for 'do not resuscitate'. the doctors cannot answer my questions yet about the quality of life he would lead if he ever becomes conscious. . .

i write this to you because i think i need to get it out of me. . . i write this to you because it is a story about falling through the cracks and disappearing despite the technology; and finding one's way to the cracks through that same technology. i write this to you because there is no adequate theory that can abstract this to intellectualization, although i think that it's theory that is holding me together in spite of it. i'm writing this obviously to share something with you about who i am, something about us, and this class; something about our lives and our humanity.

thanks for listening.

I read this message late on a Sunday night. I am stunned. It is not the kind of thing I expected to read when I logged on to my account to catch up on the weekly online class discussion, as I usually do on Sunday nights in anticipation of our Monday night class meetings. As Sammy indicates at the beginning of the message, he was to have posted a "commentary" for the week, a response to one of the assigned readings or related course topic. His previous contributions to class discussions have been extensive, engaged, and enthusiastic about the new online technologies that are the focus of much of our reading and writing and talking in the course. He is knowledgeable about the issues and about the technology itself, a self-described "techie" who can talk theory as easily as he can list systems specs. He has shown himself to be well-read and smart, eager yet sincere in his engagement with the ideas and the technology. But none of it has prepared me for this message.

I sit for a long while in front of the computer screen in a room in my home that we call the study. Everyone else is asleep. I am tired, too, and my head feels numb as I reread parts of Sammy's message and think about how I should respond—or even *whether* I should. I am deeply touched by his story, and at the same time I am uneasy that he posted it to the class email list. I wonder what his classmates will think. I wonder what he will think if my response focuses on the issues he refers to in the final paragraph of his message rather than on the troubling experiences he has described. I wonder whether I should email him directly instead of posting an "official" message to the class list. I wonder why he has posted this message to a list that otherwise has focused exclusively on academic discussion of our course topics. And I think about my own father, who never left as Sammy's father did, yet who always seems distant. I intend to write a short message to the email list, but I am unable to compose even a sentence that seems appropriate. How should I write myself into the story, the conversation, that Sammy has begun? How will my students expect me to do so? Finally, after a painfully slow half hour, I give up, turn off the computer, and go upstairs to bed.

The next morning I sit down again at the computer to prepare for the evening's class. A night's rest and a few cups of coffee have cleared my head. I reread Sammy's message and quickly compose the following response, which I post to the class email list:

> Well, it may be the time of the semester, the fact that we have become a sort of academic pseudo-community finally, the fact that we have been reading and talking about this stuff rather intensely for a few months, or perhaps the book itself—it may be any or all of those things that prompted the intense response to Taylor and Saarinen's book. I hope tonight we'll have a better idea about why the reactions to it have been so strong. Meanwhile, Sammy's earlier post about his father highlighted, for me at least, the limits of theory in our individual and collective efforts to negotiate the inevitable complexities and anguish of

our lives. (Thanks, Sammy, for your willingness to share your thoughts with us.)
More later. Bob

The message feels inadequate. I worry that I have taken a stance that will sound too tentative and perhaps even cryptic to the students, who cannot know how profoundly Sammy's story relates to my own sense of self as son and father and teacher. And only vaguely do I anticipate the intense debate that my phrase, "the limits of theory," will provoke in the following weeks.

As always, there is context. My mention of Taylor and Saarinen in my message is a reference to their book *Imagologies* (1994), which the students were to have read for this week. By this point in the semester, we have read a number of books and articles all dealing in some fashion with literacy and technology. These readings have provoked a range of responses from the students, and much of our discussion has explored not only the arguments of the authors we've encountered but our own beliefs about literacy, technology, and education. Often those beliefs have manifested themselves in resistance to new technologies and to new ways of conceptualizing literacy within emerging technological contexts such as the Internet. *Imagologies*, which offers a glib, in-your-face kind of enthusiasm for these new technologies, has provoked pointed responses from some students, as I'd expected. For *Imagologies* sticks a brash, glitzy tongue out at the staid, conventional academic discourse that most of us in the class are accustomed to, attacking and even dismissing some of our most deeply felt beliefs about the value of writing and reading in our lives and challenging us to imagine a future in which curling up with a good book is unimaginable. Taylor and Saarinen (1994) envision a postmodern future in which any remaining vestiges of the Enlightenment are obliterated and in which literacy becomes a very different way of communicating through language and image.

> Since image has displaced print as the primary medium for discourse, the public use of reason can no longer be limited to print culture. To be effective, writing must become imagoscription that is available to everyone ("Communicative Practices," section in *Imagologies*, p. 4)

This is a discomfitting vision for some, and the online discussion for this week reflects the uneasiness and even anger that this book has provoked. Michelle, for instance, a straightforward journalist in her 30s who is working in her spare time toward a masters degree, has steadfastly resisted the idea that computers are changing how we read and write. As the arts and entertainment editor for a large daily newspaper in Albany, she deals with computers and media and the Internet every day, but she doesn't like what she sees. To her, the kind of argument Taylor and Saarinen make in *Imagologies* is flashy and superficial and doesn't suitably deal with the substance of literacy as she knows it, and she makes that clear in her online commentary for the week. A few other students agree with Michelle; others, though, offer enthusiastic support for Taylor and Saarinen's vision. And the online discussion assumes a by-now-familiar shape as the students stake out their positions: Michelle's neo-luddite suspicion of the new technologies, Laura's skeptical curiosity about them, Ben's quiet conviction of their usefulness, Bill's Marxist warnings, Sarah's thoughtful reminders of the human implications of our uses of technology.

I expected Sammy to chime in with his sophisticated enthusiasm. Instead, he becomes a vulnerable, uncertain son.

My response to Sammy's message grew in part out of my sense of Sammy as an engaged and enthusiastic student of theory and advocate for technology. Up to that point, Sammy had constructed—through his online and in-class comments, through his responses to the readings and his written assignments, through his intense conversations with classmates that he regularly engaged in after class each week—a "public" self of a kind that is not unusual in a university setting, especially in a graduate program. He had written himself into our classroom discourse—and by extension the broader professional discourse—as an engaged, well-read scholar-in-training. His online message about his father, however, constructed another kind of self that seemed to diverge from the engaged and confident student he had been up to that point. Obviously, the background and experiences that he describes in his message were always part of that engaged and confident student; they were part, that is, of the *self-interest* that inevitably but more or less invisibly shaped the writing and reading he did for the class. But his message about his father reflects not only the complexity of any act of self-construction through writing or reading but also the contingency of that act: the uncertain yet inevitable ways in which that act occurs within various discourses within a specific institutional and cultural context. When Sammy constructs an "academic" self, he doesn't stop being the son of an abusive and absent father, even if that aspect of his identity is hidden from those who interact with him in an academic setting; rather, his self-constructions are mediated by the discourses in place in that academic context, just as, for instance, Celina's construction of herself as an African-American woman is mediated by the academic context within which she writes. In Sammy's case, the conventions of academic discourse work against the kind of self-disclosure that he made to the class on the email list, even though the experiences he describes in that narrative inevitably shape the writing and reading he does within those conventions. As he makes clear at the end of his message, his own academic inquiry into theories of literacy in cyberspace relate in complex ways to his struggle to construct a sense of himself as a son and an independent man.

In this sense, as a writer and reader in a graduate course, Sammy is no different from Mr. Green writing in the context of the prison writing course or Celina in the undergraduate writing workshop. What *is* different in his case is the technological medium within which Sammy writes and shares his narrative. The online class list represents not just a technology for writing and distributing a text but a unique way of interacting with other writers and readers. It may represent a new way of writing and reading that alters how students are able to construct themselves in their writing and reading. Indeed, technologies like email complicate our very conceptions and practices of literacy and thus have the potential to alter the meaning of literacy in our lives. As more of us—students and teachers alike—venture into cyberspace both within and outside school settings, there is a growing need to understand the ways in which new literacy technologies might be redefining the value of literacy in our culture and our lives.

TECHNOLOGIES, LITERACIES, AND IDENTITIES

In their wonderfully hip article, "Postings on a Genre of Email," Michael Spooner and Kathleen Yancey (1996) debate the question of whether electronic mail represents a distinct genre of writing or simply a different medium in which existing genres are used and perhaps adapted. At one point they assert that school-sponsored writing

> has as part of its effect the projection and production of particular forms of student identity. This production is necessarily tied up with other major identity formations, such as gender, and connected to broader social power dynamics. For us, rhetoric is as much concerned with the formation of identities as the construction of texts. (p. 269)

In other words, "rhetorical situations project and produce forms of identity." But they (or more accurately, *one* of the two main "voices" in the article) immediately qualify the point, asserting that "rhetorical situations are not defined by the mechanical process through which they travel, so much as by the social purposes of the rhetors" (pp. 269–270); further, "the purpose that an extant genre serves rarely disappears at the appearance of a new mechanical device. More likely, the new device is bent to the old rhetorical purpose" (p. 270).

As Spooner and Yancey remind us, literacy, and specifically school-sponsored literacy, is wrapped up in "identity formation." They suggest in this passage that genres of school-sponsored writing circumscribe the identities that students can construct. Those genres, of course, cannot be separated from the many larger discourses that shape schooling and school-sponsored writing: academic discourses, disciplinary discourses, popular discourses relating to writing and reading and a whole array of social and cultural issues such as gender and race. As we have seen in the writing of students like Mr. Green and Celina and Larry, students construct themselves through their writing within—and sometimes against—these discourses. How they construct themselves through their writing, I have suggested, is always to some extent a negotiation among the roles available to them within the discourses in place in particular situations and the *self-interest* they bring to specific rhetorical tasks.

But that process of negotiation also is related to the technologies in use in a given rhetorical situation. If the technology is simply a neutral medium for writing, as the quotation from Spooner and Yancey (1996) suggests, then that technology becomes incidental to the process. From this perspective, Sammy's post is simply a compelling personal narrative that has been distributed via email rather than, say, on paper during our class meeting; the self Sammy constructs in that narrative thus has nothing to do with the technology, and the writing is not different in any sense except how it was distributed. No doubt, it would have been possible for Sammy to write this same text on paper and physically share it with his classmates. But why did he do it via email? Was it simply because it was easier and more convenient? More important, did the medium itself *change* Sammy's message, either in terms of how he wrote it or how it was read by his classmates? Did it *mean* something different—to him and to them—because it was posted as an email message rather than distributed on paper? In short, did the technology alter or shape his specific act of writing in any substantive way?

Sammy's final paragraph provides one way to approach these questions. In that paragraph, he explains that "i write this to you because it is a story about falling through the cracks and disappearing despite the technology; and finding one's way to the cracks through that same technology." For Sammy, it seems, the technology itself could not change his difficult personal situation, but it can be a vehicle for "finding one's way" through that situation. He implies further that the technology of email—online electronic writing—somehow enabled him to *do* something in this act of writing that more conventional print technologies did not. His classmate Laura pushes this point further, in a way that speaks to the social purposes and the rhetorical situation that Spooner and Yancey (1996) cite. In a private email message that she sent to me that same evening that I read Sammy's message, she wrote:

> Sammy's post has me thinking a great deal about this amazing medium. no other mode of communication would have generated that particular message to that particular audience . . . i cannot go to class monday night without seeing him through the lens of that posting. i'm sure some class members found it an inappropriate use of the listserv, but is it? seems to me to be putting to the test some of what we've all been discussing all semester. . . i'm intrigued.

Laura suggests that the medium of email itself must be seen as integral to Sammy's specific text at that specific moment—that is, that his local act of writing was enabled and shaped by the technology in a way that would not have been the same in another medium: No other medium, she writes, could have generated Sammy's message. She focuses on Sammy's text as an *act* of communication, on what it *does* rather than on its form. And what it does, at least for her, is to alter her sense of Sammy as writer and person and (to push it just a bit further) her relationship to him as reader: "i cannot go to class monday night without seeing him through the lens of that posting."

It is easy to rebut the analysis I am offering here and adopt the stance that Spooner and Yancey (1996) define: Sammy's text is nothing new; he's just using a "new device . . . [for] the old rhetorical purpose" (p. 270). He has written a more or less conventional confessional narrative for an audience that happened to have access to email, which he employed to distribute that narrative. The unconventional use of the genre (that is, the distribution of a personal narrative in an academic situation that called for a conventional academic text) has little to do with the technology he used; had he distributed it to his audience in paper form, it would have been just as unconventional given the rhetorical situation and the expectations of his readers within that situation. In fact, one could argue that Laura's reaction was really more a function of the compelling nature of Sammy's story than of the medium.

Some scholars interested in electronic literacy and computer-mediated communication (CMC) would support such an analysis of this text. After the enthusiastic embrace of computer technologies as something akin to a revolution in teaching writing by advocates of CMC in the 1980s, skepticism has crept back into the professional discourse surrounding technology and literacy education; many critics, even those who openly support the use of computer technologies in teaching writing and reading, now counsel caution in our understanding and adoption of these technologies in the context of literacy instruction. (See Hawisher & Selfe, 1991, for a discussion of this reconsideration of earlier scholarship on computer technologies in literacy instruction. See Grusin, 1996, for a useful critique of prevailing theoretical analyses of online literacies, especially hypertext.) This caution is justified and necessary. But if literacy is, as I have been arguing, primarily local, and if specific instances of writing amount to acts of self-construction on the part of writers seeking to define roles for themselves within the discourses that shape their lives, it is hard to dismiss texts like Sammy's as simply electronic versions of conventional writing. For if the technology in use in a specific rhetorical situation shapes the way in which the writer can enter the discourses in place in that situation, if that technology somehow shapes the act of writing—and reading—such that it facilitates or enables or limits the roles the writer can assume and thus the self he or she can construct in a particular instance, then that technology seems to me to warrant a closer look. Even if email simply provided Sammy with an opportunity to write that he might not otherwise have had, then that technology would seem to be a crucial part of the context that gave rise to and influenced Sammy's act of writing.

We know from scholarly inquiry and empirical research that tools, including computers, can profoundly shape how their users engage in and understand the acts for which they are using tools. Furthermore, the history of literacy technologies, especially the printing press, indicates that technological developments shaped not only how texts were produced and distributed but also how reading and writing were engaged in, understood, and valued. Some scholars have even argued that print technology may have played a key role in the development of contemporary notions of the self, notions that may be in a process of redefinition in part because of the growing use of computer technologies for communication. Indeed, we have a growing body of evidence that online technologies may be changing how we read and write and, more important, how reading and writing function in our lives. Jay David Bolter's (1991) well-known assertion that we have entered "the late age of print" (p. 1) suggests that our students will face new challenges as literate beings trying to find their ways into the discourses that affect their lives. We need to examine these propositions in an effort to understand the relationship between emerging literacy technologies and the writing and reading our students do and will be asked to do both in and outside the classroom—and to understand better how writing and reading function in their lives in an increasingly technological world.

The Logic of Tools and the Technology of Writing

My 14-year-old son, Adam, sits down at our computer to begin work on a project for his eighth-grade social studies class. As part of a "global studies" unit, he is to prepare an oral presentation and submit an accompanying written report on an Asian nation of his choice. He chooses Nepal.[2] After accessing our Internet account, Adam immediately directs the browser to a search engine and begins looking for World Wide Web sites related to the culture of Nepal. His search-tries yield thousands of web sites, and he begins revising his searches to narrow down the list of potentially relevant sites. Once he is satisfied that the list of sites is manageable, he begins "visiting" these sites. With a barely perceptible movement of his right hand on the mouse, colorful images accompanied by text begin appearing on the screen as various web sites "load" onto the computer's hard drive. Except for slight movements of his right hand on the mouse, Adam is motionless, his left hand resting near the keyboard on the small desk, his head cocked slightly toward the monitor on his right, his eyes fixed on the slowly sharpening images on the screen. Every so often, he clicks the mouse in order to mark a specific web page he has visited. These "bookmarked" pages are sites that he has tentatively deemed useful for his project. Later, he will return to these sites to copy information and images from them. For now, he seems to skim each site on the screen, deciding whether to mark it and then moving on to a new site. He "reads" in this way for perhaps half an hour, after which time he clicks another icon on the computer screen to open a word processing program. Again using the mouse, he begins copying and pasting text and images from web sites into a file in the word processing program, from which he will draw later as he constructs the text of his project. His "reading" is in large part a function of his knowledge of the computer programs that he is using (a web browser and a word processor) and his ability to manipulate them to copy, store, and (later) reorganize text and images. He works in this fashion for half an hour more before stopping. When he is finished, he has compiled a large word processing file containing thousands of words and perhaps a dozen images, all relating in some way to his topic of Nepal. He has not touched a book or a pencil or a piece of paper. He has not made an outline or completed a notecard. He has not yet "written" anything in a conventional sense. Tomorrow, he will begin drafting "new" text for his required paper, incorporating bits of information and chunks of the text he has copied from the World Wide Web. When he is finished with that paper (which is an increasingly dated metaphor), he will print it out and submit it to his teacher in this traditional print form. But for now, he is finished "reading" and he turns off the computer. As he gets up from the chair, he picks up a pencil from the desk and, reaching into his backpack next to the chair, he grabs his notebook, which he will use to complete his math homework.

I shared the preceding description with the K–12 teachers who attended a conference for English teachers in the fall of 1997 and asked them whether Adam's reading and writing in this description is *different* in any substantive way from the reading and writing that they believe they teach in their English classes. Little consensus grew out of the discussion that ensued, but one common response emerged: Adam is still reading and writing in the conventional sense, decoding the meaning of text on the screen, but he is using a different (and admittedly powerful) tool. In other words, the only substantive difference between Adam's reading and writing and the reading and writing of a student doing research with more traditional pencil and paper in a library full of books is the tools each uses. This seemingly simple idea that the computer is really just a neutral tool is, as C. A. Bowers (1988; see especially pp. 23–29) points out, a common one not only among educators but in our society generally; it is one I encounter often in my discussions with teachers about the uses of technology in teaching writing and reading. Computers, many teachers tell me, are tools: They do not *change* literacy; they simply facilitate it.

Yet as Bowers and a number of other scholars have demonstrated, tools have the potential to shape not only human activity but consciousness as well; moreover, many scholars have examined language itself as a tool. Drawing on social theorists Martin Heidegger and Don Ihde, Bowers (1988) discusses how technology mediates human experience, showing that

> the essential nature of the technology selects the aspects of the experience that will be amplified and reduced. Thus technology is not simply a neutral tool, ready at hand, waiting to be directed by a human being. In effect, it acts on us (through selection and amplification), as we utilize it for our instrumental purposes. Eyeglasses, for example, select and am-

plify our sense of vision; similarly the pencil amplifies our ability to record our thoughts in a manner that allows us to achieve distance and view them objectively. The essence of each technology also determines what aspects of experience will be reduced; the pencil, for example, cannot communicate our voice or bring greater acuity to our ability to see or smell. (pp. 32–33)

As Bowers goes on to demonstrate, the potential of the computer for the *amplification* and *reduction* of experience is mind-boggling. But the resistance on the part of many educators to this vision of the power of technology to shape experience and consciousness can prevent those same educators from considering the far-reaching implications of technologies like the computer for writing and reading. Moreover, what Bowers calls "the conduit view of language" (p. 27) as a straightforward conduit for information contributes to this resistance. If we find it hard to accept the idea that a technology like the computer can *change* the nature of our experiences as readers and writers, we find it even harder to describe literacy itself—and language generally—as a technology. Yet the idea that language and literacy can best be understood as technologies is widespread among scholars interested in literacy. Peter Berger (1969) argues that "the tool (say, an agricultural implement) may even enforce the logic of its being on its users, sometimes in a way that may not be particularly agreeable to them," having to plant crops in straight rows, for example, and he goes on to assert that "man invents a language and then finds that both his speaking and thinking are dominated by its grammar" (p. 9).

The ways in which the grammar or structure of a language, especially in written form, can dominate, as Berger puts it, or at least influence, human thought have been the focus of a great deal of inquiry—and heated scholarly debate—for many years. Marshall McLuhan (1962/1995), who is perhaps best known for his explorations of visual media, especially television, in the 1960s, analyzed the relationship between written language—specifically, alphabetic literacy—and what he called "the forms of thought and the organization of experience in society and politics" (p. 97). In *The Gutenberg Galaxy*, McLuhan (1962/1995) draws on philosophical, scientific, anthropological, and sociological studies to try to show how forms of thought and social organization result from the phonetic alphabet. It is beyond the scope of this chapter to offer a summary that would do justice to McLuhan's complex analysis of this dynamic among phonetic literacy, thought, and social organization, but his analysis highlights the complex nature of literacy and its role in our social and individual lives and can help us make sense, I think, of the potential impact of computer technologies on literacy. McLuhan emphasizes two central qualities of writing as a technology. First, writing can "separate" words from the person. That is, whereas oral language emanates physically from a speaker, written language is physically separated from the writer. Second, writing transforms language from an aural phenomenon to a primarily visual one: my words are now *seen* rather than *heard* (unless they are being read aloud, in which case they are both seen and heard). This quality of writing is crucial, McLuhan says, because it means that writing alters the relationship of our senses to the meaning of language, emphasizing the visual rather than the aural. In this way, according to McLuhan, writing abstracts meaning from sound and translates it to a visual code.

McLuhan (1962/1995) goes on to try to show that this separation of meaning from sound that is made possible by the phonetic alphabet leads to new social dynamics. Because writing now makes it unnecessary to speak directly to another person in order to express a thought and therefore to act through language, the interdependence of people is no longer a primary effect of language. New forms of social organization are therefore possible. Moreover, new perceptions of our world—and *conceptions* of it as well—arise from the fact that we now use our senses differently, since writing emphasizes the visual rather than the oral and sets up "new ratios or proportions among all the senses" (p. 130). This reasoning leads McLuhan to conclude that "from the invention of the alphabet there has been a continuous drive in the Western world towards the separation of the senses, of functions, of operations, of states emotional and political, as well as of tasks" (p. 137). Writing, in short, changes how we live among each other.

These are enormous claims, and the audacious scope of McLuhan's (1962/1995) analysis surely must have prompted some of the resistance to his ideas. But McLuhan's insistence that we look carefully at the complex connections among literacy, technology, and human consciousness, however problematic his conceptions of those terms, has resonated with other influential thinkers, such as Walter Ong (1982), who argues in his well-known book *Literacy and Orality* that "more than any other human invention, writing has transformed human consciousness" (p. 78). Like McLuhan, Ong sees writing itself as a technology, and technologies, according to Ong, "are not mere exterior aids but also interior transformations of consciousness, and never more than when they affect the word" (p. 82). Ong extends McLuhan's emphasis on the essentially visual character of writing and places great importance on the way in which writing separates thought from the knower, the way it externalizes ideas.

> By separating the knower from the known . . . , writing makes possible increasingly articulate introspectivity, opening the psyche as never before not only to the external objective world quite distinct from itself but also to the interior self against whom the objective world is set. (p. 105)

This technology of writing, Ong would have us believe, reshapes the way we think such that it changes our conceptions of ourselves and our world.

These, too, are strong claims, and Ong's even more ambitious (and problematic) assertion that alphabetic literacy gives rise to forms of abstract analytic thought that are not possible—or at least not common—in oral language and thus in oral cultures (that is, cultures without a script literacy) has drawn vociferous criticism, and justifiably so. Deborah Brandt (1990) offers one of the most cogent critiques of this view, which she calls "a 'strong-text' explanation of literacy" (p. 13). Such a view, writes Brandt, gives "little consideration to the processes of writing and reading, to questions of how people actually accomplish literate acts in daily life." Brandt argues that alphabetic literacy by itself does not necessarily lead to the kinds of abstract thought that Ong associates with writing; rather, the social and cultural contexts within which literacy is learned and practiced shape the relationship between writing and thought—"what literacy does to you, in other words, depends upon what you do with it" (p. 25). For Brandt, these "strong-text models may account at some level for the potential of literacy— that is, they may account for what writing makes possible as a technology that oral language does not. But that is not the same thing as establishing what makes possible the human acts of writing and reading" (p. 28).[3]

Brandt forcefully reminds us that we cannot understand how literacy functions or its potential effects on how we think or how we organize our lives without accounting for the social and cultural contexts within which literate acts occur and within which technologies of literacy develop and are used. At the same time, there is little doubt that writing as a technology has the potential to effect momentous changes in how human beings understand and interact with their world and with each other. Despite the problems Brandt identifies in strong-text theories of literacy, attempts like Ong's to examine the connections between literacy and thought can be valuable at a time when radically new communications media, including television and now computer technologies, have emerged to become so integral to contemporary life in developed societies. Adam may still be part of a minority of students who have access to the technology he used for his Nepal report, but the kind of computer-based reading and writing he did for that report is becoming increasingly common as these technologies become more widespread and as more and more teachers incorporate them into their curricula.[4] In this sense, the vignette of Adam's work on his Nepal report may serve as an example of the kinds of changes in literate practice that are being precipitated by the growing uses of computer technologies. Indeed, a look at the history of literacy technologies reveals how important the emergence of new technologies can be in terms of how literacy functions in our individual and social lives and shapes our sense of self.

Lessons from the History of Print Technology

The English teachers' response to my description of Adam's web-based research is, I think, a reflection of how deeply embedded print technology is, not only in our ways of writing and reading but in our conceptions of literacy as well. Print is so thoroughly ensconced in our culture that we rarely notice that it is one literacy technology among many; we overlook the fact that the "logic" of print has shaped our Western culture and its practices and values and conceptions of literacy far more deeply than Bowers's eyeglasses have shaped our eyesight. Even a cursory look at the history of print technology reminds us that it is a techology with specific and often far-reaching effects on our social, cultural, economic, and political lives.

Elizabeth Eisenstein (1983a), in her meticulously documented account of "how printing altered written communication" (p. 22) among the already literate (in addition to spurring the spread of literacy among the nonliterate) and "how printing may have affected prevailing world views" (p. 25), resists cause-and-effect explanations of the kind McLuhan (1962/1995) and Ong (1982) propose about the relationship between alphabetic literacy and abstract thought; instead, her research reveals the complexity of the relationships among literacy, print technology, economics, politics, culture, and intellectual developments, and demonstrates that one apparent effect of literacy in a specific sociocultural and economic context may have been absent or different in another— that how literacy technologies shaped these aspects of human life was *local*. One key feature of print technology that Eisenstein (1983b) examines is standardization. She shows how print not only gave rise to the production of standard editions of specific texts but also made it possible for many different readers in different regions to have access to the same text. She concludes that the

> [I]mplications of standardization may be underestimated. . . . I am think-
> ing not only about textual emendations and errors [which could be eas-
> ily corrected in all subsequent editions and copies], but also about calen-
> dars, dictionaries, ephemerides, and other reference guides; about maps,
> charts, diagrams, and other visual aids. The capacity to produce uniform
> spatiotemporal images is often assigned to the invention of writing with-
> out adequate allowance being made for the difficulty of multiplying iden-
> tical images by hand. (p. 52)

Standardization affected not just scholarly, scientific, and philosophical texts but legal and economic documents as well. Print technology
meant that legal statutes, for instance, could be standardized and widely
distributed in ways that were not possible prior to the development of
the printing press. More important, Eisenstein asserts, are the "much
less conspicuous, more ubiquitous changes" associated with standardization of texts: "Increasing familiarity with regularly numbered pages,
punctuation marks, section breaks, running heads, indexes, and so forth
helped to reorder the thought of *all* readers, whatever their profession
or craft" (p. 73, emphasis in original). Despite her professed skepticism
about some of McLuhan's assertions, she recognizes that his attempt
to link literacy with thought can be useful in helping us understand
the effects of a technology like the printing press on literacy practices.
Referring specifically to the potential effects of the organization of
printed texts on thought, she writes:

> Editorial decisions made by early printers with regard to layout and pre-
> sentation probably helped to reorganize the thinking of readers.
> McLuhan's suggestion that scanning lines of print affected thought pro-
> cesses is at first glance somewhat mystifying. But further reflection sug-
> gests that the thoughts of readers are guided by the way the contents of
> books are arranged and presented. Basic changes in books format might
> well lead to changes in thought patterns. (1983b, p. 64)

Think of Adam searching the web for information for his Nepal report, and Eisenstein's tentative conclusions about the effects of print
technology on literate behaviors as well as literate practices may shed
light on the kinds of changes our students may be experiencing with

new computer technologies. That is precisely what some contemporary scholars interested in electronic writing and visual media wish to do.

Jay David Bolter (1991), for instance, asserts that in the "writing space" of the computer, we have "a textual medium of a new order" (p. 6). Bolter emphasizes the malleability of electronic text, which, he claims, alters the relationship between writer and reader: "The conceptual space of electronic writing . . . is characterized by fluidity and an interactive relationship between writer and reader" (p. 11). For Bolter, the primary distinction between electronic text and print text is that the latter is fixed whereas the former is not. The fixed nature of print text, which gives rise to the standardization that Eisenstein describes, forces a kind of logic not only on the relationship between writer and reader (the former exercising a measure of control over a text that the latter cannot) but also on the relationship between writer and text and between reader and text. A printed text, which can exist in many identical copies, becomes a fixed object that is at once the product of the writer's efforts and separate from them; similarly, the reader can interpret that text but cannot change it as such. Electronic writing, Bolter says, "has just the opposite effect. It opposes standardization and unification as well as hierarchy. It offers as a paradigm the text that changes to suit the reader rather than expecting the reader to conform to its standards" (p. 233).

These claims oversimplify the matter to some extent, since electronic text can mean many different sorts of computer-generated documents: hypertext (which itself exists in several forms), word processing, desktop publishing, multimedia, synchronous computer-mediated communication (such as MOOs, online chat rooms, and the talk functions of programs like *Daedalus*), or asynchronous computer-mediated communication (such as newsgroups or listservs of the kind I used in the class Sammy was in). All these forms of electronic writing have somewhat different capabilities and characteristics that may help shape the writing itself, how it is used, the role of the reader, and so on, which makes it risky to generalize about "electronic writing." Moreover, some of these forms of writing blur the distinction Bolter makes between electronic writing and print text. For instance, a text that is created using desktop publishing technologies or a document like Adam's evolving Nepal report, while it exists as a file within a particular software program, possesses some of the characteristics of electronic text that Bolter describes, such as malleability. Once that text is produced through a printer, however, it becomes a print text, used in conventional ways that such texts have been used for centuries. A hyptertext, by contrast, never exists in print form and is more overtly "interactive" in the sense that a reader must actively select paths through the text—thus helping determine the shape or organization of the text—in a way that he or she would not with a print text. In short, as several critics have noted (e.g., Grusin, 1996), Bolter and other enthusiasts for computer-based writing technologies may overstate the case somewhat.

Nevertheless, if the history of technologies such as the printing press is any guide, and if scholars like Bolter are even partly on track, we may indeed be entering a new era of literacy characterized by new ways of reading and writing. Adam's work on his Nepal report may be similar in many ways to the work he would have done on that report had he had no access to the World Wide Web or a word processing program, but it also may portend substantive changes in the ways in which students—and the rest of us—read and write and how we construct ourselves through our reading and writing in new technological contexts. And an email text like Sammy's, partly because it exists in such an overtly interactive textual medium, may underscore these changes in ways that Adam's text does not. In both cases, the writer constructs himself in his text in ways that may not be possible with conventional print technologies.

NEW TECHNOLOGIES, CHANGING SELVES

During the second week of the semester, months before Sammy posted his message about his father to our class email list, a student identified only as "Thinkbooks" posted the following message as part of a discussion about several assigned readings[5]:

After reading Boone and Bolter, I wondered if technology/ electronic writing offered the hope (or in some views promise) of increased "literacy." That is, will hypertext, electronic writing, and/or hypermedia allow more people access to what is commonly thought of as written language. So that if you are currently "severely deficient" in your reading and writing skills or if you just plain old can't read or write, will computer technology offer you an in? . . .

I do not believe that learning to read and write is a goal in and of itself. But I do believe that they are important keys to getting access to people, places, information, institutions, systems (social, educational, political) etc, particularly for those who are already marginalized because of poverty and/or race, gender, etc. I think

hypermedia could very well level the playing field so that scholars, experts, professionals and academics will have to "give up"
some of their discourse in lieu of symbols and icons and pictures
and sounds that are present in electronic writing. Also, with the
currently limited "on screen space" of hypertext and the ability
to click past/in and out of parts of text, writers will be encouraged
(if not forced) to make it short and sweet. As a result, long,
complex "discursive" language and text formatting will be
impractical. More people who otherwise had limited access to the
discussion/conversations that occur in written form both because
of the alphabetic writing and the language (discourse, Standard
American English v. Non-Standard English, etc.) will be able to
engage in the discussion/conversations, to be heard as it were.
Maybe I have overstated and/or oversimplified the possibilities
and implications and paint too optimistic a picture, but I do
believe there is promise. I'm interested in what others think.

In a class discussion a few days later, Sammy referred to this message
and then, stopping himself in mid-comment, asked, "Who is 'Thinkbooks,' by the way?" After a long moment during which the students
in the room looked over and around their computers at each other,
Celina raised her hand. An audible "ahhh" arose from the students.
During the murmuring that followed, Celina smiled a slightly embarrassed smile while her classmates expressed surprise. It was early enough
in the semester for the students in the class to be unfamiliar with each
other, but it was obvious that some of them had assumed that "Thinkbooks" was someone else.[6]

In the following weeks, "The Thinkbooks Incident" became a reference point in our discussions about several issues we were addressing in the course, especially regarding identity as it relates to literacy
in online environments: Why did the students in the room react with
surprise when Celina revealed herself as Thinkbooks? What did their
reaction say about how they read her online text? About the relationship of such a text to in-class discussion and to the students' formal
writing for the course? Sammy offered the following thought in our
online discussion:

> i can't help but fixate on our "Ahhh" when we had found out
> the "identity" (which, when we think about it, we didn't "find
> out" anything about Celia) of Thinkbooks. which i think ties in
> neatly, or rather, not so neat, into our notions of subjectivity, of
> identity. do we go scurrying to find photographs of so and so an

author? does anyone have a photo of Blanchot? did any of us feel compelled, mutter a satisfactory "Ahhh" when we had a picture of Deleuze in our hands, for our eyes to see? why the intense interest and reaction to Celia? was it a relief? a surprise? what made it a surprise? was it because she is/was a "she"? is "Thinkbooks" a decidedly male word? was it because she is black?

Without realizing that he has gotten Celina's name wrong (a wonderfully appropriate if unintentional irony), Sammy raises a series of questions about subjectivity that theorists have wrestled with in recent years as the use of computer-mediated communications technologies (such as email) has proliferated. Postmodern theorists in particular have embraced these technologies as expressions of what philosopher Jean-Francois Lyotard (1984) has called "the postmodern condition." Specifically, online discourse such as occurred on our class email list reflects the fragmented, unstable subjectivities of the postmodern world, a world in which the self is not autonomous but contingent. Theorist Mark Poster (1990) claims that

> in electronically mediated communications, subjects now float, suspended between points of objectivity, being constituted and reconstituted in different configurations in relation to the discursive arrangement of the occasion. (p. 11)

Electronic writing, he claims, "disperses the subject so that it no longer functions as a center in the way it did in pre-electronic writing" (p. 100). As composition theorist Lester Faigley (1992) puts it, electronic technologies

> have dislocated traditional subjectivities of classroom writers, inviting them to take on multiple identities. The dispersed subjectivities in classroom discussions using networked computers may be related to larger changes involved in the increasing use of electronically mediated language in our culture. (p. 200)

While some scholars have argued that such claims are overstated (e.g., Grusin, 1996), the connection that theorists such as Poster and Faigley make between electronic writing and subjectivity emerges from a much older link between print literacy and the idea of the individual. In *The Gutenberg Galaxy*, McLuhan (1962/1995) argued provocatively that print technology, because it gave rise to an "interiorization" by which people could read silently and independently instead of interacting directly with each other through oral language, encouraged and then reinforced individualism. Walter Ong (1982) has made the rather extreme case that "the highly interiorized stages of consciousness in which the individual is not so immersed unconsciously in communal structures are stages which, it appears, consciousness would never reach without writing." Writing, Ong argues, "introduces division and alienation, but a higher unity as well. It intensifies the sense of self and fosters more conscious interaction between persons" (p. 178). But even if such broad claims can be challenged, as indeed they have been, there seems to be little doubt that print literacy made possible and encouraged new ways of writing and reading and, perhaps more important, new *uses* for writing and reading and text that influenced and even reshaped our collective notions of the self. Eisenstein (1983a) provides evidence that the standardization associated with print technology in the fifteenth century was accompanied by "a heightened appreciation of individuality" (p. 133). According to Eisenstein, the increased power of the press that emerged as a result of print technology gave rise to "the heightened recognition accorded individual achievement" (p. 131). Scribal culture, she writes, which existed prior to the widespread use of the printing press,

> worked against the concept of intellectual property rights. It did not lend itself to preserving traces of individual idiosyncracies, to the public airing of private thoughts, or to any of the forms of silent publicity that have shaped consciousness of self during the past five centuries. (p. 131)

Print literacy, in short, *did* allow for all these developments and encouraged a consciousness of self that, centuries later, has become deeply embedded in American culture.

It may well have been that deeply embedded sense of self that, despite their own sophisticated understanding of prevailing theoretical critiques of such a notion, lay beneath my students' collective expression of surprise when Celina revealed herself as Thinkbooks. That "ahhh" may have represented the uneasy and confusing period of transition that we are in: a time when postmodern sensibilities challenge modernist traditions, an era of a redefined and increasingly technologized self that continues to struggle for a contingent and circumscribed autonomy, a period when we embrace *identity* even as we deny individuality. It also may have been an expression of a need on the part of the students to connect themselves with other selves through their writing and reading—that is, to construct themselves through their construction of others as readers and writers. In her response to Sammy's post, Sarah touches on that very possibility.

> I think Sammy raises an interesting question asking why the "ahhh" when we attached the text of thinkbooks to an embodied subject. . . Interestingly, a parallel incident occured in the class I'm teaching when a student announced that Shel Silverstein is black. Another student (who happens to be African American) got really excited about this, and kept exclaiming, "I can't believe it. . ." It was an interesting moment, particularly because we'd just spent a couple weeks looking at texts that disrupt traditional notions of the Author, and all of sudden, the identity of the author became very important for this student, changing, she said, how she thought about a writer who'd been important to her childhood literacy. What becomes interesting, then, is that tension between the theorizing that we did in class about our understanding of the author and the ways in which the author suddenly came back that moment as an embodied, racial being. . . . As for our discovery of thinkbooks, I think the "ah" is a productive moment to theorize because it seems to have called into question assumptions about how we read seemingly "authorless" texts (or whom, perhaps, we assume to be the "author") as well as how we read each others' bodies in a pedagogical site.

Sarah here speaks to our apparent need as readers (a need that grows out of the prevailing notions of literacy and individuality that I discussed in Chapter 2) to have some sense of a "real" person behind the text we are reading, particularly when that text touches us in some profound way, as Shel Silverstein's poems seemed to have done for Sarah's student. She reminds us that specific acts of writing and reading can be intimately wrapped up not just in our own sense of who we are but in our sense of connection to the "self" we are reading. For Sarah's student, her relationship to Silverstein as author of the poems she so enjoyed was changed by the knowledge that she and Silverstein share the same racial background. She would from that point on read his poetry differently and thus construct meaning from it differently. Her excited response to the knowledge that Silverstein is African-American gives us a glimpse into how the meaning she constructs relates to her own sense of self, to her own background and experiences as reader and writer and person—to her *self-interest*.

What Sarah did not address in her comment but what was at the center of "The Thinkbooks Incident" is the fact that Celina was using a technology that enabled her to communicate directly with others who "knew" her without revealing specific details about herself. In other words, the online textual environment of the email discussion list seems to have enabled Celina to construct "who" she would be in that discussion in a way that would have been impossible in a face-to-face classroom discussion. A few weeks later, when I asked her about the incident, she explained that she often used nongendered, non-racial pseudonyms when participating in online discussions, because she wanted her readers to focus on her comments and not on her race or gender, which, she believes, influence how her readers read her comments. In a sense, Sarah's student's reaction to the knowledge that Shel Silverstein is African-American bears Celina out: we read texts in ways that reflect our sense of who the author is, which is a function of our own sense of self.

Theorists such as Bolter, Poster, and Taylor and Saarinen have tried to show how these new technologies irrevocably change the way we make meaning through text and thus how we understand ourselves. Bolter (1996) traces the connection between theoretical conceptions of the self, particularly those of Descartes and Kant, and print technology and then goes on to argue that the new computer technologies undermine those conceptions. In a passage that recalls McLuhan's analyses, Bolter writes:

> The Cartesian definition of self was by no means created by the technology of print. However, print technology did offer a writing space in which this definition could flourish. Print emphasized and rewarded the individuality and uniqueness of the author. And in subordinating images to words, print technology encouraged a rhetoric in which abstraction was privileged at the expense of the senses and sensory information. (p. 111)

But electronic technology, Bolter says, "is helping to change the communicative balance between word and image in our media." He invokes Kenneth Gergen (1991), who "has argued that a 'postmodern' definition of the self is emerging, a self that is fragmented, empathetic, and anti-Cartesian: 'technologies of social saturation' are responsible" (p. 112). These technologies, such as radio, television, print, and the computer, are, according to Bolter, "means of representation and self-presentation. They are media for presenting ourselves to ourselves and to others, and as such they invite a definition or redfinition of the self" (p. 111). This new self, Bolter says, is "no longer the relatively permanent and univocal figure of the printed page. The electronic self is instead unstable and polyvocal" (p. 111).

"The Thinkbooks Incident" seems to demonstrate Bolter's claims, for Celina's "electronic self" does indeed seem unstable and polyvocal in this instance. If we consider her online post in the context of her other writing for this course (and for the course described in Chapter 4), we can indeed see something of the polyvocal self that Bolter refers to: African-American woman, student, neophyte academic, daughter, citizen, aspiring educator. And when we consider her racial identity and how it is invoked or hidden in the specific acts of writing she has done, the "instability" of her identity seems to emerge; that is, the self she constructs varies from one instance of writing to another. In the electronic environment of email, Celina quickly can compose different selves for different audiences (or for the same audience). In this sense, electronic writing seems to afford her a new and different way to write herself into the discourses in place in a specific situation. At the very least, the new computer-mediated communications technologies challenge our conventional ways of reading and writing and thus influence how we construct the sense of self that, I have argued, lies at the center of our acts of writing and reading.

This unstable, contingent, and polyvocal self exists in *all* writing, as we saw, for example, in the case of Mr. Green, one of the African-American students in my prison classroom, described in Chapter 3, and in Celina's writing for the workshop course discussed in Chapter 4. As writers of conventional, print-based academic essays, both Mr. Green and Celina construct identities that are complex and contingent and relate to the contexts within which they write; both are attempting to write themselves into the discourses that shape their subjectivities and to claim agency within those discourses. However, in an online environment, the immediacy of those discourses to both writer and reader and the speed with which writer and reader can enter them may change the ways in which a student writer constructs himself or herself in a text. Moreover, the conventions of the academic essay value a coherent "voice" and a "focused" text, features that reflect a traditional conception of the autonomous self. As Myron Tuman (1992) has argued, traditional writing instruction is founded on "one of the principal tenets of print literacy, that of the writer as isolated individual" (p. 91), and the academic essay is the signature example of writing as authorial expression. Even as Mr. Green's essay reflects his attempts to construct a self within several discourses, as I demonstrated in Chapter 3, the form of the essay seems to work against that attempt. There is an inherent tension between the effort to construct a self within varied discourses, which position a writer variously and give rise to his or her multifarious subjectivity, and the conventions governing the form of the essay, which demand a unified authorial voice. We saw the same tension in Celina's essays in Chapter 4.

But the context of online writing may alter the conditions that give rise to this tension, freeing the writer to an extent from the kinds of conventions that circumscribe the writing of an essay or other conventional texts. In her email messages, Celina need not strive for the unified voice and coherent self that the academic essay asks for; she can shift quickly among various voices and engage various discourses variously. Moreover, her audience is more immediate and "present" in the sense that they have almost instant access to her text and can respond to it directly via the same medium of email. Online writing in a networked environment seems to highlight this social nature of writing in ways that can be obscured in print, especially in academic discourse. In this sense, online writing can make the discourses that student writers encounter more "visible," more immediate, and thus reveal more dramatically the ways in which all their writing is really about constructing the self within discourse. Celina is writing herself into specific discourses in her conventional essays as well as in her email message, but the electronic context allows her to do so differently than in print.

The key point here is that, although online writing may indeed be changing how we construct ourselves through writing and reading, literacy remains at heart a local act of self-construction. Thus, the important question for me in this instance is the same question I have asked about the other students I've described in preceding chapters: Why did Celina write what she did in this particular case? The answer to that question inevitably will address the specific nature of the context within which Celina wrote, a context that includes the use of the electronic environment of email as well as the physical context of the classroom where we met and talked within the broader context of the graduate course she was enrolled in and the institution of the university. As several scholars have noted recently, online discourse does not exist separately from these offline contexts (e.g., see Romano, 1993; Takayoshi, 1994; Yagelski & Grabill, 1998). The fact that Celina wished to "hide" her racial and gender identity online underscores the power of those offline contexts and discourses, which so profoundly shape the ways in which her classmates understand race and gender and thus influence how they read her words. When she writes online, she may have an enhanced ability to move among these discourses and to position herself in ways that may be difficult or even impossible in print forms, but she does not escape those discourses. She continues to try to write herself within and against them. Her classmates, including Sammy, do the same.

Indeed, the lack of reaction to Sammy's post about his father underscores this point in a rather revealing way. Among the 10 or 12 responses to that message that were posted in the following weeks, none addressed the traumatic personal circumstances that Sammy described. Instead, most of them focused on one line in the brief message I posted the day after Sammy's message appeared: "Sammy's earlier post about his father highlighted, for me at least, the limits of theory in our individual and collective efforts to negotiate the inevitable complexities and anguish of our lives." Two students, Bill and Ken, challenged what they took as my implicit attack on the kind of theory that they engage in as doctoral students in English. Their challenges, of course, must be understood within the context of the course (the readings, discussions, disagreements, and so on) and the department we worked in at the time, which was characterized by ongoing debates about "theory" and "pedagogy." But what was striking about the messages they posted during this discussion is the decidedly conventional academic approach each took to the discussion and the overtly theoretical voices they constructed in their messages. In one sense, their approach was not surprising, since they ostensibly were engaged in relatively sophisticated discussion in the context of a graduate course in English that dealt with such theoretical matters directly. But given the deeply personal and highly emotional nature of Sammy's message about his father, the use of formal academic language and overt academic argumentation seemed stiff and forced, despite their obviously sincere engagement with the question of the "limits of theory." They remained well within the bounds of conventional academic discourse, drawing on the discourses of Marxist theory and other schools of academic thought in making their case against what they saw as my dichotomizing of theory and experience; they constructed conventional academic selves that inevitably obscured and even ignored the compelling issues about father–son relationships, about medical ethics and familial identity, that Sammy wrote about. In this sense, their online identities as they constructed them through their email messages seemed consistent with the identities they constructed in class—identities that were in many ways appropriate and conventional in that context.

I would argue that those identities—as complex as they clearly are—reflect the power of discourse to shape our sense of self and our efforts to construct selves in public spaces like classrooms or the Internet. For Ken and Bill, the impulse to maintain identities as academic "theorists," whatever the source of that impulse as it emerged from their respective *self-interests*, seemed to shape how they would engage—or not engage—Sammy's post. For Sammy, a need to confront a traumatic personal problem seems to have pushed him to construct a public self by both drawing on and challenging the conventions of academic discourse and embracing other discourses of social dysfunction and self-disclosure on which he seems implicitly to draw. These needs and impulses exist exclusive of the electronic technologies that these students used, but they were confronted and expressed within the context of those technologies in ways that perhaps would not have happened in other, more conventional contexts. Laura was right, I think, that "no other mode of communication would have generated that particular message to that particular audience." But the crucial point is that it was "that *particular* message to that *particular* audience"—that local instance of constructing selves through writing.

If computers as tools for literacy are indeed changing how we understand ourselves and reshaping how we interact with each other and our worlds, they nevertheless also reaffirm the deep and never-ending need of readers and writers to construct themselves in ways that enable them to claim some sense of control over their lives. Myron Tuman (1992) has made a sobering case for caution in our understanding and uses of computer technologies in teaching writing and reading, reminding us of "the inevitable intellectual and social dislocations (the losses as well as the gains) represented by the radical restructuring, if not the demise, of print literacy" (p. 80). To understand these transformations, we must "consider the wider social context in which people read and write—namely the school and the workplace" (p. 80). He cautions that we must understand changes in literacy and literacy instruction as occurring within the context of "a new post-industrial age" whose new ways of valuing literacy will affect our students in different ways—not always for the best. And he reminds us, finally, that the struggle to be fully human, as Freire (1970/1984) puts it, must remain at the center of our understanding of literacy and technology.

> [T]he utopian promise of literacy . . . lies not in technological innovations themselves, no matter how spectacular and how liberating they may seem, but in the same practical task that in its undistorted form has motivated reading and writing in the age of print, that of remaking our world and ourselves in accord with an imagined rendering, a verbal projection, of what we human beings are capable of becoming. (Tuman, 1992, p. 130)

That task, a treacherous and essential one, is always local.

Chapter 6

"A Wider Project of Possibility and Empowerment"

Teaching Literacy as a Local Act

The history of literacy is a catalogue of obligatory relations. That this catalogue is so deeply conservative and, at the same time, so ruthlessly demanding of change is what fills contemporary literacy learning and teaching with their most paradoxical choices and outcomes.
—Deborah Brandt, "Sponsors of Literacy"

Yet in attachment flowers fall, and in aversion weeds spread.
—Eihei Dogen, Shobogenzo

On an unusually humid afternoon in June, I am sitting outside a gourmet coffee shop located implausibly near a busy intersection in the rumpled, blue-collar town of Queensbury in upstate New York. Sipping my coffee, I listen with Abby as Kim Marker tells the story of the English Regents exam that Abby walked out of 2 years earlier. The exam is required for earning a Regents high school diploma in New York State, but Abby's need for a cigarette during that test was apparently more pressing than her desire to earn graduation credit in English. Because Abby didn't complete that Regents exam, she enrolled the following summer in an English class designed for students who hadn't passed the exam, and Kim's story becomes one of a determined teacher who refused to give up on a recalcitrant and troubled but bright young woman. She describes some of the essays Abby wrote for that summer class: hard, disturbing stories about a difficult young life. As she does so, she looks at Abby with a blend of pride and care colored by painful memories that the two of them share. Abby fills in details to complete a picture of a student for whom family difficulties and drugs overshadowed a latent curiosity about social and political issues and led to truancy, discipline problems, and missed academic assignments. It's a depressingly familiar tale, and from its familiar outlines emerges a vague sense that school was somehow important to Abby even if it was deadly dull and seemingly irrelevant to the problems she was facing in her life. She is still indignant about the treatment she received at the hands of some of her former teachers, but she also speaks of times when there were opportunities for engagement: a history class that encompassed a unit on the Holocaust; an interesting discussion in English class. She and Kim recall some of the books they read for English class during the pivotal junior year that followed Abby's failed Regents exam.

"*Catcher in the Rye* was good," Abby says at one point, recalling that story of adolescent angst.

But most of the other books Kim mentions—familiar titles that appear in the English curriculum guides of thousands of schools across the country—Abby deems as irrelevant or admits she didn't read, and she begins to sound like so many bored teen-agers faced with the prospect of reading "great books," the greatness of which escapes them. Nevertheless, it is obvious that, 2 years after that junior year, a year after her graduation, reading and writing are an important part of Abby's life. She mentions some of the books she has read recently: *I Never Promised You a Rose Garden*, by Joanne Greenberg, the bootstraps story of a mentally ill teen-aged girl who finds a measure of self-understanding; *Way of the Peaceful Warrior*, by Dan Millman, the story of the spiritual journey of a world-class athlete; *Solar Storms*, by Linda Hogan, a novel about the struggle of a Native-American community to preserve its traditions. These are not, it is clear, titles that Abby has stumbled on haphazardly; they relate to important ongoing struggles in her life. She talks, too, of reading poetry and writing some as well. Soon we are discussing books like three professional critics, and Kim asks Abby if she'll read a book that she is planning to use in her classes during the coming school year. "I'd like to hear how you think the students will react to it," she says to Abby. The bored, troubled, resistant student becomes book critic and curriculum adviser. Kim always knew that critic was there, even in the face of Abby's resistance to her academic work. And she must know, too, that it wasn't literacy that Abby resisted but the curriculum Kim was obligated to deliver.

As I listen to this story, I wonder how many other Abby's sit in our English classes—interested and intense young people who are justifiably bored by our boring curricula. Abby refers to the standard "book reports" that she was required to write in her English classes, and with her former English teacher listening, she questions the purpose of such assignments. For her—and for so many other students—there seemed to be little point to such assignments, which all too often turn potentially compelling stories into rote academic exercises. Holden Caulfield's troubles as described in *Catcher in the Rye*, Abby suggests, are troubles that many teens endure, but that vital connection is lost in assignments that require students to reduce that rich and disturbing story to "themes" and "style" and "character development" in canned, formulaic book reports or critical essays.

The pedagogical problem that Abby is describing as she shares these thoughts is a function of the disconnection between school curricula and students' lives. The narrowness of the implicit conception of literacy that drives the curriculum to which Abby was subjected became, for her and her peers, dullness: a continuous, tedious exercise in esoteric ways of reading and writing that seem of little use outside an academic setting. This is not to say that academic ways of reading and writing cannot benefit students; but it is to say that the kinds of writing and reading that are valued in schools tend to have little meaningful connection to the many kinds of reading and writing students will be asked to do outside school—and to the kind of literacy envisioned by theorists like Paulo Freire. This disconnection emerges even more strikingly as Abby drifts into the story about why she remained in school after her sophomore year, despite the failed Regents exam, serious truancy problems, and a stint in rehab.

"My dad paid me," she says with a slight laugh.

She goes on to explain that after her disastrous sophomore year, she had no desire to return to school, which remained for her a place of boredom run by suspicious and unsupportive but powerful adults. But her father offered her money ("$80, I think.") if she brought home a good report card in her junior year. That offer kept her going to class at the beginning of the year. But her real motivation came later, when a friend of hers, a young man who had dropped out of school, was arrested for possession of a controlled substance. Because of New York State's harsh drug laws, this young man was facing the possibility of a long jail sentence without parole despite having no prior criminal record. In the end, Abby's friend apparently pled to a lesser charge and served a few years in state prison before being released on parole, but the experience left Abby with a deep sense of outrage about what she sees as the unfairness of the American judicial system. That outrage seems only to have deepened in the years since her friend was busted. She speaks in angrier, more excited tones as she describes the recent case of a local man convicted of molesting several foster children in his care. He was sentenced to 3 years' probation for the crime.

"How much damage did he do to those kids?" she asks indignantly. "And he gets probation. My friend does some drugs by himself and gets sent to prison." She begins to talk about the role of money in the judicial system.

"My friend couldn't afford to hire an expensive lawyer," she says and she leaves the implication of that fact unarticulated, hanging heavily in the thick air.

She stayed in school that year, she says, because she decided then that if she could become a lawyer, she might be able to address those same injustices that sent her friend to jail but left the child molester on probation. This is the same young woman who 2 years earlier insisted that she was irrelevant, as I described in Chapter 1, and when I remind her of that day, she tells me that "you can't change the system, but you can fight it and help people like my friend." As part of that fight, Abby has written to her Congressman about these two cases to express her view about what she believes are unfair laws governing drug use and sexual abuse. She also has written to the local newspaper about other issues that concern her. Here, for instance, is part of what she wrote about an initiative to prohibit skateboarding and street football in her town:

> It may be true that drug use and violent crimes among adolescents are on the rise, but not all teenagers fall into these categories. If the law prohibits teenagers from recreational activities such as skateboarding on the streets and playing football on the side streets where they live . . . , all it will be doing is opening up more opportunities for adolescents to find other ways to entertain themselves, possibly in unhealthy or even threatening ways. . . . If we are unable to have hobbies that require the use of a street in our town, what and where else is there for us to do and go? We all need to work together and stop this war that seems to be going on between our youth and our elders.

As I read this passionate attempt to write herself into a public debate of local importance, I am struck by the savvy with which she is able to harness her passion to craft a letter that is both emotional and controlled. I assume she exhibited the same kind of savvy when she wrote her application to the local community college she now attends and when she applied for the few jobs she has held since graduation. A failed Regents exam in English apparently did not reflect her ability to use written language for these purposes; but now instead of book reports she is writing letters to legislators and editors and admissions counselors.

She checks her watch and realizes that she is late for her current job at a local pizza shop. She will continue to work in the fall when she returns to the community college to pursue a degree in criminal justice, which she hopes to complete at a 4-year college, and she tells me that she has already been writing to colleges for admissions information. As she starts to leave, I ask her if she thinks that the writing and reading she did in high school prepared her for addressing the kinds of social and legal problems she has been describing and the life she is trying to build for herself.

"No."

LITERACY INSTRUCTION AND STUDENTS' LIVES

In telling part of the story of her life as a student and citizen, Abby has unequivocally answered the question I posed in Chapter 1, "Does literacy matter?" Yes. It matters in terms of her ongoing effort to understand herself and make sense of her life in the context of family troubles, adolescent struggles, social dysfunction, institutional pressures, and a desire to belong. It matters in terms of her efforts to negotiate the day-to-day challenges of life in contemporary capitalist America. And it matters in terms of her attempts to address social and political injustices that she sees as limiting that life. In the poetry she writes for herself, in the reading she does about personal and cultural struggle, in the letters she has sent to her Congressman, and in the papers she writes for her community college classes, Abby strives to construct a self that is, in Paulo Freire's phrase, fully human: one who exercises some measure of control over her social and economic existence in the face of obvious institutional and financial obstacles and less obvious social and cultural limitations; one who claims some measure of autonomy within a tangled network of social and cultural forces; one who struggles to accept herself even as she demands acceptance from others. She writes herself into the political and legal discourses that circumscribe her existence in contemporary American society in overtly local ways. Her letters to her Congressman and to her local newspaper represent her efforts to use writing to make her voice heard on local problems that relate to much larger issues, to contribute to the endless stream of discourses through which her—and our—political and legal existence is constituted. This young woman who once protested to me that she doesn't matter engages regularly in literate acts as a way to insist that she does. Literacy matters because Abby matters. There can be no more compelling motivation for a teacher of writing and reading, I believe, than that.

But if Abby's story suggests that literacy matters in individual lives, it also reveals the mismatch between the ways in which literacy as a local act—as a social and individual construction of the self within discourse—functions in the lives of our students and the ways in which literacy is conceptualized and taught in our classrooms. Although there is little doubt that some of what Abby learned about writing in school now serves her in her efforts to use literacy to negotiate the challenges she faces in her life, it also seems clear that what she was asked to do as part of her school literacy curriculum seemed to have little direct bearing on those challenges, especially as she made the transition from "student" to "adult." The formulaic writing assignments she was asked to complete did not encourage her to understand writing as a way to act in the world, and the literary assignments she was given fostered a narrow view of reading as a kind of esoteric cultural "enrichment" rather than as a way to make sense of a difficult and confusing world. Her school experiences highlight the fact that the self implicitly defined by school-sponsored literacy is divorced from the conflicted and fragmented self that must be negotiated within the complex world of discourse outside school. Instead, as education researcher Jean Anyon (1980) and others (e.g., Heath, 1983) have shown, literacy learning in schools is part of the norming function that schools serve as they convey implicit beliefs about knowledge and behavior and authority; further, school-based literacy learning, as Abby's experience suggests and as I will try to demonstrate momentarily, continues to reinforce the same narrow conceptions of literacy that I described in Chapter 2, which works against the kind of critical literacy Freire envisions.

Just a few weeks after my conversation with Abby over coffee in the summer of 1998, the Modern Library released its list of the 100 Greatest Books of the Twentieth Century. (See Lewis, 1998, for one of many press reports about the list that appeared in July 1998.) The correspondence between that list, which was compiled by a panel of esteemed writers, and the list of the most frequently assigned books in American secondary schools compiled in an extensive study by Arthur Applebee (1993) is striking. More striking still was an alternative list of students' choices of the 100 Greatest Books of the Century, which was released a day or so after the Modern Library's list appeared. That student list looked as though it was copied from Applebee's study and seemed an almost perfect illustration of Freire's famous banking metaphor for education: students earnestly parroting their teachers' pronouncements about what constitutes worthwhile reading. Predictably, the popular media became obsessed with the Modern Library's list for a few days until distracted by another "event." There were the expected complaints from columnists about which books were excluded, which were first and last, which are really read and which aren't, and the usefulness or uselessness of such lists. Educators examined the wisdom (or lack of it) in these lists. Commentators commented on what such lists might say about the state of contemporary American education. But I saw no commentary on the divergence between that list of "greatest" books and the literacy needs of Abby and her peers.

For a great many of our students, our pedagogies and curricula don't serve those needs. All the public attention directed at the Modern Library's great book list both underscored the problematic conceptions of literacy that continue to drive education and missed the point that literacy education, focused as it is on "great" books, has little to do with the lives our students must lead. In the din, educators often seemed to be in the uncomfortable position of agreeing that these books are "great" and defending their effectiveness as the persons our society holds responsible for making these books available to students. In our professional discussions, we educators speak passionately of empowering our students, and I have little doubt that teachers and scholars and critics on all sides of the ongoing debates about education reform engage the matter sincerely. Yet our public discussions about literacy education often are framed by these same insufferably reductive lists of great books and the attendant political polemics and self-serving theoretical arguments that we complain about in the media. Meanwhile, students like Abby encounter great books in their English classes and then emerge from those classes to fend for themselves in a confusing and treacherous world of political and economic and legal discourses that circumscribe their lives. The gaping distance between what we teach in our classes and our students' needs as literate beings in a world largely defined by literacy constitutes our most serious failure as educators; closing that gap is our most pressing challenge.

My exploration of literacy as a local act of self-construction in this book is, I hope, a step toward closing that gap. I have tried to illuminate some of the ways in which we might productively think about literacy and its often ambiguous yet crucial place in our students' lives; I hope I also have begun to reveal some of the weaknesses in our conventional approaches to—and our scholarly treatments of—literacy instruction despite the good work of so many committed educators. In the remainder of this chapter I want to examine more closely the implications of my perspective on literacy for the teaching of reading and writing. In doing so, I will not provide a description of a particular pedagogical approach nor will I specify an English curriculum for secondary and postsecondary schools. In the end, the details of any pedagogy and curriculum must be worked out locally in order to serve the needs of specific groups of students and teachers working together in specific contexts. What I offer here instead is something akin to a meditation on what a conception of literacy as a local act—as a *human* activity—might mean for literacy educators as they struggle to develop pedagogies to help their students claim agency as writers and readers in a world shaped by discourse. In offering this meditation, I will make two key points: first, that literacy, not literature, should be at the center of the English curriculum in secondary and postsecondary education and that literacy as such must have some connection to the ways in which writing and reading function in our students' lives as people and citizens outside our classrooms; and second, that our pedagogies should grow out of a conception of literacy as a local act such as I have described in this book and thus should incorporate exploration of the ambiguous but powerful role literacy can play in our lives. In making these points I will traverse some of the familiar ground over which scholars interested in critical pedagogy and cultural studies have tread and I will engage, to a limited extent, some of the arguments about "personal" writing that periodically reappear in our professional discourse. But my interest here is not in entering these debates as much as in trying to tease out what my understanding of literacy might mean for teachers who wish to make their teaching more relevant to their students' lives.

Literacy and Literature

In the fall of 1993, amid the glare of media coverage of the pending congressional vote on the North American Free Trade Agreement (NAFTA), I observed a high school junior English class on *Huck Finn* taught by one of my student teachers, Melissa.[1] As the public debates about NAFTA intensified, Melissa's students were engaged in a different sort of discourse, one that seemed decidedly unfamiliar to them, in which they were discussing the themes of that widely recognized "great book." At one point, the students were asked to consider a passage in which Huck explains his reasoning for a subterfuge he has engineered. After rereading the passage aloud, Melissa posed standard questions about how it developed themes of morality and honesty and revealed Huck's character as a moral agent. Listening to Melissa's students struggle to answer her questions, I wondered what they might make of the many articles and flyers and related documents that proliferated as the public debate on NAFTA headed toward the culminating congressional vote. As a political and cultural event, NAFTA reflected the many new and difficult challenges facing those students as readers and writers—as consumers and producers of texts—in a rapidly changing society. As a "text" of enormous complexity and importance, NAFTA represented both the value and power of literacy as it functions within the American economic and political system and the so-called world economy. It was a text whose meanings resided within the economic, political, legal, and cultural discourses within which NAFTA occurred—and whose meanings played out in countless ways as the millions of people somehow involved in the event engaged in various activities surrounding it. For many of those people—politicians, lawyers, union activists, small business owners, factory workers, consumers—NAFTA was implicitly about the ways in which literacy amounts to acts of engagement in the political and economic systems within which they live.

By contrast, Melissa's lesson on *Huck Finn*, which she taught to an eleventh-grade English class in a public high school in rural Indiana, pointed up the same limited conception of literacy that informed the classes Abby complained about. The lesson was structured around teacher-led discussion of specific passages in the novel, in this case the chapters describing Huck's and Jim's encounter with some thieves on the river. Melissa posed two kinds of questions to her students, the first focusing on what happened in these chapters ("And what does Huck do when he meets these men?"), and the second intended to elicit some sort of interpretation ("Why does Huck lie about the wreck to the caretaker on the barge?"). During the discussion, Melissa did most of the talking. The 30 students in the room were generally quiet, perhaps politely so for Melissa's sake as I looked on. A few periodically volunteered brief answers to Melissa's questions. The others either listened quietly or seemed to drift into that bored adolescent reverie I have seen so often in high school classrooms. There were a lot of uncomfortable silences, which Melissa filled by rephrasing her questions or, in barely noticeable exasperation, answering them herself.

As the hour dragged on, the thrust of Melissa's lesson became clear: She wanted to focus attention on specific passages in order to help her students see how Twain constructs the elaborate metaphor of the river and how that metaphor relates to some of the moral issues typically associated with this novel. She used literary terms like *motif* and *symbol*; she talked about *characterization* and development of *themes*. Her primary purpose, one that seems so commonsensical to those of us who have made the study of literature part of our professional lives, was to illuminate the ways in which this text holds together as a work of literary art. Although most of the lesson focused on what David Bloome (1987) calls *cataloguing*, that is, "a listing of parts that count as a whole" as opposed to *analysis*, or "a process of segmenting the whole into parts in order to gain insight into the nature of the whole" (p. 132), Melissa's goal was to open up the literary complexity of this text to her students, to help them see beyond the plot. When she directed her students' attention to the passage about the thieves, for instance, she urged them to think about how Huck understands "honesty" and what his motivations for "lying" might be: "In what ways did Huck 'help' the thieves?" "Are the 'lies' he tells on the river different from his 'lies' on shore?" On the surface at least, Melissa's efforts fell short. The frantic page turning that followed each of her questions suggested that few of the students had even read the passage, and fewer still seemed able or willing to engage the text in ways that Melissa encouraged. The lesson plodded to the period's end, at which point Melissa hurriedly assigned chapters for that night's reading.

Admittedly, I am presenting *my* brief version of what happened in Melissa's class that day. Melissa's version, which she offered in conversation with me and her cooperating teacher after the class, revealed her frustration about the students' apparent lack of enthusiasm. She had few concerns about the content and purpose of her lesson, and I raised no objections to her unit, since she had virtually no control over the curriculum. But she was unhappy with what she perceived to be the students' unwillingness to engage the material she was presenting. I made some suggestions about how she might draw her students into the story, which explores difficult issues of racial and moral conflict. Her students have experienced such conflict, I pointed out. (There recently had been a racial incident at the school involving some White students and a Latino student.) In short, I suggested a shift in the focus of the lesson from identifying literary techniques to exploring social, psychological, and ethical issues; I argued that connecting those issues to the social and cultural contexts within which the students live would help make the novel relevant to their own lives. Her cooperating teacher, however, disagreed and offered yet another version of what happened in that class. He believed that the students' silence reflected a lack not of engagement but attentiveness. They were quietly learning the material, he argued. Later he told Melissa, "You can do all the namby-pamby personal connecting you want, but the students still have to learn this material for Friday's test." For him, what was most important about the lesson was that the students remember specific "material" from the story and then reproduce that material in brief written answers on the week's test.

There was really nothing out of the ordinary about Melissa's lesson or about her cooperating teacher's concerns about the week's test. The lesson was very much like dozens I've observed, like hundreds I've taught, like thousands taught every schoolday. And the cooperating teacher echoed sentiments I've often heard in conversations with teachers: the importance of covering specific material; the need for students to learn particular kinds of (textual) information about "important" novels, poems, or stories. Indeed, it is the very commonness of the experience that concerns me, since it is this kind of lesson that represents a significant portion of most students' literacy learning, as it did for Abby.

Teaching Relevant Discourses

What might students learn about reading and writing in a class like this? Implicitly, given the way Melissa focused her students' attention on aspects of this text, her students are likely to have learned that aesthetic texts like *Huck Finn* differ from other texts and therefore must be read differently, although the students are not likely to have learned *why* that is the case. In addition, they might have learned that Melissa, like all teachers, knows how to read texts like *Huck Finn.* Her students likely will never "see" the sophisticated process by which she has come to interpret this text. They are rarely, if ever, given models of *how* to read such a text; they merely see a kind of end product in the form of their teacher's seemingly effortless interpretation. Thus they may come to believe that a text "contains" an objective "hidden meaning" that a teacher can see but that they cannot. As John Mayher (1990) puts it in his critique of traditional approaches to literature instruction, "The products rather than the processes of literary analysis tend to be presented (and tested); students [are] rarely encouraged or allowed to encounter texts on their own to develop their authority as readers" (p. 28).

Researcher David Bloome (1987) has explored the ways in which teachers convey to students such problematic assumptions about what it means to read a text like *Huck Finn.* Bloome's description of a reading lesson in an eighth-grade language arts classroom illuminates an activity characterized by what he calls "text reproduction," that is, reading or rereading aloud. According to Bloome, "What reading the text seemed to do [in this classroom] was to establish the dominance of text reproduction as a definition of problem solving and of interacting with text" (p. 134). Bloome goes on to describe the teacher-led discussion of a story ("The Saint," by V. S. Pritchett) about a religious sect, a discussion similar to the one Melissa led about *Huck Finn*. Bloome concludes that

> the discussion framed students as passive responders to text that was unrelated to their experiences . . . almost all of the students were or had been intensely involved with religious enterprises (e.g., Sunday school), and a handful belonged to religious sects that were similar to the religious sect described in 'The Saint.' In neither the discussion of [a related class trip] nor 'The Saint' were the mediating frames established through teacher–student interaction grounded in student experience. (p. 141)

In other words, when it came to reading a literary text, personal experiences seemed irrelevant; so, too, were the social and cultural contexts within which those experiences occurred. Similarly, what seemed to matter in Melissa's class was not understanding how experience mediates the construction of meaning (how, for example, the students' own attitudes about and recent experiences with racial tension might shape their reading) or how race and class influence meaning making (that is, how Melissa's lower-middle-class, rural, White students might understand Jim differently than their Latino or Latina classmates and how such understandings relate to the discourses that shape conceptions of matters like race); rather, what mattered was how Twain's text functioned as a work of literary art. What was implicitly taught, then, was text as object, as container of predetermined meaning, rather than meaning as a function of the constructive activities of reading and writing within specific social, cultural, political, and historical contexts. Thus, despite her genuine concerns for her students' understanding of such matters, Melissa implicitly encouraged what Bloome calls "a passive, 'alienated' stance toward extended text" (p. 146).

Such a stance reflects a view of literacy that Deborah Brandt (1990) has called the "strong-text" theories of literacy, which "give little consideration to the processes of writing and reading, to questions of how people actually accomplish literate acts in daily life" (p. 13). This strong-text view of literacy is akin to the functionalist conception of literacy driving public discussions of education reform that I described in Chapter 2, in which reading and writing are understood as the straightforward transfer of ideas or information through a text, the meaning of which is autonomous. Through her lessons on *Huck Finn*, Melissa implicitly presents to students a *meaning* as if it stands apart from the contexts in which the text was written and in which it is read; the text embodies this meaning, and thus it too stands apart from context. The fact that Melissa's students are asked to reproduce aspects of this meaning on a written exam only reinforces the notion that there is a single valid meaning to this text, which the students are expected to learn. For those students, then, reading the assigned text becomes a matter of "finding" the right meaning or learning it from the teacher; writing becomes a matter of reproducing this right meaning accurately on an exam. Texts become what Brandt (1990) calls "decontextualized pieces of language," and decontextualization, according to Brandt, "comes to be seen as the essential interpretative move that literacy requires. Because texts are abstract objects, conceptual, logical, literal, and detached, so too does literacy come to be characterized in the same terms" (p. 25).

Melissa's role in reinforcing such a view of literacy is in large part predetermined. Although her training as an English education major exposed her to the idea that literacy is a social and cultural activity in ways that Brandt and others (e.g., Heath, 1983; Scribner & Cole, 1981; Street, 1984) have illuminated, her many years of experience in classrooms much like her own and the pervasiveness of functionalist views of literacy work against her best efforts to make reading and writing more meaningful to her students. It's also important to note that Melissa herself believed that she was doing something other than what I have tried to describe here. She asserted that she was exposing students, through the study of literature, to rich and profound ideas that would help them understand the complexity of their world. In other words, Melissa did not intend the study of literature to be primarily about the text as a static literary artifact.

Not all teachers teach texts in the way I'm suggesting Melissa and her cooperating teacher did, and a good case can be made that some elements of traditional literary study in schools can be beneficial to students in terms of their development as literate persons. Gladys Knott (1987), in reviewing literacy instruction in secondary schools, concluded that, despite the superficial nature of much of the reading that students are asked to do in secondary schools, "there are secondary schools in which literary instruction and the role of literacy are meaningful components of secondary education" (p. 363). No doubt this is true. And certainly Melissa was striving for such meaningful study. Yet the evidence we have suggests that the kind of lesson I observed in Melissa's class is common practice in secondary English classrooms nationwide. Bloome (1987), for example, reported "recurrent patterns" of "text reproduction" (p. 146) and similar practices across the middle school classrooms he observed. And in one of the most comprehensive national studies of the teaching of literature in American secondary schools, Applebee (1993) concluded:

> The typical lesson is a mixture of seatwork, in which students focus on "what is happening" in the works they are asked to read, and teacher-led whole-class discussion that tries to meld their individual understandings into an acceptable, commonly agreed upon whole. In a pattern that owes much to New Critical traditions, discussion usually is tied quite closely to the individual text and the way in which the text "works" to convey an author's meanings. In some classes, this leads students into thought-provoking engagement with the text and with one another; in many others, it turns literature into an exercise in puzzle-solving, in which the task for the student is to find the meaning that the teacher sees hidden there. (p. 194)

In short, the typical secondary school English program continues to be what John Mayher (1990) calls a "commonsense" language arts curriculum that does not "help students find a means of more fully developing *critical powers* of literacy" (p. 41, emphasis added). Despite reform efforts, there is little evidence that our secondary school English curricula are being changed in ways that will prepare students to become critical readers and writers who can participate meaningfully in a complex and changing political system, who can find ways into that system as Abby is struggling to do—who can, as Mayher puts it, "both critique and participate in the power structure of the world in which they live" (p. 41). The 50% or so of these secondary school students who go on to postsecondary schools enter college or university programs in which "writing" is separate from "literature," a distinction that further reinforces a functionalist perspective on literacy, nothwithstanding the extensive theoretical and pedagogical work of composition scholars.

Not surprisingly, then, students like Melissa's are unlikely to encounter pedagogies that foreground the acts of reading and writing texts as complex individual efforts to engage the discourses that shape their lives and to participate in those discourses. What this might mean for these students as they confront the enormous variety of texts that somehow influence their lives can, I think, be seen in the ways in which NAFTA was constructed through many different kinds of texts and in the challenges those texts present to readers trying to make sense of NAFTA.

Around the time I visited Melissa's classroom, I came across an article written by corporate executive Dean O'Hare (1993) in a lengthy advertising supplement about NAFTA in the *New York Times*. O'Hare's piece of approximately 350 words, in which he uses terms like "secure business relationships," "level playing field," and "multilateral trade agreement" to argue that NAFTA will result in sustained job growth for American service companies, is the kind of text that proliferated during the intense NAFTA debates—and the kind of text Melissa's students would never see in their English class. Most of them were lower-middle-class White students living in a rural region with few job opportunities and little hope for better wages than those earned by their parents, who were able to take advantage of agricultural and manufacturing jobs that have largely disappeared from that region. A little more than half of them eventually would go on to postsecondary schools, many to 2-year technical colleges where they would learn "marketable" skills; many of the rest would try to find employment locally. NAFTA and the many texts like O'Hare's that focused on that agreement were decidedly relevant to the social and economic existence of these students. Will they be able engage such texts in a way that is useful to them as they decide about their futures and perhaps cast votes in local or national elections? Will their reading of these texts amount to critical participation in a discourse that affects the economic conditions within which they live? To do so requires an understanding of text—and of literacy—that is very different from the "passive, 'alienated' stance toward extended text" that Bloome (1987, p. 146) describes and very different from how Melissa's students are taught to engage and understand a text like *Huck Finn*. Their school-sponsored literacy learning largely ignores the various discourses—social, cultural, political—within which NAFTA as a text and a political event occurred. The only discourse that matters in their English class is the discourse of *Huck Finn* as a work of literary art, a discourse that is presented—implicitly—as separate from other economic, political, cultural, and institutional discourses.

In the end, little of what Melissa's students learn in their "reading" of *Huck Finn* will encourage those students to understand the ways in which a text like a political advertisement about NAFTA grows out of a specific set of circumstances within the extraordinarily complex context of a congressional debate about an international trade agreement. Nor are they likely to be asked to consider how the "meaning" of an apparently simple text like O'Hare's can be seen as a function of complicated historical, social, economic, and political contexts or that the text represents a sophisticated rhetorical act with an array of purposes and a number of different (sometimes conflicting) audiences. It may be unreasonable to expect these students to have knowledge of economic principles and the intricate political procedures of the U.S. Congress. But it is not unreasonable—indeed, it is crucial—to expect them to understand what it means to read texts such as O'Hare's article about NAFTA, to understand that such texts represent rhetorical acts that can affect their lives. These students, who are being schooled in a kind of passive literacy, are the very same students who will soon enter a world of work that is being reshaped by agreements like NAFTA. In order to participate meaningfully in the political processes by which such developments occur, they must be able to negotiate meanings of texts in ways that enable them to act knowingly as voters, as citizens, as consumers. In order to claim the kind of political agency that Freire and others call for, they must be able to participate in what James Berlin (1992) calls "the network of intersecting discourses" (p. 21) that shape their economic and political lives. Can they do so as a result of their experiences with reading and writing in school? If those experiences with written language, with text, are limited to the kind of lesson I observed in Melissa's class, if they resemble the school experiences Abby describes, the answer is no.

Melissa's students—all our students—have a stake in the public discourses surrounding an event like NAFTA, just as Abby has a stake in the public discussions surrounding her town's ban on skateboarding. To ignore those discourses—to ignore NAFTA as "outside" school literacy—is to deny students the potential for political agency. If our literacy curricula are to help students acquire such agency, literacy instruction should be based on the activities of reading and writing as social and cultural practices within powerful existing and evolving discourses rather than on the more traditional content of language arts, which tends to focus on knowledge of formal grammar, specific textual forms, and a canon of literary works. Students should be given a range of experiences with a variety of texts within a variety of rhetorical contexts that foreground the inherently situated and constructive nature of reading and writing, so that students are not simply *doing* reading and writing as teacher-directed exercises but coming to an understanding of how these activities grow out of specific social, cultural, historical, and political contexts (see Yagelski, 1994b). Moreover, traditional approaches to studying canonized literary texts, which are based on outdated assumptions about literature and literacy and which present texts like *Huck Finn* as inviolate works of literary art that are to be analyzed for structure, style, literary technique, and so on, should be replaced with a curriculum in which students are encouraged to read various texts not only to learn the texts themselves but to learn how to read texts for a multiplicity of purposes, to learn how texts—and the acts of writing and reading them—amount to participation in various and sometimes competing discourses.

We will serve our students best, I believe, if we teach them a way of understanding and engaging in literacy that enables them to imagine themselves as active participants in their world; to do so is to help them find ways to write themselves into the discourses that affect their lives and thus to begin to close the gap between school-sponsored literacy and the vital role of literacy in their lives as citizens. Texts like *Huck Finn* can be an important part of such an effort; the study of literature by itself, however, especially in the context of lessons like Melissa's, is little more than a futile exercise that reflects outdated and exclusionary Arnoldian beliefs about the value of literary art in a "civilized" culture, an exercise that leaves students virtually powerless in a postmodern world shaped by texts like NAFTA.

Technologies and a Literacy of Possibility

It should be clear, too, that such a shift in the focus of the English curriculum must encompass the evolving new technologies of literacy, especially online technologies like the Internet. The growing importance of these technologies as means of communication as well as vehicles for political and economic interaction represent both new responsibilities and new opportunities for literacy educators. In Chapter 5 I explored the ways in which these new technologies may be changing how we understand and use literacy in our lives. Important public matters like NAFTA can bring these changes into relief. Consider one recent illustration of this point.

In July 1998 a news story about a federal court case involving privacy on the Internet, an issue of growing economic and political importance in the late 1990s, was reported by some news organizations. I learned of the court decision in a brief spot on National Public Radio, but I could find no mention of it in any of the newspapers I normally read. A search of the Internet, however, quickly yielded several sources of information about the case, which involved a man named William Sheehan, who accused several major credit reporting agencies of failing to remove inaccurate information from his credit report. The search also yielded the Internet address of the web site that Sheehan had set up, which became the focus of the lawsuit against him. That web site was Sheehan's attempt to publicize his version of the story of the companies' injustice against him. On the site, he railed in decidedly unflattering (and sometimes profane) language against the companies and included personal information about some company executives (such as addresses and telephone numbers and even maps to their homes). Not surprisingly, the companies filed suit and won a temporary injunction to force him to shut down his site. But the U.S. District Court judge who heard the case removed the injunction on the grounds that Sheehan's web site was proteced by the First Amendment. One article about the case that was published in the *Columbian*, a regional newspaper from Washington state that I accessed online, noted, "Historically, people have used newspapers, magazines and leaflets to exercise their constitutional right to free speech"; it quoted Aaron Caplan, an attorney from the American Civil Liberties Union: "A decision like this one makes very clear that the same types of First Amendment protections apply when you distribute your leaflet electronically" (Associated Press, 1998, p. B2).

Sheehan's case demonstrates rather dramatically the potential power of the web to enable someone to act on his or her own behalf or perhaps in the service of some cause. Sheehan easily could have written a letter to the editor of his local newspaper or perhaps even printed a flyer in order to publicize his complaints against the credit reporting companies, conventional strategies that many citizens have used. But such strategies, which rely on traditional print technologies, could not match the potential of the electronic "publishing" that Sheehan employed to disseminate his message and present himself as victim. By launching a web page on the Internet, Sheehan instantly reached a potential audience of millions, the same audience that companies are soliciting so vigorously in search of "e-commerce" profits. Sheehan's antagonists recognized that power and its potential to damage their own businesses and thus tried to deny him that forum through legal channels. In his decision, the judge in the case cited a 1971 U.S. Supreme Court case "in which an organization critical of the business methods of a real estate broker passed out leaflets that gave the broker's home telephone number and asked readers to call him there. The U.S. Supreme Court ultimately ruled that the public's interest in the distribution of the leaflets outweighed the broker's interest in privacy" (Associated Press, 1998, p. B2). The clash between the conventional print technologies (in the form of leaflets) and the emerging electronic literacy technologies (in the form of the World Wide Web) is stark in this instance, and the case thus provides a rich example of how these new literacy technologies are not only challenging our traditional ways of communicating and interacting through literacy but also providing new models of literacy as a means of acting in the world (see Gurak, 1997, for a related discussion).

There is challenge but also opportunity for literacy educators in these developments. Online technologies like the Internet provide teachers with vast resources for exploring issues like privacy and free speech—resources that are largely unavailable via conventional means; moreover, these technologies can be a powerful vehicle by which we can help students explore how literacy functions in our changing world and provide opportunities for them to engage the extant discourses in the context of issues like NAFTA or Internet privacy. We ignore these opportunities at our students' expense.

Not long before I learned of the Sheehan case, my son Aaron learned about Thomas Paine's famous leaflet, *Common Sense*, in his eighth-grade social studies class. That text, originally published by a commercial printer in Philadelphia as an 80-page pamphlet some 6 months before the signing of the Declaration of Independence in 1776, is estimated to have sold 120,000 copies in 3 months and as many as 500,000 in total (Downs, 1970, p. 26). It is one of the most dramatic instances of the power of print technology to communicate widely and thus to help shape important civil and geopolitical events. In Aaron's social studies class, that text was presented to the students as an example of one person's influence on world affairs: the brave, individual political pamphleteer as American hero. Yet in this same school district, which boasts state-of-the-art computer technologies and a flashy web site for its high school, students have extremely limited access in school to these technologies, which represent possibilities for their own direct engagement with a changing world and which go far beyond Sheehan's self-interested web site—possibilities that approach the potential of Thomas Paine's famous pamphlet. The power and dangers of online technologies are obscured by simplistic uses of the computer as a tool to accomplish the same outdated and limited curricular goals that Melissa so diligently pursued in her class on *Huck Finn*. The important intersections between our students' personal lives and their political existence in a changing technological environment, intersections that emerge dramatically in a comparison of the Sheehan case and Paine's *Common Sense*, thus are ignored.

We do have numerous examples of promising uses of computer technologies for accomplishing pedagogical goals that capitalize on these opportunities for literacy learning (e.g., see Rickley, Harrington, & Day, 1999; Selfe & Hilligoss, 1994). But even as a few visionary teachers find ways to incorporate new technologies into progressive literacy curricula, the same narrow conceptions of literacy that I discussed in Chapter 2 circumscribe general attitudes toward computers as technologies for literacy and thus work against the kind of vision of literacy that I have tried to lay out in this book. As I noted in Chapter 5, education theorist C. A. Bowers (1988) warned more than a decade ago about the implications of a view of computers as "a tool that is culturally neutral" (p. 28) and urged educators to consider more carefully "how this technology mediates the cultural transmission process . . . [and] how the professional judgments of the teacher in the instructional uses of the microcomputer relate to the larger question of political empowerment and cultural reform" (p. 52). My experiences in schools and a growing body of evidence (e.g., see Center for Applied Special Technology, 1996) suggest that teachers, under pressure to use the sexy new computer technologies as schools rush to embrace these technologies, are largely unmindful of the relations among technology and politics and culture that Bowers invokes. As a result, computers are more likely to become a means by which the status quo is maintained and limiting notions of literacy are reinforced than vehicles for truly empowering literacy pedagogies.

In a prescient 1985 article, Richard Ohmann wrote that "computers are an evolving technology like any other, shaped within particular social relations, and responsive to the needs of those with the power to direct that evolution" (p. 680). As such, computers as technologies for literacy have the potential to limit as well as to empower, and Ohmann, by describing the ways in which computers "routinize" and "dehumanize" (p. 682) already menial jobs in places like fast food restaurants and supermarkets, shows that computers can contribute to

> the degradation of labor and the stratification of the workforce. . . . [H]ow about the young people behind the fast-food counter, whose computer keyboards no longer carry numbers and letters, but pictures of food items, so that the work can be done by someone who is both computer-illiterate and just plain illiterate? Predictions that 50 to 75 percent of jobs will be "computer-related" by 1990 sound intimidating, but how many of those jobs will call for even the slightest understanding of computers? (p. 683)

Ohmann concludes that those with certain kinds of valued computer and literacy skills will benefit from "the computer revolution" while "those who do no more than acquire basic skills and computer literacy in high school will probably find their way to electronic workstations at McDonald's" (p. 683).[2] What's more, the racial and socioeconomic distribution among these categories is likely to be unequal. In 1998, the *Chronicle of Higher Education* reported that among households whose annual income totaled less than $40,000, "27.5 per cent of white households had computers, but only 13.3 per cent of black households had computers"; Whites are also more likely than Blacks to have access to the Internet (Kiernan, 1998, p. A38). (At the time the mean annual income for a family of four in the United States was approximately $35,000.) Such figures demonstrate that literacy technologies, like literacy itself, reflect complex and often ambivalent circumstances in which some of our students clearly will be at risk.

As teachers of writing and reading at a time when new technologies are redefining the role and value of literacy in our society, we must, I believe, address the reality that new literacy technologies may help marginalize some of our students and benefit others, that their uses of computer technologies are part of the complex processes by which they struggle to write themselves into the discourses that shape their lives— discourses that are themselves partly a function of technology. Obviously, I believe that a pedagogy based on a conception of literacy as a local act of self-construction, as I have laid out in this book, can help our students find ways into these discourses and acquire more than the basic computer literacy that Ohmann decries. Such an approach could include, for instance, assignments asking students to examine cases like Sheehan's in order to explore how literacy and technology functioned in the context of the legal, economic, and political forces in place in that situation; such an assignment might entail critique of the various texts that played a role in the case, including Sheehan's web site, legal documents, press reports, and so on, so that students might consider how literacy defined, limited, empowered, or disempowered and how someone like Sheehan used literacy—and online technologies—to accomplish personal goals that intersected with legal and economic interests. The rhetorics and discourses employed in the case might be examined in order to foster an understanding of the contingent, interested, and conflicted nature of discourse and of literacy. And students should be encouraged to engage in acts of writing and reading with technology that encourage the same careful, critical examination of the role of literacy in their own lives—including building their own web sites and using the technologies available to them to accomplish specific goals relevant to their own lives as young men and women, as citizens and consumers, as people of specific racial and ethnic and socioeconomic identities.

As my own uses of online technologies to learn about the Sheehan case suggest, these technologies can provide students with extensive access to an enormous variety of documents representing the many discourses that come into play in a case like Sheehan's. Thus, they offer teachers a powerful means by which to facilitate substantive learning about literacy and technology. They also offer new possibilities for students to imagine ways of participating in their changing and increasingly technological world. But to take advantage of these possibilities, teachers will have to do more than teach their students to read great books like *Huck Finn* as works of art or texts like *Common Sense* as emblems of American individualism. They will have to adopt a complex and sometimes unsettling conception of literacy and technology and embrace an understanding of the ambivalent role of literacy in the lives of their students.

TEACHING THE AMBIVALENCE OF LITERACY: THE PERSONAL AND THE POLITICAL

As I write these unequivocal statements about how we *should* teach literacy, I am still hearing the echo of Elspeth Stuckey's (1991) troubling question, "What to do? What to do?" (p. 97). For despite my assertion in Chapter 1 that Stuckey's despair about the role of literacy educators in effecting systemic change is ultimately unwarranted, she won't let us forget that even if we "empower" a group of students like Melissa's, for example, by teaching them ways of reading and writing as I have outlined here, we send them off into a world in which economic and political agreements like NAFTA may leave them without the realistic prospect of sustaining work and thus without viable "power" in an uncertain and changing economy. Indeed, some of Melissa's students came from families affected directly by NAFTA: They had brothers or fathers or mothers whose jobs disappeared as factories were relocated to Mexico or other developing nations with low wages and no unions. In such an economic context, the power of literacy can work *against* our students as well as *for* them, and the distinction is rarely clear-cut. Our most heartfelt injunctions to our students about the importance of succeeding in school are meaningless in an environment in which their diplomas—which implicitly certify their literacy skills—may have limited value. As Deborah Brandt (1998) reminds us, even "as we assist and study individuals in pursuit of literacy, we also [should] recognize how literacy is in pursuit of them. When this process stirs ambivalence, on their part or on ours, we need to be understanding" (p. 183). Literacy education, to be empowering in ways that Freire calls for, in ways that I hope for, in ways that teachers strive for, cannot deny this ambivalence.

Hannah's essay about her encounter with her guidance counselor (which appears in Chapter 2) provides one example of an opportunity to explore this ambivalence in the context of the "localness" of literacy in a way that might deepen her understanding of the complex role of literacy in her life as a student, a worker, a citizen, and a woman. As I suggested earlier, Hannah's resistance to the notion that her essay was a kind of declaration of received views about individual opportunity is related both to her implicit acceptance of prevailing cultural values and to her sense of writing as a relatively straightforward matter of getting the story right. In this sense, we can view her essay about her school experience as her effort to write herself into the powerful American story of personal success. That perspective can help me as her teacher understand how Hannah has approached her subject, how she sees herself within the story she tries to tell, and why she made some of the decisions she made about the text (e.g., why she didn't follow up on the social class distinctions that she describes at the beginning of her essay). It is helpful for Hannah, too, because it opens up ways of thinking about her experience that illuminate its complexity and its relationship to the broader contexts within which she lives. But it isn't enough to stop there, since by itself such an understanding of her essay doesn't necessarily lead to an awareness of the tricky and powerful ways in which discourse shaped her experience as well as the essay she is writing about it. In order to write herself into that American fable of success, Hannah must accept the terms by which she is defined within the discourses of American education and of American capitalist culture, terms that can be seen as limiting her in the first place. In other words, whereas she bristles at being categorized by her teachers according to social class affiliation, suggesting that she should be judged instead on her own merits and performance, it is ostensibly on the basis of that individual performance in school that her guidance counselor pronounces her unfit for a 4-year college education. Such a pronouncement denies any connection between her social class status and the opportunities available (or denied) to her in and out of school; it ignores how she is positioned within the discourses that shape those contexts. Thus, her insistence that she can do it on her own unwittingly reinforces the terms by which she has been judged unable to do it on her own; she ultimately embraces the same ideology of individual opportunity that helps limit her in the first place.

As her teacher, I want first to help Hannah see that her essay is such a construction of herself as the heroine of her American success story. If I can help her see that, then I can help challenge her sense that she is simply telling it like it is, presenting what "really" happened, describing a static reality that she must somehow adapt to rather than influence or change. Like Freire, I want to present to students a view of the world as constructed through language, and I want Hannah to see that she participates in that construction. Such a view, seemingly straightforward but frustratingly difficult for many students to acquire, is crucial if literacy is to become something more for a student like Hannah than a means by which her own agency is limited. Initially, I might encourage this view by asking straightforward but provocative (and perhaps uncomfortable) questions about what she has written: questions about how she was categorized and treated by her teachers and counselor, questions about why she believes the blame for not attending a 4-year college was hers, questions about the source of her belief in self-reliance, questions about her economic and social existence outside school. I might also present alternative interpretations— most likely in the context of class discussions and readings—that clash with her self-construction in order to open up the possibility that hers is not *the* story but *a version* of events that she experienced. Any of these versions, I want her to see, will be constructed within complex and sometimes competing discourses that shape how we understand those events. Eventually I want to move her to a revision in which she doesn't simply "improve" this essay as a text but reexamines and reinterprets her experience through writing. And I want her to see that revision also as a self-construction, as part of her effort to write herself into those discourses, the power of which I hope she has begun to appreciate. If I am successful in this effort, Hannah will learn something about herself and her experience and how each is constructed through written language; ideally, she also will have learned something about how literacy functions more generally.[3]

Such an approach to Hannah's essay is similar in many respects to approaches proposed by some advocates of cultural studies or critical pedagogies (e.g., Berlin, 1996; Shor, 1987). Like such advocates, I want my students to begin to see their connection to the broader discourses and social forces that shape their lives and to understand how the ideas they present in their essays are inextricably linked to those discourses and forces. But I also want to emphasize the *self* in a way that I think many cultural studies and critical pedagogy proponents don't. As I have suggested earlier, in much of our current thinking about pedagogy, the individual writer/reader often seems obscured—paradoxically—by our collective focus on social, cultural, ethnic, gender, and racial identity. It is important for Hannah to see herself in terms of social class and gender and race and to examine how these aspects of her identity might have figured into the experience she describes in that essay—how her counselor's advice, for example, might have differed had she been African-American or upper middle class or male and how that advice relates to broader discourses about gender and opportunity. It is also important to highlight the fact that many of Hannah's classmates can be described according to these same categories, yet their individual interactions with the social and institutional forces that affect them differ from hers. In other words, Hannah's story of her "success" as a working-class, White, rural woman is different in significant ways from the stories her classmates who are also White, working-class, rural women tell about themselves. And those differences matter, even if the success story is basically the same, because those differences reflect Hannah's unique effort to construct herself in her writing; they reflect her *self-interest*, which, as Paul Smith (1988) points out, is ultimately the seat of her agency within the discourses that she cannot escape or control. As a teacher of writing, I don't want to lose sight of those differences because they help me understand how Hannah's essay and those of her classmates came to be. In this sense, those differences can be a window into the idiosyncratic ways in which Hannah and her classmates write themselves into the discourses that shape their ideas about themselves and their roles in society; they also become a powerful teaching tool not only in my attempts to understand the decisions by which Hannah created her essay but also in my effort to help her understand more fully how her essay relates to the discourses within which she is constructed and through which she constructs herself. And this is perhaps the central insight that a conception of literacy as a local act can provide for teachers of writing and reading: that these differences in our students' literate acts matter, not because they reflect unique, autonomous individuals, but because they help illuminate the individual ways in which students construct their multifarious, contingent, and complex selves within the discourses that in turn inevitably shape those selves.

In this sense, Hannah's essay about herself provides an opportunity for me to help her see how she constructs herself as an "individual" even as she questions, through her writing and reading, her ideas about individuality and about herself. Her "personal" writing thus can become a place to examine—and perhaps resist—the ways in which she is written by discourse and to explore ways to enter and engage discourse with a measure of critical awareness. And it can be an occasion for learning about how literacy is not neutral but is in large part a function of the settings within which she writes and reads. The long-standing professional arguments about the use of personal writing in our pedagogies often obscure the fact that, as Hannah's essay amply demonstrates, any personal essay is also always political and social and cultural. Hannah cannot write about herself in a vacuum but draws on social, cultural, political, institutional, and economic discourses, among others, as she constructs her tale of personal success. (For a discussion of this intersection of the individual and the social in a slightly different context, see Yagelski, 1994c.) Conversely, pieces of writing that are overtly "analytic" or "expository" also are always "personal" in the sense that an individual writer engages the discourses in place in a particular writing situation in particular ways that reflect his or her self-interest, as we saw, for example, with Celina's essay about Black language in Chapter 4. The distinctions we make among kinds of writing in our more traditional pedagogies can sometimes prevent students from understanding and engaging in literacy as a local act of self-construction by focusing on genres and forms as distinct from the various institutional settings and discourse conventions that give rise to them in the first place.

I want to emphasize that the kind of personal writing I am describing here is distinct from a "personal growth" model of writing instruction common in schools and from the kinds of self-exploratory writing sometimes used in critical pedagogies as a vehicle for cultural critique. The purpose of the kind of personal writing I asked Hannah to do is to help students explore the nature of literacy as an individual and social activity, as a political and ideological matter, and as an act of self-construction within discourse; furthermore, it is to help them acquire the means by which they can put such an understanding into practice as they engage in literate acts in their lives in and outside school. I wish to enable them to examine and participate in acts of writing and reading that represent ways of participating in the world as students, citizens, consumers, workers, and persons trying to understand and negotiate these many roles. It seems reasonable to expect that students should leave our classrooms with some experience of what it means to write and read for specific legal or political or economic purposes and to have some sense of how literacy functions in varied contexts, how it can serve or hinder their own purposes in specific situations, and how it helps shape the roles they adopt and the selves they construct. Such experiences, I believe, must go beyond the sometimes narrow ideological goals of critical pedagogies and cultural studies. It is not enough, in my view, to have students engage in cultural or political critique in order to help them see the ways in which they are positioned, circumscribed, limited, and even oppressed by the cultural, economic, legal, institutional, and political forces to which they are subject. And it is not enough simply to identify types of "oppression" with specific institutions or with a capitalist economic system, as enlightening as such identification might be. We also must help students imagine *themselves* as writers and readers within a world where change is possible, a world constructed through discourse that they can engage, participate in, and, in infinite local ways, shape and influence. Our efforts for pedagogical or curricular reform, in short, ultimately must have at their center a complex conception of literacy that retains a focus on the struggles of individual writers and readers like Hannah to find their ways into discourse.[4]

Our efforts also must unflinchingly confront the ambivalence that Deborah Brandt refers to. Encouraging Hannah to gain the kind of understanding I explained above and helping her acquire the ability to put that understanding into practice, as empowering as that can be, does not change in any substantive way the kind of situation about which Hannah has written. In other words, those same forces that helped create the difficulties she described in her essay remain in place, in large part a result of the same literacy that I am helping Hannah acquire. While her enhanced literacy skills and knowledge may help her negotiate such situations more effectively, they do not, ultimately, guarantee the success she seeks. In describing similar struggles among their own college students, Linda Finlay and Valerie Faith (1987) acknowledge this dismaying reality. Their students, they write

> fear and distrust the culture that runs the schools, a culture that they perceive as subordinating individual activity to the needs of a consumer economy [but] . . . their education is complicated by their awareness that they have become accomplices in maintaining this culture and its values. They want those consumer goods, they want the college degree for earning power, political power, social power of many kinds. (p. 82)

Hannah wants all this, too, but she may not get it. And if she doesn't, the reasons will have as much to do with the power of literacy to limit as with its potential for empowerment. It is our ethical charge as literacy educators to acknowledge that fact and to help our students understand it, too. I don't believe this acknowledgment needs to be the source of the despair that Stuckey describes, but we cannot ignore the paradoxical nature of literacy's power, since we are implicated in its role in our society and, more important, since our students' lives are so deeply shaped by literacy. Like Finlay and Faith, we can seek possibilities for resolving this dilemma in our students' writing, which is "where this struggle between the philosophical and ethical perspectives of their human selves and their social selves emerge[s]" (p. 82). These local acts of writing carry both our heaviest responsibilities as educators and our best hopes for our students' empowerment as literate human beings.

THE UNCERTAIN POSSIBILITIES FOR CHANGE

In the early 1990s I was part of a group of faculty at Purdue University charged with revising the curriculum for education students. As part of our effort to make the core curriculum for all secondary education majors more effective in preparing them for the challenges of classroom teaching, we reviewed teacher education programs at several other universities. One of those programs, called A Community of Teachers, is run by Tom Gregory at Indiana University. The program is based on Gregory's overriding belief that, when it comes to substantive education reform, small is not only beautiful but essential. For Gregory, education can be effective and fulfilling, for both teachers and students, only if those teachers and students can feel and function as part of a community based on mutual support and shared goals and beliefs. Complex bureaucratic institutions such as large public high schools or universities, Gregory believes, work against the formation and maintenance of such communities in part because they must exercise such extensive behavioral control in order to exist. A primary function of such large institutions is to preserve the institution itself, and students' and teachers' needs are met only to the extent that they coincide with the institution's efforts to maintain the status quo. The norming function of such institutions thus creates a virtually insurmountable obstacle to substantive systemic reform or personally empowering education. So Gregory has set up his program, as best he can, outside the normal bureaucratic channels of the large education school at Indiana University and has intentionally kept the program small.[5]

Gregory's program is similar in some ways to the projects of other reformers who have called for change on a local scale.[6] But what struck me most about Gregory's efforts, as I learned about them when I met him on the Indiana University campus one warm spring afternoon in 1993, is his unwavering focus on the potential of individual teachers and students working together. During a day of meetings and informal discussions, my Purdue colleagues and I listened to the impassioned descriptions of Gregory's program by his students and a few of the teachers with whom he works. What emerged from them was a strong sense of possibility. They told stories of individual teachers working with individual students, of their idiosyncratic struggles in the context of a collective effort. As best they could they tried, as a group, to make space for each other even as they relied on each other and made demands of each other. Their answers to our probing questions about such thorny matters as state regulations, school boards, curriculum mandates, resistant administrators, suspicious parents, and standardized testing indicated that this program is no panacea. It has encountered a host of problems and had its share of setbacks. But it seemed to me to be a program built on a belief in possibility with a human face, an effort to enact a vision of education as a decidedly human endeavor that is always local.

I was heartened by Gregory's program that day and sustained by its promise in the following months as my colleagues and I pushed a frustrating path through the Purdue bureaucracy in our own reform initiative. I won't tell the story of that initiative here, since it is an all-too-familiar one with the kind of ambiguous outcome so common in such efforts. But my memory of our visit with Gregory is shaded by the irony that our meetings that day all took place within the halls of the same sprawling bureaucracy that Gregory sought to escape; that education bureaucracy ironically gave rise to and facilitated the Community of Teachers program, whose very existence was a statement against that same bureaucracy. "Alternative" is thus an ambivalent badge: it implies that whatever counts as the status quo remains in place.

I feel the weight of that badge as I try to conclude this discussion. I'm not certain that any of the changes I'm suggesting in this chapter are realistic on a large scale, given the monumental obstacles to change in institutionalized education and the overwhelming complexity of these issues of literacy and literacy instruction in our culture. Nor am I convinced that my particular take on these matters can make the kind of difference in our students' lives that I have suggested it can, since so much depends on circumstances well beyond our control as teachers. I am thinking of a man in my prison class who suddenly stopped attending class meetings only a few weeks before the semester's end. His unexplained absence puzzled me, since he had been a diligent student who seemed committed to completing the course successfully. When I asked about him, I learned that he had been sent to "the hole"—to solitary confinement—for some kind of infraction. I learned, too, that while so confined he was allowed to have no books or paper or pens or any of the things he would need to complete his work for the course. There was no literacy of possibility in that cell, and his "empowerment" through literacy would not have made that cell and the system it represents disappear. I am thinking, too, of a young woman in one of the writing workshop courses I taught years later at the State University of New York at Albany. She worked hard in the course through the eleventh or twelfth week, when she stopped attending class. Just before the semester ended I learned that she had dropped out of school because of complications with her pregnancy, which was in its first trimester. She had struggled to hold down a part-time job to pay for school, but her medical condition and tenuous financial and social status made that impossible, at least for the moment. The physical and economic difficulties of being a single mother of limited means forced her to put her literacy education on hold. In the face of such obstacles, my pedagogy of personal empowerment and my framework for understanding literacy as a local act and vehicle for individual agency seem feeble indeed.

At the same time, without a means to acquire the literacy that inevitably affects their lives, these same students have virtually no hope of changing the limiting circumstances within which they are struggling. Like Hannah, like most of us, these two students both believed deeply in the possibilities that literacy represents for changing *their own* lives, even as their lives underscored the ambivalent role of literacy within a social and economic system that seemed to deny them hope. Both acted on that belief in spite of their circumstances (or perhaps because of them): The prison student returned from solitary confinement a day before the semester's end to complete all the required work in the course; the young mother returned to school a year later to try to finish her degree. Ideally, our pedagogies will merit the trust our students place in us to help them acquire literacy in ways that will enable them to fulfill those possibilities; ideally, too, our curricula will be structured to enable us, as teachers, to do so. Inevitably, the two—pedagogy and curriculum—are linked, and thus teachers who see literacy as a means to empowerment must always see their own teaching within the broader context of reform movements that address the complicated matter of literacy's role in society. Local systemic change, in the form of school-based reform initiatives and programs like Gregory's, represents, I believe, our best hope for substantive improvement in the ways in which we prepare our students for literate lives. Such initiatives link our individual struggles to a larger collective one and thus give greater scope to our efforts to help our students claim some measure of agency as literate persons in a complex and difficult world. They give us hope that our work with students can turn personal empowerment into something greater.

An even more powerful hope for change lies in the day-to-day interactions we as teachers have with individual students in the classroom: in exchanges about their writing and reading and its importance in their lives; in our efforts to understand the ways in which they construct themselves through literacy. I am fond of offering this exhortation to the student teachers with whom I've worked, but it was one of them, a woman named Lynn, who taught me its difficult truth. She left the English education program at Purdue, where she had been outspoken, energetic, and diligent in her work as a student teacher, to teach high school English in a small, rural Indiana school district, where her classroom had a bible discreetly placed in the teacher's desk. Lynn's passionate Freirean views about literacy education ran headlong into the deep conservatism of that little community, and she soon found herself questioned, challenged, scrutinized, and even harrassed. Few of her colleagues and even fewer parents supported her attempts to enact her progressive pedagogy; some were openly hostile. They wanted her to continue the kind of "basic" writing and reading instruction that had characterized English classes in their school for many years. But some of her students felt differently, and their enthusiasm for the kinds of reading and writing and thinking she asked them to do convinced her that her pedagogy could make a difference. A year or so after she left Purdue, Lynn returned for a visit, during which she spoke to some of the English education students and shared stories of her year in that small district. Over lunch she described to me the difficulties she encountered almost daily: complaints from parents and colleagues, arguments about lesson plans and assigned books, questions from the principal, a school board appearance, even a few harrassing phone calls. She told success stories, too, of enthusiastic students who embraced the new ideas she presented to them. But these stories seemed overshadowed by the problems she faced, and I wondered why she didn't pursue other job opportunities. You won't change that town, I told her; you can't change its beliefs by yourself. Maybe, I suggested, the kind of curriculum that has been in place in the school was the right curriculum for that community. Go to a place where your perspective on literacy is valued, I advised. But then who will give these kids what they get in my class? she asked.

In some ways, Lynn's story is as much an American fable as the essay Hannah tried to write, a problematic story of teacher-as-hero of the kind Lil Brannon (1993) has critiqued. But it also highlights the complex connections among literacy, education, community, culture, and ideology that always characterize the teaching of writing and reading. In her fervor, Lynn wasn't able to make sense of all of this, and her passion about her teaching may have blinded her to some of the problems she herself caused and to the ways in which she inadvertently might have compromised her students within their community. At the same time, Lynn's willingness to place her students at the center of her work was not only admirable but, I think, crucial. In time, she would become more aware of the complexity of her role as their English teacher, an ambivalent role indeed, but it would be her sincere commitment to her students' literacy learning that would facilitate that awareness and deepen her sense of the conflicted power she holds as a teacher of writing and reading.

The challenges we face as teachers of literacy, as Lynn came to learn, are great. As I noted in Chapter 1, these challenges seem even greater in an increasingly technological and multicultural world where old paradigms no longer obtain, a rapidly changing world that seems to ask ever more of those responsible for literacy education.[7] And so in the end I can make only one call: that teachers of writing and reading reexamine their own attitudes toward literacy and literacy instruction and their roles in the lives of the students they teach in this changing world. I have argued that an understanding of literacy as a local act of self-construction within discourse can illuminate our work with students as writers and readers and help us help them gain access to a literacy that enables them to claim agency for themselves in this complex and difficult world shaped by discourse. But such an understanding of literacy will manifest itself in countless ways as individual teachers work with their student writers and readers. As they do so, those teachers, I hope, will explore and question their roles in the lives of those students within the broader context of the economic and political system within which they teach and in which they inevitably are implicated; and I hope they will keep in view the ambivalence of their work as literacy educators. For Abby and Hannah and Celina and Mr. Green and Larry and the many other students whose lives intersect with ours in our classrooms, that might make all the difference.

Postscript

Literacy and Pedagogies of Hope

Our culture may find itself alienated from its textual tradition, but human beings are never "textless"—we cannot help making text, formulating our images into phrases, our dreams into lives.
—Linda Sexton, Ordinarily Sacred

One of the tasks of the progressive educator, through a serious, correct political analysis, is to unveil opportunities for hope, no matter what the obstacles may be.
—Paulo Freire, A Pedagogy of Hope

A few months after my meeting with Abby and Kim at the coffee shop (described in Chapter 6), I find myself on a plane en route to an educational testing company to do some consulting. My job is to help the company determine whether the writing examinations it offers are accurate and fair—to serve, in a way, as censor, someone with a say in what counts as "correct" or "appropriate" or "effective" writing, which is to say, "mainstream, academic writing." It is some indication of the value such writing has in our culture that the company can afford to fly me and several other consultants from around the country to work with them for a few days. On the plane, among business travelers and vacationers, I read a first-person account of a journey through Mexico and the American southwest (Kaplan, 1998). The author describes the marginal existence of many of the people he encounters along the U.S.–Mexican border, people whose prospects are dimmed by depressed local economies shaped by the same NAFTA agreement that affected the lives of Melissa's students (also described in Chapter 6). I am certain most of those people will never encounter the test on which I will be working. It seems somehow miraculous that I am reading about them as I jet across the sky toward my writing-test consulting work; it is troubling that many of them likely will never have an opportunity to read that article.

I have at times in the writing of this book been rendered nearly wordless by such thoughts. My writing has given rise to an uneasy sense that literacy as I have experienced it and used it is at once a necessity and a luxury. The literacy that represents empowerment for me is in part a function of my middle-class status in a capitalist economic system that places a certain value on the uses of writing and reading in which I routinely engage. These stories I tell of my literacy history are middle-class stories, tales of the importance and also of the ambivalence of literacy, to be sure, but tales of privilege, too. Millions—here and in other nations—have no access to this kind of literacy. And that reality has left me at times hard pressed to resist Elspeth Stuckey's (1991) angry despair about our roles as literacy educators.

But my privileged story of literacy is supplemented by insistent images of hope that emerge from the student writers and readers I have worked with. In *A Pedagogy of Hope*, Freire (1994) emphasizes an "ontological need" for hope among progressive educators (p. 8). "While I certainly cannot ignore hopelessness as a concrete entity," he writes, ". . . I do not understand human existence, and the struggle needed to improve it, apart from hope and dream" (p. 8). Shortly after finishing Chapter 4 of this book, in which I describe Larry, I spoke with him by telephone. I learned that he had completed his degree and, after struggling briefly with a few unsatisfying jobs, found his way into a communications position in the New York State Legislature. When I congratulated him, he sheepishly confessed that he still didn't think his writing was good enough for his job, which demands much writing that is overtly public and political. In some ways, he still seemed to be struggling with the same attempt to construct a viable, valuable self in his writing that seemed to characterize his work in my course. But his professional success and his satisfaction with his work belie his own doubts. Despite so many apparent obstacles, Larry somehow finds a way to write himself into discourse. And in a profound sense, it is his continuing belief that he can make a difference that seems to be the engine driving his literate life.

Hannah shares that belief. Her struggles with school, which she described poignantly in the essay reproduced in Chapter 2, continued at SUNY–Albany. During the semester in which she disappeared from my class, she had been informed that she would not be granted admission to the education program that she so genuinely wanted to enter; her goal of becoming a teacher, she was told, was unrealistic. It was the same kind of judgment that had once been made of her by her high school guidance counselor. So she dropped out of college, existing on restaurant jobs but never giving up her belief that she could become a teacher. In some ways, the same cultural values of individual opportunity and hard work that I describe in my discussion of her essay in Chapters 2 and 6 as limiting her also enabled her to construct a self who could achieve her goals; those same problematic values that enabled a guidance counselor to dismiss her as inadequate also sustained her. Within a few months, she gained acceptance to an education program in another college, and at this writing she is preparing for her student teaching semester. When I spoke to her, her enthusiasm and commitment to her career were obvious, although her experiences have left her a bit less sanguine about the world. Nevertheless, despite her travails, I detected not a hint of doubt in her voice.

"Without a minimum of hope," Freire (1994) writes, "we cannot so much as start the struggle" (p. 9). Nor can we continue it. I am certain that Larry and Hannah will gain a more sober perspective on literacy and its possibilities as they gain more experience with its ambivalent workings in the world. As their teacher, I have tried to present such a perspective to them. But that effort should never entail a destruction of the hope that so clearly has sustained them and must sustain us.

Notes

CHAPTER 2

1. Jay David Bolter (1991) links this conception of writer to the technology of print. He writes that "19th-century critics believed that poets had special visionary powers: that belief carried over into our times, and the poet's vision is now supposed to apply to important social and political questions. The technology of print helps to sanction this belief" (p. 149). I agree, and in Chapter 5 I will address more directly Bolter's point that these conceptions are intimately related to the technology of print.

2. Despite recent efforts to measure student progress "in context" through large-scale portfolio programs, such as the one in place in the state of Vermont, most standardized measures still reduce writing to a set of definable (and limited) skills and, in part because they are so widely used and because they are relied on for all kinds of decisions about students' abilities (or lack thereof), continue to reinforce the limited notions of literacy that I am describing in this chapter.

3. A "local diploma" in New York State at the time referred to a diploma that did not meet state standards for designation as a Regents diploma. In effect, a local diploma signified that a student met minimum state requirements for graduation from high school but did not meet more rigorous standards generally assumed to be intended for college-bound students. New York State has since changed its requirements and standards, so that all students are required to meet the (supposedly more rigorous) standards for a Regents diploma in order to graduate from high school.

CHAPTER 3

1. In her work in the late 1980s, Flower tried to incorporate a more social conception of writing into her cognitive framework (e.g., Flower, 1988; Flower et al., 1990). In her most recent work, she seems to have moved closer to the position of some of her critics in reconceiving "cognition" as socially mediated (see *The Construction of Negotiated Meaning* [1994]), a move I find useful, as I suggest later in this chapter.

2. I need to distinguish here between "critical literacy" as a pedagogical agenda for change, as a means to empowerment, and a critical or postmodern

conception of literacy as a framework for explaining acts of reading and writing. The distinction is blurry, but it seems to me that if Knoblauch and Brannon (1993) are right that critical literacy "remain[s] suspect as a theoretical enterprise and will be considered dangerous" (p. 23) by many segments of American society, then such a view of literacy must not only represent a call for fuller and freer participation in American society but must also have explanatory power, a way to help us understand what literacy is and how it functions. In this chapter I am primarily interested in this second sense of the term *critical literacy* as a way of understanding how literacy functions in individual lives, and I wish to explore how it might provide a framework for examining specific acts of writing and reading.

3. I use the term *poststructuralism* to refer to theories of language, often associated with Jacques Derrida, that define meaning as a function of language. Such a perspective sees all meaning as contingent and largely outside the control of the writer. I use *postmodernism* as a broader term to refer to a general set of assumptions about language and epistemology that grow out of poststructuralist theories. (See Faigley, 1992, for an overview of the term *postmodernism*.) These assumptions focus on three key concepts: representation of reality, legitimation of truth-claims, and subjectivity. From a postmodern perspective, as I conceive of it here, reality is essentially what it is represented to be, which is a function of language and discourse. Truth is always contingent and unstable, and competing versions of reality are legitimated through and within discourse. And, as this chapter tries to make clear, subjectivity as well is contingent and unstable and constructed through discourse.

CHAPTER 4

1. I am referring here primarily to the debate, well known among scholars in rhetoric and composition, between David Bartholomae and Peter Elbow about the nature of "academic" writing and "personal" writing. (See Bartholomae, 1995; Elbow, 1995.) For a very provocative alternative view of the tricky role of the personal in student writing, see Morgan (1998). My own argument in this chapter is consistent with Morgan's concerns about the sometimes disturbing nature of students' personal writing, and his description of his students' writing supports my point that our students' academic writing should be seen as part of their ongoing effort to construct themselves as students and as people.

CHAPTER 5

1. I required the students in this course to participate in the online discussions throughout the semester; they were to log onto their accounts at least once each week, read the messages posted to the class mailing list, and post at least one message of their own. This use of email and other forms of

college-level computer-mediated communication (CMC), such as newsgroups, to extend class discussions has by now become quite common among many college, level writing teachers. (See Wells, 1993, for a good overview of the pedagogical uses of these technologies.) Although generalizations about the voluminous research on the uses of asynchronous and synchronous CMC in the teaching of writing are tentative at best, there is evidence to indicate that CMC can help instructors accomplish a variety of pedagogical goals and can offer some advantages in fostering student participation and encouraging collaboration and critical reflection among students in ways that may be difficult or impossible in conventional face-to-face classroom interactions. See Yagelski and Grabill, 1998, and Yagelski, 1999, for further discussion of CMC as a pedagogical tool; see also the latest review of research in the journal *Computers and Composition*.

2. Consider how this description of Adam's work on this project reflects aspects of his *self-interest* and how that self-interest shapes his "reading" and "writing." For instance, why Nepal? For one thing, like his father, Adam is very interested in mountaineering, especially in the Himalayas; for another, his own experience includes many trips to mountain regions along with discussions with his father about Eastern philosophy. All these (and more), I'd argue, are part of the self-interest that shapes his literate behavior and the self that he will construct in this text.

3. There is wonderful irony in this criticism, given the point McLuhan (1962/1995) makes about the way in which writing separates speech from the person and thus changes language from an *act* to a thing. Brandt argues here that writing, like oral language, is always an act implying a context that may not be physically apparent but that is essential in any case for writing to carry meaning.

4. Among the many sources of evidence for this assertion are a variety of reports from the National Center for Education Statistics, including *Student Use of Computers* (December 1995), available online at http://nces.ed.gov/pubsold/CoE95/95txt.html, and *Advanced Telecommunications in U.S. Public Elementary and Secondary Schools, Fall 1996* (February 1997), available online at http://nces.ed.gov/pubs/97944.html.

5. The readings referred to in this post are Elizabeth Hill Boone (1994) and Jay David Bolter (1991).

6. This is the same Celina I describe in Chapter 4; 2 years after she took the course referred to in Chapter 4, Celina enrolled in our graduate program at SUNY–Albany and later took the graduate course I describe in the present chapter.

CHAPTER 6

1. The discussion in this section and the following section ("Teaching Relevant Discourses") originally appeared, in slightly different form, in Yagelski (1997).

2. Several recent studies suggest that Ohmann's predictions were more or less on the mark. See Conte (1997), which cites several studies indicating that "wage differentials have increased partly because demand for high-skilled workers is rising more rapidly than demand for low-skilled ones" and that "workplaces where computers are used account for as much as half of the relative increase in the demand for high-skilled workers since 1970" (p. 18).

3. I think it is important to acknowledge that this can be uncertain and treacherous ground for both student and teacher. Dan Morgan (1998) has written about the ethical uncertainties that accompany our invitations to students to write about themselves in the way Hannah has written about herself, and I don't want to minimize these uncertainties. Although Hannah's essay does not describe the kind of horrifying experiences that Morgan describes (suicide attempts, sexual abuse, criminal activities), it does reinforce Morgan's point that our students' "personal" writing is often not about writing itself as much as it is about their difficult lives; their writing is a way for them to confront—or deny—difficult aspects of their lives and to make some sense of their experiences. I think it is crucial for writing teachers to recognize that fact and to approach essays like Hannah's with empathy, to read such essays and comment on them not just as pieces of writing but as their students' attempts to describe and make sense of their lives.

4. There are innumerable ways for teachers to begin to accomplish such goals. Two worthwhile collections that offer examples of pedagogical approaches similar to what I have in mind are Shor (1987) and Downing (1994). I am also heartened by the recent trend in composition studies and in English education toward developing ways of fostering "civic literacy" among students and the related move to incorporate "service learning" into writing courses.

5. See Gregory (1993) for a discussion of his ideas about education reform. The Community of Teachers Program is still in place; information about the program is available on its website at http://education.indiana.edu/~tched/community/.

6. Ted Sizer's Coalition of Essential Schools is, to my mind, the best example. Sizer's vision for substantive reform rests on the idea that change can best be effected at the level of the school building rather than by district or state. Each "essential school" must espouse the principles of Sizer's coalition but must find its own way to enact those principles. I am thinking also of Pat Carini's Prospect School in Vermont, an "alternative" K–8 school whose curriculum and pedagogy rest on Carini's innovative ideas about the intellectual development of the child.

7. It barely needs mentioning that the bewildering demographic shifts we are experiencing at the end of this millennium intensify the challenges facing literacy educators. To cite just one obvious example, Mike Rose (1995) describes a southern California high school where "there are forty-two nationalities represented on campus and thirty-eight languages spoken" (p. 36). In the writing center at my own university of approximately 15,000 students,

we will in a single academic year work with students representing more than 80 different languages. Clearly, these kinds of changes present daunting challenges for teachers of writing and reading just in terms of practical classroom matters, and that's to say nothing of the even more complex cultural, ethnic, socioeconomic, and political issues that emerge as our population becomes ever more diverse.

.

References

Anyon, J. (1980). Social class and the hidden curriculum of work. *Journal of Education, 162.* Reprinted in G. Colombo, R. Cullen, & B. Lisle (Eds.). (1995). *Rereading America* (pp. 45–60). Boston: Bedford Books.

Anyon, J. (1997). *Ghetto schooling: A political economy of urban educational reform.* New York: Teachers College Press.

Applebee, A. N. (1993). *Literature in the secondary school: A study of curriculum and instruction in the U.S.* Urbana, IL: NCTE.

Arnove, R. F., & Graff, H. J. (Eds.). (1987). Introduction. *National literacy campaigns: Historical and comparative perspectives* (pp. 1–28). New York: Plenum.

Ashton-Jones, E., & Thomas, D. K. (1990). Composition, collaboration, and women's ways of knowing: A conversation with Mary Belenky. *Journal of Advanced Composition, 10,* 275–292.

Associated Press. (1998, July 20). Internet ruling called first amendment victory. *The Columbian,* p. B2.

Bartholomae, D. (1985). Inventing the university. In M. Rose (Ed.), *When a writer can't write: Studies in writers' block and other cognitive process problems* (pp. 134–165). New York: Guilford Press.

Bartholomae, D. (1990). Producing adult readers, 1930–50. In A. A. Lunsford, H. Moglen, & J. Slevin (Eds.), *The right to literacy* (pp. 13–28). New York: Modern Language Association.

Bartholomae, D. (1995). Writing with teachers: A conversation with Peter Elbow. *College Composition and Communication, 46,* 62–71.

Baudrillard, J. (1983). *Simulations.* New York: Semiotext(e).

Berger, P. (1969). *The sacred canopy.* New York: Doubleday Anchor Books.

Berlin, J. (1992). Poststructuralism, cultural studies, and the composition classroom: Postmodern theory in practice. *Rhetoric Review, 11,* 16–33.

Berlin, J. (1996). *Rhetorics, poetics, cultures.* Urbana, IL: NCTE.

Bizzell, P. (1989). Review of *The social construction of written information. College Composition and Communication, 40,* 483–486.

Bleich, D. (1988). *The double perspective: Language, literacy, and social relations.* New York: Oxford University Press.

Bloome, D. (1987). *Literacy and schooling.* Norwood, NJ: Ablex.

Bolter, J. D. (1991). *Writing space: The computer, hypertext, and the history of writing.* Hillsdale, NJ: Erlbaum.

Bolter, J. D. (1996). Virtual reality and the redefinition of self. In L. Strate, R. Jacobson, & S. B. Gibson (Eds.), *Communication and cyberspace: Social interaction in an electronic environment* (pp. 105–119). Cresskill, NJ: Hampton Press.

Boone, E. H. (1994). Introduction: Writing and recording knowledge. In E. H. Boone & W. D. Mignolo (Eds.), *Writing without words: Alternative literacies in Mesoamerica and the Andes* (pp. 3–26). Durham, NC: Duke University Press.

Bowers, C. A. (1988). *The cultural dimensions of educational computing: Understanding the non-neutrality of technology.* New York: Teachers College Press.

Braddock, R., Lloyd-Jones, R., & Schoer, L. (1963). *Research in written composition.* Urbana, IL: NCTE.

Brandt, D. (1990). *Literacy as involvement: The acts of writers, readers, and texts.* Carbondale: Southern Illinois University Press.

Brandt, D. (1998). Sponsors of literacy. *College Composition and Communication, 49*, 165–185.

Brannon, L. (1993). M[other]: Lives on the outside. *Written Communication, 10*, 457–465.

Center for Applied Special Technology. (1996). *The role of online communications in schools: A national study.* Peabody, MA: Author. Available online at http://www.cast.org/publications/stsstudy/index.html

Clifford, J. (1991). The subject in discourse. In P. Harkin & J. Schilb (Eds.), *Contending with words: Composition and rhetoric in a postmodern age* (pp. 38–51). New York: Modern Language Association.

Collins, J. (1993). "The troubled text": History and language in american university basic writing programs. In P. Freebody & A. R. Welch (Eds.), *Knowledge, culture and power: International perspectives on literacy as policy and practice* (pp. 162–186). Pittsburgh: University of Pittsburgh Press.

Conte, C. (1997). *The learning connection: Schools in the information age.* Washington, DC: Benton Foundation.

Cook-Gumperz, J. (1986). Introduction: The social construction of literacy. In J. Cook-Gumperz (Ed.), *The social construction of literacy* (pp. 1–15). Cambridge, NY: Cambridge University Press.

Cooper, M. M. (1989). Women's ways of writing. In M. M. Cooper & M. Holzman (Eds.), *Writing as social action* (pp. 141–156). Portsmouth, NH: Heinemann/Boyton-Cook.

Cooper, M. M. (1991). Dueling with dualism: A response to interviews with Mary Field Belenky and Gayatri Chakravorty Spivak. *Journal of Advanced Composition, 11*, 179–185.

Curtis, M., & Herrington, A. (in press). *Persons in process.* Urbana, IL: NCTE.

Delpit, L. (1995). *Other people's children: Cultural conflict in the classroom.* New York: New Press.

Downing, D. B. (Ed.). (1994). *Changing classroom practices: Resources for literary and cultural studies.* Urbana, IL: NCTE.

Downs, R. B. (1970). *Books that changed America.* New York: Macmillan.

Eagleton, T. (1991). *Ideology: An introduction.* London: Verso.

Eisenstein, E. L. (1983a). On the printing press as an agent of change. In D. R. Olson, N. Torrance, & A. Hildyard (Eds.), *Literacy, language, and learning:*

The nature and consequences of reading and writing (pp. 19–33). Cambridge: Cambridge University Press.

Eisenstein, E. L. (1983b). *The printing revolution in early modern Europe.* New York: Cambridge University Press.

Elbow, P. (1995). Being a writer vs. being an academic: A conflict in goals. *College Composition and Communication, 46,* 72–83.

Eliot, T. S. (1985). Tradition and the individual talent. In N. Baym et al. (Eds.), *The Norton anthology of American literature* (2nd ed.; Vol. 2, pp. 1201–1208). New York, Norton. (Original work published 1919)

Emig, J. (1971). *The composing processes of twelfth graders.* Urbana, IL: NCTE.

Faigley, L. (1992). *Fragments of rationality: Postmodernity and the subject of composition.* Pittsburgh: University of Pittsburgh Press.

Feenberg, A. (1991). *Critical theory of technology.* New York: Oxford University Press.

Finders, M. (1997). *Just girls: Hidden literacies and life in junior high.* Urbana, IL: NCTE.

Finlay, L. S., & Faith, V. (1987). Illiteracy and alienation in American colleges: Is Paulo Freire's pedagogy relevant? In I. Shor (Ed.), *Freire for the classroom: A sourcebook for liberatory teaching* (pp. 63–86). Portsmouth, NH: Heinemann.

Flower, L. (1988). The construction of purpose in writing and reading. *College English, 50,* 528–550.

Flower, L. (1994). *The construction of negotiated meaning: A social cognitive theory of writing.* Carbondale: Southern Illinois University Press.

Flower, L., & Hayes, J. R. (1981). A cognitive process theory of writing. *College Composition and Communication, 32,* 365–387.

Flower, L. S., & Hayes, J. R. (1984). Images, plans, and prose: The representation of meaning in writing. *Written Communication, 1,* 120–160.

Flower, L., Stein, V., Ackerman, J., Kantz, M., McCormick, K., & Peck, W. C. (1990). *Reading-to-write: Exploring a cognitive and social process.* New York: Oxford University Press.

Flynn, E. A. (1988). Composing as a woman. *College Composition and Communication, 39,* 423–435.

Flynn, E. A. (1991). Politicizing the composing process and women's ways of interacting: A response to "A Conversation with Mary Belenky." *Journal of Advanced Composition, 11,* 173–178.

Foucault, M. (1972). *The archaeology of knowledge and the discourse on language* (A. M. S. Smith, Trans.). New York: Pantheon.

Foucault, M. (1977). What is an author? In D. F. Bouchard (Ed.), *Language, counter-memory, practice: Selected essays and interviews* (pp. 115–138). Ithaca, NY: Cornell University Press. (Originally published in *Bulletin de la Societe Francaise de Philosophie, 63,* 1969, 73–104)

Fox, T. J. (1990). *The social uses of writing: Politics and pedagogy.* Norwood, NJ: Ablex.

Freire, P. (1984). *Pedagogy of the oppressed* (M. B. Ramos, Trans.). New York: Continuum. (Original work published 1970)

Freire, P. (1988). The adult literacy process as cultural action for freedom and education and conscientizacao. In E. R. Kintgen, B. M. Kroll, & M. Rose (Eds.), *Perspectives in literacy* (pp. 395–409). Carbondale: Southern Illinois University Press.

Freire, P. (1994). *A pedagogy of hope* (R. R. Barr, Trans.). New York: Continuum.

Freire, P., & Macedo, D. (1987). *Literacy: Reading the word, reading the world.* Westport, CT: Bergin & Garvey.

Gergen, K. J. (1991). *The saturated self: Dilemmas of identity in contemporary life.* New York: HarperCollins.

Giroux, H. A. (1987). Introduction: Literacy and the pedagogy of political empowerment. In P. Freire & D. Macedo, *Literacy: Reading the word, reading the world* (pp. 1–28). Westport, CT: Bergin & Garvey.

Goldblatt, E. C. (1995). *'Round my way: Authority and double consciousness in three urban high school writers.* Pittsburgh: University of Pittsburgh Press.

Graff, H. J. (1979). *The literacy myth: Literature and social structure in the nineteenth-century city.* New York: Academic Press.

Graff, H. J. (1987). *The legacies of literacy.* Bloomington: Indiana University Press.

Gregory, T. (1993). *Making high school work: Lessons from the open school.* New York: Teachers College Press.

Grusin, R. (1996). What is an electronic author? Theory and the technological fallacy. In R. Markley (Ed.), *Virtual realities and their discontents* (pp. 39–53). Baltimore: Johns Hopkins University Press.

Gurak, L. J. (1997). *Persuasion and privacy in cyberspace: The online protests over Lotus Marketplace and the clipper chip.* New Haven: Yale University Press.

Harkin, P., & Schilb, J. (Eds.). (1991). *Contending with words: Composition and rhetoric in a postmodern age.* New York: Modern Language Association.

Hawisher, G. E., & Selfe, C. L. (1991). The rhetoric of technology in the electronic writing class. *College Composition and Communication, 42,* 55–65.

Heath, S. B. (1983). *Ways with words: Language, life, and work in communities and classrooms.* New York: Cambridge University Press.

Himley, M. (1991). *Shared territory: Understanding children's writing as works.* New York: Oxford University Press.

Hirsch, E. D. (1987). *Cultural literacy: What every American needs to know.* Boston: Houghton Mifflin.

hooks, b. (1989). *Talking back: Thinking feminist, thinking black.* Boston: South End Press.

hooks, b. (1994). *Teaching to transgress: Education as the practice of freedom.* New York: Routledge.

Hourigan, M. M. (1994). *Literacy as social exchange: Intersections of class, gender, and culture.* Albany: State University of New York Press.

Hull, G., & Rose, M. (1989). Rethinking remediation: Toward a social-cognitive understanding of problematic reading and writing. *Written Communication, 6,* 139–154.

Jarratt, S. C. (1991). Feminism and composition: The case for conflict. In

P. Harkin & J. Schilb (Eds.), *Contending with words: Composition and rhetoric in a postmodern age* (pp. 105–123). New York: Modern Language Association.

Kaplan, R. D. (1998, July). Travels into America's future. *Atlantic Monthly, 282,* 47–68.

Kiernan, V. (1998, April 24). Report documents role of race in who uses the world-wide web. *Chronicle of Higher Education, 44,* A38.

Knoblauch, C. H. (1991). Critical teaching and the dominant culture. In C. M. Hurlbert & M. Blitz (Eds.), *Composition and resistance* (pp. 12–21). Portsmouth, NH: Heinemann.

Knoblauch, C. H., & Brannon, L. (1993). *Critical teaching and the idea of literacy.* Portsmouth, NH: Heinemann.

Knott, G. (1987). Literacy instruction in secondary school classroom contexts. In D. Bloome, *Literacy and schooling* (pp. 354–371). Norwood, NJ: Ablex.

Kozol, J. (1985). *Illiterate America.* New York: Doubleday.

Lewis, P. (1998, July 20). "Ulysses" on top among 100 best novels. *New York Times.* (available online at http://www.nytimes.com/library/books/072098best-novels.html)

Lyotard, J. (1984). *The postmodern condition: A report on knowledge* (G. Benington & B. Masumi, Trans.). Minneapolis: University of Minnesota Press.

Macdonnell, D. (1986). *Theories of discourse: An introduction.* New York: Basil Blackwell.

Malcolm X. (1992). *The autobiography of Malcolm X.* New York: Ballantine Books. (Originally published in 1964 by Grove Press)

Mayher, J. (1990). *Uncommon sense: Theoretical practice in language education.* Portsmouth, NH: Boyton-Cook/Heinemann.

McLuhan, M. (1995). The Gutenberg galaxy: The making of typographic man. In E. McLuhan & F. Zingrone (Eds.), *Essential McLuhan* (pp. 97–148). New York: Basic Books. (Originally published in 1962 by University of Toronto Press)

Mills, S. (1997). *Discourse.* New York: Routledge.

Morgan, D. (1998). Ethical issues raised by students' personal writing. *College English, 60,* 318–325.

O'Hare, D. (1993, July 21). NAFTA: Mexico, a market that is ready for services. *New York Times,* pp. C10–C11.

Ohmann, R. (1976). *English in America: A radical view of the profession.* New York: Oxford University Press.

Ohmann, R. (1985). Literacy, technology, and monopoly capital. *College English, 47,* 675–688.

Ohmann, R. (1995). English after the USSR. In C. Newfield & R. Strickland (Eds.), *After political correctness: The humanities and society in the 1990's* (pp. 226–237). Boulder, CO: Westview Press.

Ong, W. J. (1982). *Orality and literacy: The technologizing of the word.* New York: Routledge.

Poster, M. (1990). *The mode of information: Poststructuralism and social context.* Chicago: University of Chicago Press.

Rickley, R., Harrington, S., & Day, M. (Eds.). (1999). *The online writing classroom*. Cresskill, NJ: Hampton Press.

Rodriguez, R. (1983). *Hunger of memory*. New York: Bantam Books.

Rogoff, B. (1990). *Apprenticeship in thinking: Cognitive development in social context*. New York: Oxford University Press.

Romano, S. (1993). The egalitarian narrative: Whose story? Which yardstick? *Computers and Composition, 10*, 5–28.

Rose, M. (Ed.). (1985). *When a writer can't write: Studies in writers' block and other cognitive process problem*. New York: Guilford Press.

Rose, M. (1989). *Lives on the boundary*. New York: Free Press.

Rose, M. (1995). *Possible lives: The promise of public education in America*. New York: Penguin.

Scribner, S., & Cole, M. (1981). *The psychology of literacy*. Cambridge, MA: Harvard University Press.

Selfe, C. L., & Hilligoss, S. (1994). *Literacy and computers: The complications of teaching and learning with technology*. New York: Modern Language Association.

Shor, I. (Ed.). (1987). *Freire for the classroom: A sourcebook for liberatory teaching*. Portsmouth, NH: Heinemann.

Shuman, R. B. (1990). Secondary school English teachers: Past, present, future. In G. E. Hawisher & A. O. Soter (Eds.), *On literacy and its teaching: Issues in English education* (pp. 36–49). Albany: State University of New York Press.

Smith, P. (1988). *Discerning the subject*. Minneapolis: University of Minnesota Press.

Spooner, M., & Yancey, K. (1996). Postings on a genre of email. *College Composition and Communication, 47*, 252–278.

Street, B. (1984). *Literacy in theory and practice*. Cambridge: Cambridge University Press.

Stuckey, J. E. (1991). *The violence of literacy*. Portsmouth, NH: Heinemann.

Takayoshi, P. (1994). Building new networks from the old: Women's experiences with electronic communication. *Computers and Composition, 11*, 21–35.

Taylor, M. C., & Saarinen, E. (1994). *Imagologies: Media philosophy*. New York: Routledge.

Tinberg, H. B. (1991). "An enlargement of observation": More on theory building in the composition classroom. *College Composition and Communication, 42*, 36–44.

Tobin, L. (1993). *Writing relationships: What really happens in the composition classroom*. Portsmouth, NH: Heinemann.

Tokarczyk, M. A., & Fay, E. A. (Eds.). (1993). *Working-class women in the academy: Laborers in the knowledge factory*. Amherst: University of Massachusetts Press.

Trimbur, J. (1994). Taking the social turn: Teaching writing post-process. *College Composition and Communication, 45*, 108–118.

Tuman, M. C. (1992). *Word perfect: Literacy in the computer age*. Pittsburgh: University of Pittsburgh Press.

Twain, Mark. (1995). *The adventures of Huckleberry Finn* (critical controversy ed.). (G. Graff & J. Phelan, Eds.). Boston: Bedford/St. Martin's.

Wells, R. (1993). *Computer-mediated communication for distance education: An international review of design, teaching, and institutional issues*. State College, PA: American Center for Distance Education.

Yagelski, R. P. (1991). *The dynamics of context: A study of the role of context in the composing processes of student writers*. Ann Arbor, MI: University Microfilms International.

Yagelski, R. P. (1994a). Collaboration and children's writing: What "real" authors do, what children do. *Journal of Teaching Writing, 12,* 217–233.

Yagelski, R. P. (1994b). Literature and literacy: Rethinking English as a school subject. *English Journal, 83,* 30–36.

Yagelski, R. P. (1994c). Who's afraid of subjectivity? The composing process and postmodernism, or, a student of Donald Murray enters the age of postmodernism. In T. Newkirk & L. Tobin (Eds.), *Taking stock: Reassessing the writing process movement in the 90's* (pp. 203–215). Portsmouth, NH: Heinemann.

Yagelski, R. P. (1997). What does NAFTA mean? Teaching text in the 1990s. *English Education, 29,* 38–58.

Yagelski, R. P. (1999). Asynchronous networks for critical reflection: Using computer-mediated communication in the preparation of secondary school writing teachers. In R. Rickley, S. Harrington, & M. Day (Eds.), *The online writing classroom* (pp. 339–368). Cresskill, NJ: Hampton Press.

Yagelski, R. P., & Grabill, J. T. (1998). Computer-mediated communication in the undergraduate writing classroom: A study of the relationship of online discourse and classroom discourse in two writing classes. *Computers and Composition, 15,* 11–40.

Zebroski, J. T. (1990). The English department and social class. In A. A. Lunsford, H. Moglen, & J. Slevin (Eds.), *The right to literacy* (pp. 81–90). New York: Modern Language Association.

Index

About the Author

Robert P. Yagelski is assistant professor of English at the State University of New York at Albany, where he directs the writing center and teaches undergraduate courses in writing and tutoring and graduate courses in rhetoric, composition, and literacy. Formerly, he was assistant professor of English education at Purdue University, where he co-directed the English education program and taught in the graduate programs in rhetoric and composition and in language and literacy. He taught English at Vermont Academy, an independent high school, where he also served as English Department chair, and has worked closely with elementary, middle, and high school teachers in several states in their efforts to improve litaracy instruction. He earned his Ph.D. in Rhetoric and Composition at the Ohio State University in 1991. His articles on literacy, writing, and writing instruction have appeared in a number of edited collections and in such journals as *College Composition and Communication, Computers and Composition, English Education, The Journal of Teaching Writing, Rhetoric Review,* and *Research in the Teaching of English.* He has also written a children's book called *The Day the Lifting Bridge Stuck.* Currently his research focuses on theoretical conceptions of literacy and on the technologies of literacy.

2712
Gift